Alfred M. Copeland

A History of the Town of Murrayfield

Earlier known as Township No. 9, and comprising the present towns of Chester and

Huntington, the northern part of Montgomery, and the southeast corner of

Middlefield, 1760-1763

Alfred M. Copeland

A History of the Town of Murrayfield
Earlier known as Township No. 9, and comprising the present towns of Chester and Huntington, the northern part of Montgomery, and the southeast corner of Middlefield, 1760-1763

ISBN/EAN: 9783337219895

Printed in Europe, USA, Canada, Australia, Japan

Cover: Foto ©ninafisch / pixelio.de

More available books at **www.hansebooks.com**

A HISTORY

OF THE

TOWN OF MURRAYFIELD,

EARLIER KNOWN AS

TOWNSHIP NO. 9,

AND COMPRISING THE PRESENT TOWNS OF CHESTER AND HUNTINGTON, THE NORTHERN PART OF MONTGOMERY, AND THE SOUTHEAST CORNER OF MIDDLEFIELD.

1760—1783.

By ALFRED M. COPELAND,
Of SPRINGFIELD, MASS.

SPRINGFIELD, MASS.:
CLARK W. BRYAN & COMPANY, PRINTERS.
1892.

Reprinted by -

HIGGINSON BOOK COMPANY
148 Washington Street, Post Office Box 778
Salem, Massachusetts 01970

Phone: 978/745-7170 *Fax:* 978/745-8025

A complete catalog of thousands of genealogy and local history reprints is available from Higginson Books. Please contact us to order or for more information, or visit our web site at www.higginsonbooks.com.

This book is photoreproduced on acid-free paper.
Hardcover bindings are Class A archival quality.

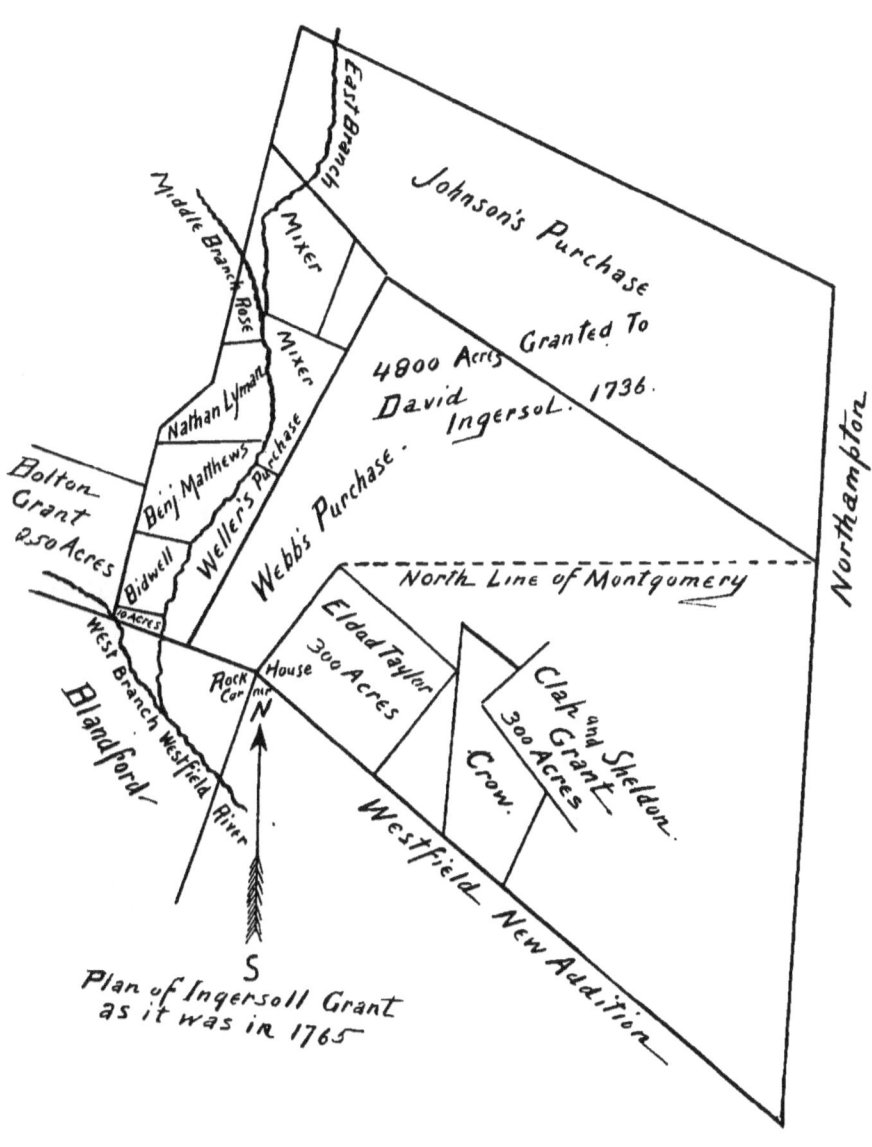

PREFACE.

About ten years ago I began gathering facts touching the history of the town of Murrayfield. I had had occasion frequently, during my residence in the town of Huntington, to consult the book of records of the original proprietors, and had traced a copy of the proprietors' plan of the town for my own use, as occasion might require in my professional work in the neighborhood; but it had never occurred to me to write a history of the town, nor to institute investigations in that direction.

Some time after the organization of "The Connecticut Valley Historical Society" I promised to write a sketch of the town of Murrayfield, in a single paper, to be read before the society; but several years transpired before I felt sure that I had found the starting point. The more I investigated, the richer the field proved. From the proprietors' records, from the registry of deeds, from the records of courts, from the records of the Colonial General Court, from original documents in the office of the Secretary of the Commonwealth, from the records of the old town and of the old church, and from inscriptions upon headstones in the old cemetery, I gathered together a greater array of facts than had at first seemed possible.

From individuals living in Chester and in Huntington I could obtain absolutely nothing touching the early history of Murrayfield. The information obtained from the most intelligent of them related to a later period.

It was often necessary to give some collateral history of the times in order to make clear many facts which the records of the town fail to explain. It seemed undesirable to attempt to present any facts unverified by authentic records. The reader will judge whether I have erred in this. At any rate, I feel sure that the sketch of Murrayfield which is here offered to the public is worthy of a careful perusal, and that I have succeeded in snatching from oblivion many valuable facts. I feel equally certain that the early history of other towns in western Massachusetts offer a rich field to the historian. The history of Murrayfield is very like that of other towns in this part of the state that were settled too late to be involved in the Indian wars.

This history of Murrayfield presents an object lesson as to the birth and growth of inland towns in New England, and so cannot but be of general interest.

ALFRED M. COPELAND.

A HISTORY OF THE TOWN OF MURRAYFIELD.

CHAPTER FIRST.

INGERSOLL GRANT IN THE OLD COUNTY OF HAMPSHIRE, MASSA-
CHUSETTS.

On page 122 of book L in the Registry of Deeds, for the old county of Hampshire, is the copy of a deed as follows:

"John Stoddard and Ebenezer Pomeroy of Northampton, and Thomas Ingersole of Westfield, all in the county of Hampshire in the Province of Massachusetts Bay in New England, Esqrs., on March the 26th, 1736, were by the Great and General Court of the said Province, specially authorized and appointed among other things to purchase rights of land of the proprietors of Upper Housatonick Township—so called—in the said county in order to the accommodating and bringing forward a settlement of the Indians above the Monument Mountain—so called—in said Housatonick Township,* and to give equivalents therefore in some of the unappropriated lands of the said province to the proprietors of whom we shall purchase the land as per the said order of the said court or assembly reference to the same being had will appear. Now we, the said John Stoddard, Ebenezer Pomeroy, & Thomas Ingersole, by virtue of the said commission & authority vested in us, have purchased six rights of land in Upper Housatonick above the Monument Mountain—so called—each right containing four hundred acres, of David Ingersole of Westfield in the county & province aforesaid. Now we, the said John Stoddard, Ebenezer Pomeroy, & Thomas Ingersole, as a committee aforesaid, have agreed with the said David Ingersole to give him an equivalent from the government for the aforesaid rights of land in the unappropriated land of the said Province, a certain tract or parcel of land of the quantity of four thousand & eight hundred acres; beginning at the northeast corner of Southfield† Equivalent land called Glasgow; north east corner & so running upon Glasgow line West 20° North two hundred & twenty perch to a marked tree on the east bank of the west branch of the Westfield River; & thence North 15° East two hundred & eighty perch; thence East 40° North one hundred perch; thence North 15° East continuing that line until five hundred & sixteen perch be completed;

---

* For a more particular account of this the reader is referred to the history of Stockbridge. The sketch of Stockbridge in Dr. Holland's History of Western Massachusetts gives some account of it.
† Suffield.

then beginning, viz: at Glasgow north-east corner, thence running south 39° east* one thousand & fifteen perch to Moss Meadow† to a tree with stones about it, which tree is Northampton south-west corner. This last mentioned line joins upon Westfield last grant; thence from said tree North 5° east, in or on Northampton line until eleven hundred and ninety-five perch be completed; & from thence in a straight line to the northernmost point of the line before mentioned which was north 15° east, and five hundred and sixteen perch; excepting three hundred acres heretofore laid out within the bounds aforesaid to Samuel Clapp & Ebenezer Sheldin. Now, we, the said John Stoddard, Ebenezer Pomeroy, & Thomas Ingersole, by virtue of the commission to us, we do hereby give, grant, convey, & confirm unto the said David Ingersole, to him, his heirs, & assigns for ever, all the aforesaid described land, saving the said three hundred acres.

To have and to hold, possess & enjoy, quietly & peaceably for ever more; and further we, the said John Stoddard, Ebenezer Pomeroy, & Thomas Ingersole, Esqrs., by virtue of said commission to us granted, and in the name, & the behalf of the said government of the said Province, we hereby covenant, promise & engage the before granted premises unto him, the said David Ingersole, his heirs & assigns, forever to warrant, maintain, secure, and defend against the lawful claims or charges of any person or persons whatsoever.

In witness whereof we have hereunto set our hands & seals this first day of June in the eleventh of the reign of George the Second, King, &c. Anno Domini 1738.

"Signed, sealed & delivered in presence of us by John Stoddard & Ebenezer Pomeroy, Oliver Partridge, Jr., Witnesses.
" Witness to Thomas Ingerso'e signed, &c., Benjamin Prescott, Wm. Pynchon.

} JOHN STODDARD & Seal.
EBENEZER POMEROY & Seal.
THOMAS INGERSOLE & Seal."

" Hampshire ss., June 1st, 1738, John Stoddard & Ebenezer Pomeroy, Esqrs., two of the subscribers to the above instrument appearing acknowledged the same to be their act & deed.
Coram, JOB WILLIAMS, Just. Peace."

"Suffolk ss., Boston, June 20th, 1738, Thomas Ingersole, one of the subscribers to the above instrument personally appearing acknowledged the same to be his act & deed.
Coram, JOSHUA WINSLOW, Just. Peace."

The southeast corner of this tract was about a mile southeasterly from the present town house in Montgomery. When the town of Norwich was incorporated in 1773, Ingersoll Grant was wholly included and formed the south end of that town. When the town of Montgomery was incorporated in 1780, a large part of this grant was included, and formed about one-third of the territory of that town. A

---

* This was an error. The course in fact was S. 49° E.
† This name should be Moose Meadow.

small mountain called "Rock House," near which was the northeast corner of Glasgow, now called Blandford, was included by the bounds of this grant.

INGERSOLL'S DEED TO WEBB.

By a deed dated April 7th, 1738—before receiving a deed from the government—David Ingersoll conveyed to Thomas Webb of Boston, a part of his grant, and described it as follows:

"Beginning 100 rods west 20° north from a certain tree which is Glasgow's north east corner, then from said tree South 39°* east 1015 perch upon Westfield line to Moss Meadow,† being the south west corner of Northampton;‡ then North 5° East 800 perch on Northampton line; then North 63° west 770 perch; then 600 perch to the place of beginning." It was called in the deed 3000 acres exclusive of the 300 acres owned by Shelden & Clapp. The quantity of land & the length of some of the lines were exaggerated.

INGERSOLL'S DEED TO JOHNSON.

By deed dated August 14th, 1738, Ingersoll sold the north end of his grant to John Johnson of Boston, a marriner, and described it as follows:

"Beginning 800 rods from the southwest corner of Northampton on Northampton west line; then North 44° West 750 perch; Then beginning at first bound running North 5° East on Northampton line 335 perch; then North 63° West 900 rods; then South 15° West 150 rods; then turning and running 250 rods to the westernmost end of the 750 perch line." The quantity of land was estimated to be 1500 acres.

INGERSOLL'S DEED TO BREWER.

Ingersoll sold the remainder of his grant to John Brewer of "No. 1 on the road between Westfield and Sheffield," and described it as consisting of 800 acres of land northeast of and adjoining Blandford. It was north of the northeasterly part of Blandford. The deed was dated July 8th, 1742, the year after the township called Glasgow was incorporated under the name of Blandford. The tract was described as follows:

"Beginning 100 rods West 20° North from a pine tree which is Blandford's north east corner, then running west 20° North 127 rods to a marked tree standing on the bank of the West Branch of Westfield River; then running

---

* This was in fact 49°.
† Moose Meadow.
‡ Northampton had not been divided at this time.

North 15° East 289 rods; then East 40° North 103 rods; then North 15° East 380 rods; then East 33° South 341 rods to stake & stones, being the north west bound of a tract of land sold by me to Thomas Webb of Boston; then running to the first mentioned bound; & bounded south by Blandford; west by the country land; North by land I sold to John Johnson of Boston, & east by land I sold to said Webb." The consideration named in this deed was eighty pounds.

BREWER'S DEED TO WELLER AND WELLER TO BIDWELL AND TO MATTHEWS.

By deed dated August 28th, 1754, John Brewer sold this tract of land to Nathaniel Weller of Westfield. By Weller it was parcelled out to various purchasers. By deed dated April 14th, 1758 he conveyed 50 acres of it to John Bidwell of Hartford, Connecticut, and it was described as follows:

"A certain tract of land of fifty acres out of the southwest part of a certain farm I bought of John Brewer of 800 acres lying northward & adjoining Blandford in said County of Hampshire; said fifty acres is bounded east on the main river* called Westfield River, & to extend west to the line of said farm, & to bound southerly on said Blandford town line, only reserving thereout ten acres† on said Blandford line, and to extend as far north on said farm as to make the said complement of fifty acres."

The deed was acknowledged before David Moseley, Justice of the Peace.

By a deed dated May 26th, 1760, Weller sold to Benjamin Matthews of Torrington, Connecticut, in consideration of 100 pounds, two tracts of this land, one containing 107 acres and the other containing 68 acres. The description is as follows:

"Bounded at the south east corner by a hemlock tree near the river, from thence running west 20° North 86 rods to stake & stones; thence North 15° East 160 rods to a heap of stones; then East 142 rods; bounded at the river by a hemlock tree with stones about it; from thence by the river southerly to the first mentioned bound, & bounded south by John Bidwell's land.

The other parcel lying a little northerly from the above described land on the second branch of the river, bounded at the north east corner on the river bank by a tree with stones about it; so running west 30° North 6 rods; then South 15° West 205 rods to a black birch tree with stones about it; then east 63 rods to a buttonwood three on the bank of the river; then running northerly by the river to the first bound containing 68 acres."

---

* This was the east branch of Westfield River, which was sometime called the main branch.

† Weller sold this ten acres to Samuel Root of Southampton, December, 2d, 1761, and described it as bounded on West Branch and by Blandford line 75 rods, and up the East Branch 21½ rods, and bounded it northerly by John Bidwell's land 75 rods, and located it between Bidwell's land and Blandford line.

WELLER'S DEED TO NATHAN LYMAN.

By a deed dated July 6th, 1760, Weller sold to Nathan Lyman of Southampton, 90 acres of this land described as

"A tract of land lying between the Branches of Westfield Great River above Great Falls, bounded at the south east corner by the river bank by a hemlock tree marked, which is Benjamin Matthews' north east corner; thence W 142 rods; thence N. 15° E. about 20 rods to a hemlock tree marked; thence E. 40° N. 103 rods; thence N. 15° E. 50 rods to a birch tree which is said Matthew's south west corner; thence 63 rods to a buttonwood staddle on the river bank; so running down the river to the first mentioned bound containing 90 acres."

WELLER'S DEED TO MIXER.

By deed dated April 28th, 1762, Weller conveyed to Isaac Mixer of Suffield, Connecticut, 75 acres, located in the northerly part of his tract on the east side of East Branch, and it was described as follows:

"Beginning at a maple tree, thence E. 25° S. 80 rods; thence N. 25° E. 141½ rods; thence W. 33° N. 100 rods to the river by the falls; thence down the river which is the main branch to the first bound a little above where the second branch enters* the main branch of said river on the West side."

MIXER'S TAVERN.

Mixer built a house and kept a tavern before 1764. Although it is not certain where this tavern was located, there is reason to believe that it was south of the land above described upon land of Weller, which Mixer afterward purchased. The records of the Court of General Sessions in 1764 contain the following record: "Isaac Mixer of a place called Westfield River Branches, or No. 9, is licensed to be an innholder and common victualler." In 1765 Mixer made another purchase of Weller's land, containing 159 acres and described as follows:

"Beginning at stake & stones about 25 rods up the river above Mixer house near the bank, then E. 25° S. 144 rods; thence S. 38° W. upon the line of Samuel Webb's land 203 rods to stake and stones; thence W. 25° N. to a spruce tree at the river; thence up the river to the first bound, lying on the east side of the 'Great River' so called; thence bounded northerly upon said Weller's land, and westerly upon the river; with the dwelling house & barn, and with a saw-mill standing on the same."

MATTHEWS' DEEDS TO HIS SON AND TO HIS DAUGHTER.

On the 28th of July, 1760, Benjamin Matthews gave to his daughter Eunice Rose, wife of Israel Rose of Granville, 30 acres from the south

* This must have been further south than at the present time (1890).

end of his sixty-eight acre tract, and to his son Gideon of Torrington, Connecticut, 50 acres from the north end of his one hundred and seven acre tract. His son and his daughter with her husband soon after located their homes in this vicinity, and he himself became a resident of Westfield about the same time.

THE OLD ROAD UP THE EAST BRANCH OF WESTFIELD RIVER.

Remains of an old road between this locality and Westfield are still in existence: it crossed Westfield river a few rods below the junction of the east and west branches by a fordway which is often used at the present time. From this fordway the old road may be traced between the river and the Boston and Albany railway which it crosses, and so continues in a northerly direction near the east bank of the east branch. This road passed Isaac Mixer's tavern, and probably continued up the river into Chesterfield and connected with a highway which was laid out from Hatfield, and passing through Chesterfield, extended to Pontusic—now Pittsfield—as early as 1760.

WEBB'S DEED TO ELDAD TAYLOR.

By deed dated April 30th, 1762, Thomas Webb and Samuel Webb, sons of the Thomas Webb to whom Ingersoll conveyed, sold to Eldad Taylor of Westfield, 300 acres of land described as follows:

"A tract of land in the county of Hampshire & lying northerly from Westfield & adjoining to said Westfield, beginning at a tree which is now fallen down with stones on it, which tree is the north west corner bound of Westfield & the north east corner bound of Blandford & from said bound to run east 39° south* 240 rods by Westfield line, & from thence to run north 39° East 200 rods, thence West 39° North 240 rods, thence south 39° West 200 rods to first bound containing 300 acres, and is bounded southerly by Westfield & the other three sides on said Webb's land." The consideration was sixty pounds.

It does not appear that any other conveyances were made from the Webbs to any one prior to June, 1762. They subsequently conveyed parcels of land, lying east of the tract sold to Eldad Taylor, to David Crow and to Thomas Crow. They also sold tracts of land to Ebenezer King, to Benjamin Converse, to James Taggart, persons who became residents of the town of Murrayfield.

JOHNSON'S LAND SOLD TO DR. SPRAGUE.

Of the tract sold by Ingersoll to John Johnson, a deed dated May 20th, 1756, was given by Johnson to Nicholas Tobb of Boston. On

---
* See the description in the deed to David Ingersoll as to this course.

the following day Tobb executed a deed of the same land to Priscilla Johnson, the wife of John; and she by deed dated September 7th, 1756, conveyed it to John Sprague, M. D., of Boston. The record does not show any conveyance of this land by Sprague prior to June, 1762.

SHELDEN AND CLAPP GRANT.

The grant to Shelden and Clapp, mentioned and excepted from the grant to David Ingersoll, was made in answer to "a petition of Ebenezer Shelden for himself and for Samuel and Mary Clapp, showing that the said Shelden and his sister Mary Clapp, in their long captivity in Canada, contracted an acquaintance with the Cagnawaga Indians, who now put them to an extraordinary charge to entertain them when they came to Deerfield; and therefore praying for a grant of province land from this court. In the House of Representatives read; and in answer to this petition ordered that the petitioners have leave, by a surveyor and chain-man on oath to survey and lay out three hundred acres of the unappropriated lands of this Province in the county of Hampshire, and return a plat thereof to this court within twelve months for confirmation, one-half thereof to the said Ebenezer Shelden and the other half to the said Samuel and Mary Clapp, Wednesday, January 12th, 1736."

This is all that appears of record. The plat, if in fact returned for confirmation, does not appear of record, so that there is nothing to show definitely its location. It was somewhere intermediate between the northeast corner of Glasgow or Blandford and the west line of Northampton as it was at that time. It was east of the 300 acre tract sold by the Webbs to Eldad Taylor, at a distance probably of about 400 rods from Rock House corner.

SHELDEN'S DEED TO CALEB STRONG.

Ebenezer Shelden, describing himself as of Deerfield, by deed dated October 29th, 1741, sold his half of this grant to Caleb Strong of Northampton and described it as follows:

"A certain tract of land lying west of the township of Northampton & east of Suffield's Equivalent north east corner now called Glasgow north east corner containing one hundred & fifty acres being one half of a grant of three hundred acres made by the General Court or assembly of Massachusetts Bay to me the said Ebenezer Shelden & my brother & sister Samuel & Mary Clapp on January 12th, 1736. The whole tract is bounded & more particularly described by a plat of the same dated June 14, 1737 & confirmed by the aforesaid court in June A. D. 1738."

STRONG'S DEED TO THE CARTERS.

Caleb Strong sold this land to William and Asa Carter of Norwich by deed dated January 7th, 1774, following substantially the description in Shelden's deed to him.

CLAPP'S DEED TO WELLS.

By a deed dated May 9th, 1774, Ebenezer Clapp and others of Northampton, and Elijah Clapp and others of Southampton, heirs of Samuel and Mary Clapp, in consideration of seventy-five pounds, conveyed to Joseph Wells of Groton, New London County, in the state of Connecticut, "a certain tract of land lying in Norwich, being one-half of a tract containing three hundred acres granted by the General Court, January 12th, 1736, to Ebenezer Shelden and Samuel and Mary Clapp," etc. This deed gave no description which could aid in locating the grant. Subsequently Wells sold to Job Halliday of Montgomery; and estates belonging to Salmon Thomas, to Hiram Halliday, and to Silas Hubbill were mentioned in the deed as abutting lands.

THE GREEN AND WALKER GRANT AND WILLIAMS GRANT.

GREEN AND WALKER GRANT.

Joseph Green and Isaac Walker, both of Boston, were copartners in the mercantile business under the style of Green & Walker. They were owners of extensive tracts of land in various parts of the Province of Massachusetts Bay. They held rights of land in Upper Housatonnock—as it was then spelled—at the time the provincial government was arranging for a settlement of the Indians above Monument Mountain. The settling committee, consisting of John Stoddard, Ebenezer Pomeroy and Thomas Ingersoll, who had been appointed for that purpose by the General Court, purchased these rights of Green & Walker and gave them in exchange therefor other tracts of land located in the county of Hampshire. One of the tracts given to make up an equivalent for their rights in Upper Housatonnock was located about 130 rods west of the west line of the town of Northampton, and consisted of 2,000 acres of land. The southwest corner of this grant, which was known as the Green & Walker Grant, touched the north line of the Ingersoll Grant. The west line was near the east branch of Westfield River, a part of which was included toward the northwest part of the grant. The pond known as Norwich Pond was for the most part within the grant, occupying the northeast corner; the north line of the grant passed across the north end of the pond.

The laying out of this grant and its conveyance to Green & Walker was reported to the General Court by Ebenezer Pomeroy and Thomas Ingersoll, two of the settling committee, at the session held May 30th, 1739, but was not acted upon until the session which began by adjournment, December 5th, 1739. A copy of the conveyance of this tract to Green & Walker by the settling committee does not appear in the Registry of Deeds for the old county of Hampshire; but the facts are recited in a deed given by Isaac Walker to Joseph Green dated October 24th, 1744. Mr. Green retained his interest in this grant until his death, which took place some time between 1764 and 1769. His widow, Anna Green, as executrix of his will, by deed dated January 30th, 1769, conveyed to George Green of Boston, the interest which her husband had in the Green & Walker grant at the time of his death, for the price of 400 pounds.

In 1764 a partition of this grant was made by Oliver Partridge, Elijah Williams, and Moses Graves, commissioners appointed for that purpose by court, who made and returned a report December 18th, 1764, and with it a plan upon which is the following minute: "A plan of 2,000 acres of land lying in Murrayfield laid out to Messrs. Joseph Green, Isaac Walker, Byfield Lyde, and John Green, surveyed June, 1739, and surveyed and marked anew October, 1764, by Elisha Hubbard, surveyor."

GREEN'S DEED TO KIRTLAND.

George Green sold 163¾ acres of his part to John Kirtland of Murrayfield by deed dated July 4th, 1772.

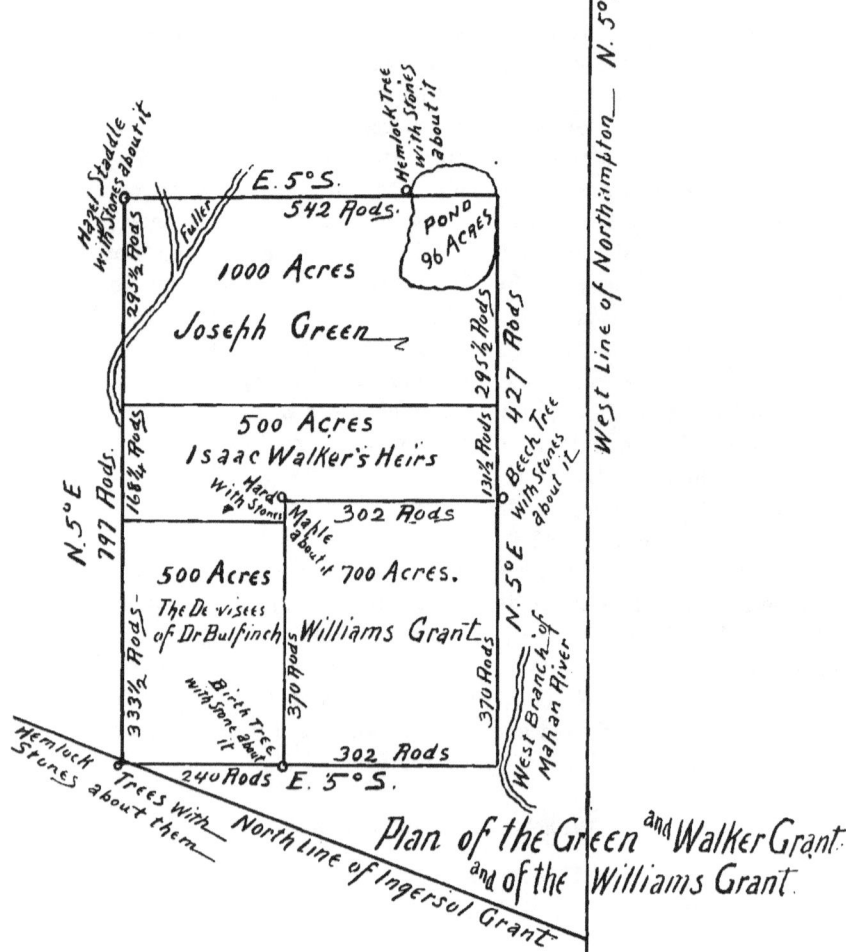

WILLIAMS GRANT.

The Williams grant contained 700 acres of land, and was granted by the General Court of the Province to the heirs of the Rev. John Williams, formerly of Deerfield, whose name is familiar to all who have read of the Indian wars in New England. The grant was made in answer to the petition of the Rev. Stephen Williams of Springfield, June 1st, 1737; it was laid out October 6th, 1737. The record of the General Court shows the following:

"On petition of the Rev. Mr. Stephen Williams of Springfield, in the House of Representatives, June 1st, 1737, read & in answer to the petition, ordered, that the petitioner have leave to survey & lay out by a surveyor & chainman on oath 700 acres of unappropriated lands of the province, in lieu of 700 acres laid out & confirmed at the session of this court held the 24th of November last which fall within a former grant & therefore is hereby vacated; & return a plan thereof within twelve months for confirmation to satisfy the grant within mentioned."

Sent up for confirmation,   J. QUINCY, Speaker.

In council June 2d, 1737. Read & ordered consented to.

The plan returned read as follows: "A tract of seven hundred acres of land lying west of the township of Northampton, viz; the southeast corner of said 700 acres being about half a mile westward of the north end of a great hill known by the name of Break-neck Hill, and said corner is near the west bank of the west branch of Mahan River, laid out to satisfy the grant of the General Court to the heirs of the Rev. Mr. John Williams, late of Deerfield, deceased.

Proportioned to a scale of 100 perch in an inch.

        EBENEZER KINGSLEY & ROGER MILLER, Chairmen.

Laid out October 6, 1737.

                          OLIVER PARTRIDGE, Surveyor."

Accompanying this was a plan of the grant.

WILLIAMS' DEED TO JOHN KIRTLAND.

The deed of the Rev. Stephen Williams, then of Springfield, to John Kirtland, yeoman, then of Norwich, New London County, Connecticut, conveyed 400 acres for 180 pounds; and as it gives a description of the whole tract I will copy the description part in full:

"A tract of land in Murrayfield in said County of Hampshire, containing 400 acres, being 4-7 parts [the whole in seven equal parts to be divided] of a tract of land in said Murrayfield containing 700 acres, which said tract of 700 acres was granted by the general court of the province aforesaid & laid out to the heirs of the Rev. John Williams, late of Deerfield, deceased, & is bounded as follows: The south east corner of said 700 acres is about half a mile westward of the north end of Break Neck Hill, at a hemlock & beech tree marked 'W'; from thence said land runs N. 5° E. 370 perch to a black birch marked 'W' with stones around it; from thence running W. 5° N. 302½ perch to a maple marked 'W' & stones; from thence S. 5° W. 370 perch to a beach tree marked 'W'; from thence to the first mentioned bound."

Kirtland had previously purchased two undivided sevenths, one by deed dated March 16th, 1768, from Samuel Woodward and his wife, Abigail Woodward, of Weston, Mass., Jacob Cushing and his wife, Anna Cushing, of Waltham, Mass., Joseph Parsons and his wife, Sarah Parsons, of Brimfield, Mass.; and the other by deed dated April 25th, 1768, from Nathan Williams, clerk, of Hartford, Conn. Each of these deeds conveyed 100 acres, and the price named in each deed was 45 pounds. Thus John Kirtland became the owner of six-sevenths of the Williams grant.

KIRTLAND'S DEED TO CLARK.

By deed dated June 20th, 1768, John Kirtland sold to James Clark, also of Norwich, Conn., a carpenter, 50 acres which he described as "being a part of 700 acres of land granted by the General Court of the Province of Massachusetts Bay, and laid out to the heirs of the Rev. Mr. John Williams, late of Deerfield, deceased, beginning at the southwest corner of said 700 acres at a beech tree marked 'W,' thence E. 5° S. 160 rods to a stake & heap of stones; thence N. 5° E. 50 rods to stake & stones; thence W. 5° N. 160 rods to stake & stones in the west line of said grant; thence S. 5° W. 50 rods to first mentioned bound." And by deed dated May 9th, 1769, John Kirtland sold 115 acres of the 700 acre tract to Daniel Kirtland, Jr., also of Norwich, Conn., and bounded it as follows:

"Beginning on the east line of a tract conveyed to me 62½ rods from the southeast corner of said grant, then W. 5° N. 134 rods; thence N. 5° E. 137 rods; thence E. 5° S. 134 rods; thence S. 5° W. 137 rods to the first mentioned bound." The two Kirtlands and James Clark took up their abode in Murrayfield shortly after the dates of these deeds.

These two grants, the Green & Walker and the Williams grants together, formed a parallelogram, the Williams grant occupying the southeast corner.

THE BOLTON GRANT.

Immediately west of Ingersoll grant and bounded south 208 rods by Blandford and east 210 rods by Ingersoll grant was a tract of land containing 250 acres and known as Bolton grant. Its south line was south of the west branch of Westfield River. Huntington village, formerly Chester village, and earlier known as Falley's X Roads, occupies a large part of the land which was comprised within this grant. This tract of land was occupied and claimed by John Bolton without legal title. He was what in our time would be called a "squatter."

FOYE'S DEED TO BOLTON AND BOLTON'S TO BURT.

In the year 1737 John Bolton purchased of John Foye, one of the original proprietors of Blandford, about 27 acres of land lying between the east and west branches of Westfield River at their intersection, and having as its northerly line the north line of Blandford. This piece of land he sold to Noah Burt of Southampton, the description of which will be of interest to persons who now own land within its bounds. The deed was dated January 30th, 1761, and is recorded in book 12 on page 208, now in the Hampden County Registry of Deeds. The grantor is described as "John Bolton, living on Province land between the branches of Westfield River between Blandford and Southampton in the county of Hampshire." The description is as follows:

"Twenty-seven acres of land in the town of Blandford, in a 500 acre lot number 38, which 27 acres I bought of John Foye. It is bounded as follows: Beginning at the east branch of the river on the line of the town of Blandford, & measured W. 20° N. to the other branch 74 rods; thence S. 10° E. by the river 40 rods; thence S. 20° E. 20 rods; thence southward by said branch or southerly to where the branches meet 66 rods; thence N. 9° E. to the first bound by the river." The price was fifty pounds.

The original proprietors of township No. 9 spoke of Bolton grant as a tract of land in the possession of John Bolton, as though there was some question in their minds as to whether Bolton was the rightful owner of it. .

BOLTON'S PETITION TO THE GENERAL COURT.

The following appears upon the records of the General Court early in 1762: "A petition of John Bolton, living in the branches of Westfield River, setting forth that in the year 1736 the Great & General Court made a grant of 200 acres of land in the township of Methuen to Capt. John Foot of Amsbury, who soon after sold the same;

that upon the line between this province & New Hampshire 127 acres of said land, purchased by the petitioner fell within the bounds of New Hampshire, and that in the year 1757 he petitioned the general court for relief, & was then encouraged by a committee of the Court to be relieved, but nothing was done; & praying that the case may be now considered. In the House of Representatives Ordered. That the Committee for the sale of Western Lands be directed to except the 250 acres of land (now in possession of John Bolton) in the sale; and that the said 250 acres be reserved to the further order of this Court.

In Council read & noncurred, & ordered that the petition be dismissed.

In the House read & concurred.

In the House of Representatives Ordered. That the Committee for the sale of lands at the westward be directed to except 250 acres of land now in possession of John Bolton & adjoining his house, & that the same be reserved for the further order of this court.

In Council read & concurred.

Consented to by the Governor."

BOLTON'S DEED TO ELDAD TAYLOR.

Bolton never was disturbed by any controversy about his title; and in 1763, on the 21st of September, he sold to Eldad Taylor thirty acres from the northeast corner of his grant, a description of which may not be uninteresting:

" Beginning at the northeast corner by a beech staddle with stones about it, thence W. 15° N. 40 rods; thence S. 15° W. 120 rods; thence E. 15° S. 40 rods; thence N. 15° E. to the first mentioned bound; containing 30 acres, & bounded west & South by Bolton's land, north by land of John Murray, & east by lands of John Moseley, Josiah Parks & John Bidwell."

BOLTON'S DEED TO BURT AND LYMAN.

By deed dated April 16th, 1764, describing himself of township No. 9, in consideration of £200, he sold to Samuel Burt and John Lyman, both of Northampton, the larger part of the grant, and described it as follows:

" Being part of a grant of land made by the General Court of said Province to the said John Bolton, which part of said grant lieth on the southerly side of said grant adjoining the town of Blandford; the length of said giant being 208 rods. The part hereby conveyed is as follows: beginning at a bass staddle with stones about it at the south east corner of land belonging to Eldad Taylor; thence running southerly 90 rods to Blandford line; thence W. 20° N. 208 rods to stake & stones standing on the bank of the west branch of Westfield River; thence running northerly on land of David Bolton 90 rods to stake & stones; thence easterly to a hemlock tree which is the southwest corner of said Taylor's land; thence easterly to the bass tree first mentioned."

THE SALE TO TEN TOWNSHIPS JUNE 2, 1762.

These five grants, Shelden and Clapp's, Ingersoll's, Williams', Green and Walker's, and Bolton's, were all included within the bounds of Township No. 9, which was sold by auction June 2d, 1762. Ten townships were sold at the same time by auction at Boston. The order under which these sales were made, and committee appointed to make the sale, was passed by the General Court February 17th, 1762.

Concerning this sale Dr. Holland, in his "History of Western Massachusetts," makes the following statement: "As the finances of the Colony were embarrassed, and money became accumulated in individual hands, private enterprise found more extended fields of operation, and land speculations came to mingle in the schemes of those who had the means to engage in them. The peace which followed the events of 1760 gave opportunity for these operations, and the General Court ordered ten townships in the western part of the colony, on the 2d of June, 1762, to be sold at Boston, by auction, to the highest bidder. They were sold by their numbers, in order, as follows:

"No. 1. East Hoosac, now Adams, to Nathan Jones, for £3200.

No. 2. A tract embracing the present towns of Peru and Hinsdale, to Elisha Jones, for £1460.

No. 3. The present town of Worthington, to Aaron Willard, for £1860.

No. 4. The present town of Windsor, called Gageboro' at first, to Noah Nash, for £1430.

No. 5. The present town of Cummington, to John Cummings, for £1800.

No. 6. The present town of Savoy, to Abel Lawrence, for £1350.

No. 7. The present town of Hawley, to Moses Parsons, for £875.

No. 8. The present towns of Lenox and Richmond, to Josiah Dean, for £2550.

No. 9. The present town of Chester, at first called Murrayfield, to William Williams, for £1500.

No. 10. The present town of Rowe, to Cornelius Jones, for £380."

THE EARLY CUSTOM OF CONVEYING TOWNSHIPS TO TENANTS IN COMMON.

"When our ancestors first came to America, it was usual, in some of the New England states, for the legislatures to grant township of land to a certain number of proprietors, as grantee's in fee, to hold as tenants in common; and a great portion of the lands of Massachusetts and Plymouth colonies were originally granted in this way by the colonial legislatures." (See 2d Dana's Abridgement, p. 698; 4th Dana's Abridgement, p. 70; Angle & Ames on Corporations, c. vi. §1; Sullivan on Land Titles, pp. 39, 40, 44-48.)

This custom did not apply to private grants, such as have been referred to and described. The plats of the Shelden & Clapp grant and of the Bolton grant were lost. Many others have been lost wholly or in part through inattention to the importance of their preservation. Those that remain are now carefully cared for in the Secretary of State's Department in the State House at Boston.

CHAPTER SECOND.

Township No. 9.

Township No. 9 was bounded north by Chesterfield, then called New Hingham, and by Worthington, then called township No. 3, in the same group with township No. 9; west by Becket, then called township No 4, but not of the same group of townships with No. 9; on the south by Blandford and by Westfield New Addition; on the east by Southampton and by Northampton. It was estimated as containing 32,200 acres of land, including the former grants. Out of township No. 9 were carved the whole of the town of Chester and the whole of the town of Norwich, including the Green & Walker, the Williams, and the Ingersoll grants. When the town of Montgomery was incorporated, about half the Ingersoll grant was included. In the year 1783 the northwest corner of this township was severed from Chester and became part of Middlefield.

The Original Proprietors of No. 9.

This township, as we have seen, was sold by auction at Boston, June 2d, 1762, to William Williams of Hatfield, for £1,500. For some reason, which does not appear, Williams did not take it, and it passed at once into the possession of John Chandler and Timothy Paine of Worcester, John Murray of Rutland and Abijah Willard of Lancaster, all in the county of Worcester, who took Williams' place in the transaction and were recognized by the provincial government as the purchasers and original proprietors of township No. 9. They did not at this time receive any instrument conveying to them an absolute title in fee; but they took it subject to certain conditions which they were to fulfill as conditions precedent, and which will fully appear further on, called conditions of settlement. Their title was not confirmed to them until the year 1766.

Names of Settlers before June 2, 1762.

Prior to the sale of this township, nineteen settlers, with their families, other than settlers within the grants mentioned in the preceding chapter, had taken possession of tracts of land within the limits of the proprietors' purchase and had settled upon them. These persons were David Bolton, James Bolton, James Clark, Abraham Flemming, Zebulon Fuller, David Gilmore, John Gilmore, Thomas Kennedy, William Kennedy, Moses Hale, William Mann, Ebenezer Meacham, William Miller, Moses Moss, Israel Rose, David Scott, Ebenezer Webber, John Webber and Jonathan Hart Webber. These persons had settled near the west and the middle branches of Westfield river. The settlers on Ingersoll grant were in the immediate vicinity of the east branch.

Leasing the Lands by Provincial Government.

In 1760 the General Court of the province empowered Benjamin Pratt, John Worthington and Joseph Hawley to look up cases of violation of the laws against purchasing lands of the Indians; and they were directed to "enter, in the name of the province, into any and all unappropriated lands of the province west of the Connecticut river, and to execute leases of any land or lands, as they might judge proper, to any person or persons." It does not appear how many of these settlers upon the unappropriated land of No. 9 held under these leases, or how many were there unlawfully.

Hampshire County.

Hampshire county at first comprised all the territory of the province of Massachusetts bay lying west of Worcester county. Berkshire county was established April 21st, 1761, at the same time the township which had been known by the name of Pontoosic was incorporated and named Pittsfield. Blandford, at first called Glasgow, was incorporated in 1741, and New Hingham was incorporated and named Chesterfield in 1762. Settlements and towns had sprung up all around township No. 9 at the time of its sale, but it was still substantially a wilderness, and settlers were attracted because it promised them homes at little cost aside from their own labor. Most of them were in low circumstances and brought little with them except great health and bodily endurance, willing hands and indomitable energy. Let us consider for a moment to what they came and what they had to contend with in this rough, wild and wonderfully picturesque region.

Topography of No. 9.

It is in the midst of the Green Mountain range. The formation is mostly mica schist, the strata standing vertical and the strike so nearly north and south as to serve some of the purposes of the compass. The highlands range from 1,000 feet to 1,700 feet above sea level, and present great diversity of surface, very little of it being level. This diversity of surface is the result of erosion. The great number of streams, mostly brooks, which find their way into the branches of Westfield river, have furrowed out valleys wonderfully diversified in depth and width. Up these valleys the settlers found it possible to build roads of convenient grade. Here and there in these highlands are hollows or basins, scooped out of the rocky foundations, perhaps by glaciers in remote ages, which retain the waters that come from melted snow, the rains, and often from springs, thus forming wet, swampy places, and occasionally quite large ponds. From these small brooks flow and make their way to larger streams, following the valleys that they themselves have made. Some of the old swamps have become so completely filled with the accumulations of vegetable mould and the material washed from the surrounding surface of the land, that they offer to the farmer spots of rare fertility. The soil in this region is for the most part composed of drift, with which at the surface is mingled vegetable mould, and in it are myriads of bowlders varying in size from large erratic blocks of granite to beds of fine gravel.

The settlers found this land, from the fertile lowlands to the cliffs of naked rock, well wooded with a thick growth of trees consisting of pine, hemlock, birch, poplar, maple, beech, chestnut, butternut, walnut, basswood, buttonball, ash, wild cherry, oak, elm and other New England forest trees; so that trees had to be felled and the land cleared preparatory to tillage and building.

Westfield River and its Branches.

The three branches of Westfield river, called east, west and middle branches, flow through the territory which was comprised within the original bounds of the township No. 9. The east branch extends through the entire width from north to south; the middle branch extends from a point about two miles east of the original northwest corner, in a southeasterly direction, crossing the township diagonally and empties into the east or main branch about two miles north of the original Blandford line; the west branch extends from a point about two miles south of the original northwest corner and flows at first in a southeasterly and then in an easterly course for eight or nine miles to a point near the original east line of Blandford, where it joins the east branch. From this point the main river is called Westfield river until it reaches the meadow lands of West Springfield and there it is called Agawam river. The writer of the sketch of Chester, in a book called the " History of the Connecticut Valley," persists in calling it "Agawam River" through its entire length, and in a note he makes the following comment: "This stream and its branches are often called the Westfield river, but there would be the same propriety in calling it Russell or Chester river, or in calling the Connecticut Springfield river. It should ever retain its Indian name." If "Agawam" were in fact its Indian name, there would be some force and some justice in this criticism, but such is not the fact. It is said by good authority that the word "Agawam" is an Indian word meaning "lowland, marsh or meadow, also a place below or down stream with reference to some place above or upstream." For some distance before this stream enters Connecticut river it flows through low meadows and there it is called Agawam river. Perhaps the Indians called it the agawam part of the river.

Westfield river and its branches are rapid streams, and during heavy rains they often are so swollen as to inundate some of the meadows through which they flow. Formerly when the soil of its watershed was kept moist by the shade of the forests, the earth readily absorbed water that came from melting snow and falling rain and retained it to flow off gradually by percolating through the soil, but now the water which falls in showers runs off rapidly from the dry, parched soil and naked rocks, and soon is lost in the streams and flows off, giving but little benefit to the soil except during long rains, after which the surface becomes soon dried, as also the soil below the surface. That this has an unfavorable effect upon the fertility and productiveness of this region is obvious to every observing and thoughtful person.

For many years after the first settlement of the town, these streams could be crossed at fordways only, and the fordways were impassable during high water, to the serious inconvenience and often to the detriment of the inhabitants.

Along the three branches of Westfield river are frequent level spots of alluvial land called "interval lands," and many of them are in terraces; sometimes there are terraces of a higher level composed of gravel and sand which may have been made during the Champlain period. These alluvial lands and terraces are much sought for by the farmers, many preferring them to the highlands. When faithfully cultivated they yield remunerative crops.

WHAT THE EARLY SETTLERS HAD TO CONTEND WITH.

The early settlers were poor as to money and as to goods; but they were rich in spirit and in fortitude. They were accustomed to hard fare and to subsisting upon the bare necessities of life, and were not afraid of the hardships of frontier life. They had no sawmills, no gristmills, no roads. Their first necessity was to clear the land and to build shelter for themselves and for their cattle. The log cabin, without glass windows and with the rudest of doors, was their shelter and home. To provide for themselves while clearing and preparing land enough to raise the necessary crops for the sustenance of their cattle and of themselves, was a necessity not to be put aside. The abundance of game in the forest, fish in the streams, of berries and of nuts helped to make up their daily bill of fare. But they had chosen this region for their abiding place and they had to make the best of it, hoping to better their condition in a short time. If hardships and the necessary privations incident to frontier life was their lot on the one hand, it was not without compensation on the other. It was a wild and beautiful country and reasonably fertile. To persons who had been accustomed from childhood, as many of them had, to the highlands of Scotland, these wild hills and deep glens, with a dark forest and ragged cliffs, were sufficiently delightful reminders of their native land to give them a reasonable degree of contentment. That Blandford was settled by Scotch people is attested by the name they gave it—New Glasgow—and by the Scotch names borne by so many of the people. Several of the early settlers of township No. 9 came from Blandford.

GENERAL CONDITION OF THE PROVINCE IN 1762.

About the close of the year 1762, the Province of Massachusetts Bay was in a prosperous condition. Its population was 250,000 whites and 5,000 blacks. There were, including the Province of Maine, thirteen counties and about 240 towns. The commerce of the country employed 600 vessels, owned chiefly in Boston and Salem, which were engaged in commerce with all parts of the civilized world, and many were engaged in the fisheries. There was an encouraging growth of domestic manufactures. The spinning wheel and loom were found in nearly every house; and fabrics, both woolen and linen, woven by the wives and daughters of Massachusetts farmers, furnished comfortable clothing independent of foreign supplies. Wealth was rapidly increasing in the colony, education was advancing, publishing houses were engaged in diffusing the productions of both native and foreign authors, some newspapers were published, and the colonists were a reading people. It is a noteworthy fact that many copies of Blackstone's Commentaries were sold in the colony, and the work was extensively read by persons outside of the legal profession. Speeches of popular orators and addresses of the General Court were sent into every town; and the writings of Chauncy, of Mayhew and of Edwards were read in nearly every house. There were 530 churches in New England and the worshippers were numerous. Matters of public concern were freely discussed from the pulpit, and there was a lively interest among the people in all matters pertaining to the public weal. One hundred and forty-two years had passed since the landing of the Pilgrims. Springfield had been settled 126 years, and there had grown up in the Connecticut valley many thrifty towns and settlements.

First Division of Lots Surveyed.

The propietors of township No. 9 employed Eldad Taylor and Charles Baker, two surveyors residing in Westfield, to survey and lay out the first division of lots in the township. They did this work in October and November, 1762, and they surveyed and laid out about 120 lots, most of them containing 108 acres each, and furnished a plat of the territory so surveyed to the proprietors. These lots were laid out in tiers extending N. 10° W. from Blandford line to the north line of township No. 9. This division of lots comprised nearly all the land lying between the west and middle branches of Westfield river.

In gathering historical facts few things are more satisfactory than original documents and records made and kept at the time of the events to which they relate. The records of the doings of the original proprietors, kept by their own clerk, begin with the following statement:

Beginning of the Proprietors' Records.

"No. 9. A township lying west of Southampton containing about 24,700 acres exclusive of grants, and of 250 acres now in possession of John Bolton, and bounded north on New Hingham and to run from the southwest corner of said New Hingham to the northeast corner of No. 4; then on the east line of No. 4 to the southeast corner of said No. 4; and from thence the same course to Blandford line; then to bound south on Blandford and Westfield; and east on Southampton, to William Williams for 1,500 pounds, who gave it up to John Chandler, John Murray, Abijah Willard, and Timothy Paine from whom have received twenty pounds and their bond for 1480 pounds."

"The above-written is extracted from a report of a committee of the General Court, accepted by the same, and consented to by the governor.

MR. JNO. COTTON, D. Secty.
Copy examined per TIMO. PAINE, Prop. Clerk."

PROPRIETORS' FIRST MEETING.

The first meeting of the original proprietors was held pursuant to a warrant issued by Josiah Dwight, a justice of the peace, in response to the following request:

"To Josiah Dwight, Esqr. one of his Majesty's Justices of the Peace for the county of Hampshire. The subscribers, proprietors of a township of land sold by the province to us in June last called No. 9, lying adjoining to Blandford, Westfield, Southampton, etc., in the county of Hampshire, desire you would issue your warrant for the calling a meeting of said proprietors to be held on the 5th day of January next at 10 o'clock forenoon at the house of Mr. William Lyman, Innholder, in Northampton in said county, to act on the following articles, viz:

1. To choose a moderator, proprietors' clerk, & treasurer, & to raise money for defraying the charges of lotting out said township & for the settlers to draw their lots & agree upon the method for calling proprietors' meetings for the future.

Worcester, November 18th, 1762.

ABIJAH WILLARD, } For themselves
TIMO. PAINE,   } and the other proprietors."

A warrant was issued as follows:

"Hampshire ss. To Timothy Paine, Esq., one of the above proprietors. [L. S.] Agreeably to the above request you are hereby required to notify the proprietors of the above-said township that they meet & assemble at the time & place above mentioned to act on the foregoing articles. Notice of which meeting is to be given by advertising the same in the several Boston weekly newspapers forty days at least before said meeting agreeably to law. Hereof fail not & make return of this warrant with your doings thereon to said proprietors at said meeting. Given under my hand & seal this 20th day of November A. D. 1762, & third year of his majesty's reign.

JOSIAH DWIGHT, Just. Pacis."

The record of the meeting is as follows:

"At a meeting of the proprietors of a township of land sold by the Province in June last to John Chandler, John Murray, Abijah Willard, & Timo. Paine, Esqrs. called No. 9., alias Murray Field lying adjoining to Blandford, Westfield, Southampton, &c., by warrant from the worshipful

Josiah Dwight, Esq. at Northampton in the county of Hampshire at the house of Capt. William Lyman on Wednesday the 5th day of January 1763, after due warning.

Voted. That John Chandler be moderator.
Voted. That Timo. Paine be proprietors' clerk.
Voted. That John Murray be proprietors' treasurer.
Voted. That the settlers in said township be admitted upon the conditions following, viz:

That each one within the space of three years commencing from the first of June last build a dwelling house on their lot of the following dimensions, viz: Twenty-four feet long, eighteen feet wide, & seven feet stud, & have seven acres of land well cleared & fenced & brought to English grass or plowed, & actually settle with family on the same & continue such family thereon for the space of six years, & shall also within three years from this time actually settle a Prostestant minister of the Gospel there & pay one-sixth part of the charge thereof, & that each settler have 100 acres of land as an incouragement, & that they give bond to the treasurer of said proprietors in the sum of fifty pounds conditioned to perform said conditions, & that upon their complying & performing said conditions the said lots be confirmed to them, their heirs, & assigns forever.

Voted. That the following persons be admitted settlers upon the following hundred acre lots & conditions aforesaid, viz.:

The Lots Drawn January 5, 1763.

Voted. That the following persons be admitted settlers upon the following hundred acre lots & conditions aforesaid, viz:

David Bolton,	No.	2	Thomas Kennedy,	No.	68
Asa Noble,	"	4	Robert Blair,	"	70
Thos. Noble, Jr.,	"	6	James Clark,	"	71
John Gilmore,	"	8	Absalom Blair,	"	72
John Woods,	"	11	Israel Rose,	"	75
Alexander Gordon,	"	13	James Fairman,	"	80
John Hammon,	"	15	Abner Smith,	"	82
John Lyman,	"	17	David Gilmore,	"	84
John Scott, Jr.,	"	19	William English,	"	86
John Smith,	"	21	Nathan Mann,	"	87
Benja. Matthews,	"	23	John Boyes,	"	90
John Laccore,	"	25	Andrew English,	"	92
John McIntire,	"	27	William Mann,	"	94
David Scott,	"	32	Jonathan Webber,	"	98
Ebenezer Webber,	"	33	John Brown,	"	100
Elias Lyman,	"	35	Thomas Morcton,	"	102
Levi Woods,	"	38	Samuel Elder,	"	104

Gideon Mathews,	No.	41	William Campbell, Jr.,	No.	106
William Kennedy,	"	45	William Moore,	"	108
Glass Cochran,	"	49	Thomas McIntire,	"	110
John Crooks,	"	51	Paul Kingston,	"	114
Abraham Flemming,	"	53	John Wood of Lancaster,	"	43
James Fairman,	"	54	Nathan Rose,	"	112
David Flemming,	"	56	Jesse Johnson,	"	116
John Webber,	"	64	James Black,	"	37"
John Crawford,	"	66			

The remainder of the record of this meeting is unimportant for the purposes of this history. Only thirteen of the nineteen settlers found on this territory by the proprietors when they took possession, were permitted to draw lots; of these only seven were permitted to hold one hundred acres, where they had begun their improvements; six were permitted only to draw lots with the other settlers, their wishes to retain the lands where they had begun improvement being disregarded by the proprietors; the remaining six of the nineteen settlers, James Bolton, Zebulon Fuller, Moses Hale, Ebenezer Meacham, William Miller, and Moses Moss were neither permitted to keep the lands upon which they had settled nor to draw lots with the others. Fuller, Meacham, and Miller remained and purchased farms; the other three went elsewhere.

The Policy of the Proprietors in scattering the Settlers over different parts of the Town.

It appears to have been the policy of the proprietors to so locate the settlers as to secure the settlement and cultivation of lots in all parts of the First Division. The wishes and convenience of the settlers were not consulted. Settlements had been begun within the territory of Ingersoll grant, which the proprietors thought a more desirable location than the territory sold to them. It was more accessible to Westfield, as well as to other more settled places in this part of the province. Much of the land lay near the river, was comparatively level and easily cultivated. Roads could more easily be built. The advantages of that part of the township which lies along West Branch, in the vicinity of what was afterwards known as Chester Factories, were offset by its remoteness from such roads as had then been established leading to the more settled towns. The proprietors owned but little available lands in the vicinity of Ingersoll grant. To make a successful settlement of their lands they were obliged to seek that part of the township which constituted the highlands, and which comprised a strip of territory about three or four miles wide lying immediately west of the Middle Branch and extending from the south to the north lines of the township. While this served the purposes of the proprietors, it was in many ways unfortunate for the settlers. They were obliged to go to and from their homes as best they could, the distance from one point of settlement to another being not only burdensome but the way also difficult. The proprietors neither laid out nor built any roads; they only made an allowance for roads by adding two acres and eighty rods to their one hundred acre lots. When the settlers came to the building of roads they found it impracticable to locate them where there would be the least grade or the shortest distance. Farm buildings had already been built and homes established where the proprietors had dictated. The people were too poor to abandon their homes and build anew, and so the roads must be laid to accommodate the location of their houses. The maintenance of these roads, as well as the original locations of them, has ever been a burden upon the town, entailing the original disadvantages upon succeeding generations; so that the citizens of what is known as Chester Hill still find themselves at great disadvantage in this regard. Their most pressing need is good roads of easy grade, and such roads are possible even in this hilly town. It is noticeable that the farms earliest abandoned are those most difficult of access. There are many good farms within the limits of the First Division of lots in township No. 9. Men have prospered and, despite many disadvantages, still do prosper upon these farms. The land is as strong in fertility as any in Massachusetts—stronger even than the alluvial lands bordering the Connecticut river. Nearly all the valuable crops grown in Massachusetts can be successfully cultivated here. All the ordinary fruits of New England, even peaches and grapes, are grown abundantly wherever the attempt is skillfully made. The atmosphere upon the highlands is as pure and healthful as man breathes in any part of the world. Above the fogs, the dampness, the cutting frosts, and the sweltering heat of the lowlands bordering the rivers, the summers are delightful, and the winters, although possibly more subject to strong winds than among the lowlands, are more even and are far less unwholesome than in the valleys, exposed as they are to sharp frosts and the chills attending the frequent thaws and the dampness, which are inseparable from the lowlands. Why should not these highlands be more populous? What explanation is more forcible than the existence of so many breakneck roads, and the lack of roads of easy grade—the building of which is, no doubt, practicable?

Where Some of the Settlers Came From.

It is difficult and perhaps practically impossible at this time to ascertain where all these settlers and purchasers of lots in township No. 9 came from. Most of them were adventurers seeking cheap lands, and most of them were poor. The Boltons came to this township from Blandford, and so did John Crooks, John Scott, Jr., and Glass Cochran. Andrew and William English, and probably the Gilmores, came from Pelham. Elias and John Lyman lived in Northampton and never settled in township No. 9. Elias Lyman gave his lot to his two sons, Stephen and Timothy, who, packing their worldly effects into a chest and carrying it between them, one hand grasping a handle of the chest and the other an axe, made their way on foot to the highlands of No. 9. Here they made their homes and became useful and honored citizens. The farms which their industry changed from a forest to fertile fields are now owned by their descendents, whose lives have reflected credit to the name they bear. Stephen Lyman took for his wife Anna Blair of Weston. Were Absalom and Robert Blair her relatives, and did they come from Weston? Timothy Lyman married Dorothy Kinney. John Boyes, John Woods, and probably James Black and Levi Woods came from Rutland, the town in which John Murray lived. John Wood came from Lancaster where Abijah Willard lived. Jesse Johnson and John Hannum came from Southampton. Abner and John Smith came from Northampton. Tradition says that John was a man of extraordinary physical strength and endurance, and that when he came to the highlands of No. 9 he came all the way on foot, carrying on his back a five-pail iron kettle. His first wife, Abigail, died August 12th, 1767, and the headstone at her grave in the cemetery on Chester Hill is the oldest in town. He married for his second wife Abiline Cors, November 10th, 1767. Gideon Matthews was a resident of Torrington, Conn., and the son of Benjamin Matthews of that place, who afterwards moved to Westfield, but never resided in township No. 9, although he drew a lot in the first division; but Gideon settled in No. 9. Israel Rose came from Granville and settled near the Middle Branch of Westfield river as early as 1760. His wife was the daughter of Benjamin Matthews. It is probable that Nathan Rose was his brother. The Nobles were Westfield men, but never became residents of No. 9, nor did they fulfill the conditions upon which they drew their lots. Ebenezer Meacham came from Enfield, Conn. It does not appear where the Webbers came from. Jonathan Hart Webber was a single man, and in 1771 he took for his wife Keziah Cooley of Springfield. Timothy Smith came from Wallingford, Conn., and on the 5th of October, 1763, he received from the proprietors a deed of 500 acres of land located between the East and Middle Branches of Westfield river, abutting mostly upon the Middle Branch and included the southerly part of Goss Hill. The price was £225, for which he gave his bond to the proprietors and secured it by a mortgage upon his 500 acres.

William Miller, who was excluded by the proprietors at the drawing of lots in January, 1763, purchased 100 acres of land toward the north part of the township, at the confluence of the east branch and a brook for many years called Miller's brook, but now called Little river. The deed was dated November 3d, 1763. This land was interval land for the most part, is still owned by his descendents, and is considered a valuable farm at this time. The price was £35.

John Boyes, Levi Woods, John Woods of Rutland, John Wood of Lancaster, John Crooks and Glass Cochran gave up or otherwise disposed of their lots. They did not become residents of the new township. Malcom Henry came from Oakham early in 1763, and on the 25th of April, 1764, took from John Woods of Rutland a deed of his lot No. 11, and settled upon it and built a house and set up the first inn in that part of the township. It was located southeasterly from the meeting-house, a short distance southerly from the road leading to Littleville. The old cellar-place and the very deep well were filled up recently by the present owner of the land.

Settlers Upon Ingersoll Grant.

Samuel Webb, son of David Ingersoll, grantee, came to township No. 9 and settled on land that he inherited from his father. Nathaniel Weller and Ebenezer King, both Westfield men, came and settled near East Branch. But these people had nothing to do with the original proprietors in the matter of their holdings. February 2d, 1763, Benjamin Matthews, then of Westfield, sold to Amaziah Dickinson of Amherst, the north end of the tracts which he bought of Weller, and described it as located in a place called "Westfield River Branches, otherwise called Murray Field, otherwise called number Nine," but Dickinson did not become a resident of this township.

John Bolton resided just over the line in Blandford on the land that was conveyed to him by John Foye, one of the original proprietors of Blandford. The land which Benjamin Matthews conveyed to his son Gideon, having been re-conveyed to him, he sold to John Mosely of Westfield, for sixty pounds, by deed dated February 6th, 1764.

A deed, remarkable for its indefiniteness, was given by Samuel Webbs, then of Scituate, to Job Clapp of the same place, April 12, 1763, in consideration of twenty-one pounds. The description runs as follows:

"Five hundred acres of land lying and being in the County of Hampshire, part of a large tract of land which I own in partnership with my brother Thomas Webbs as tenants in common & undivided, the said 500 acres to be as good for quality as the whole tract is one acre with another. The whole of said tract of land is particularly bounded & described in a deed of bargain & sale which David Ingersoll gave to my father, Thomas Webb, bearing date April 7th, 1738."

The First Houses Built by the Settlers.

None of the first houses built by the settlers now remain. There were people living a few years since who saw some of these old houses and remembered how they were constructed. Many of the old cellar-places remain and mark the spot where the houses stood. The cellar walls and the foundations of the houses were made of rough stones and without mortar. Around many of the old cellar-places lilacs and rosebushes now grow and blossom; these are fragrant and beautiful mementos that were planted by female hands as expressions of their love for the beautiful, and were emblematic of the refinement and sweet influence of mothers and sisters whose loving and tender sympathy shed a holy fragrance in those old homes. These old houses were rudely constructed. A huge stone chimney was built up through the center of the house with a spacious fireplace in each of the principal rooms, and in cold weather they were liberally supplied with fuel, which was cheap and close at hand; and even then often it was only with the aid of screens and high-backed settles that the inmates of these houses could keep themselves comfortable while hovering round the blazing fire. Few of these houses could boast of glass windows. The doors were large and heavy and fastened with great wooden latches, which were lifted from the outside by pulling a string called the latch-string, passing through a small hole in the door just above the latch. At night the door was made secure by drawing in the latchstring. To say, "You will find the latchstring out," was an invitation to come and an assurance of welcome.

Conditions of the Early Settlers as to Household Conveniences.

In these days of gaslight and of electricity, tallow candles are regarded with contempt, and one would commiserate the misfortune of those who are compelled to use them; but in the days of these early settlers they were a luxury, almost the acme of household convenience. A lighted pine knot served them for a torch to go about at night. But the bright fires in their ample fireplaces lighted up their apartments more cheerfully than are the rural homes of to-day. The preservation of the household fire was a matter of great concern. To lose it involved a journey to the nearest neighbor to borrow live coals. The nearest neighbor was often at quite a distance—half a mile or more. The tinder box was not always available. It is said of one of the early settlers that he brought the household fire with him, when he came with his family, carefully and successfully preserving it during a journey occupying several days, and it was preserved, without once going out, for many years. Yet these people were neither fire worshipers nor ancestor worshipers.

Whatever furniture and other articles for domestic uses were at their command, must have been rude enough. But few of these articles, if any, have been preserved. Of clocks perhaps there were none; at any rate, they were in but few houses. People unused to timepieces learn to judge quite accurately of the hour of day by the experience of long observation, although unable to clearly explain how they do it. The noon hour was determined by a noon-mark cut upon the doorsill or upon the window sill, serving in fair weather like a dial to inform the housewife when to sound the dinner signal. The poverty of these people in 1763, in the matter of household conveniences, may be estimated from their condition in this regard a quarter of a century later. The late John J. Cook of Huntington, in relating to me the experience of his father, Pearly Cook, who came to this township about twenty-five years later than the time we are considering, told me that his father came alone, a young, unmarried man, and was obliged to build a rude house at first and live like any frontiersman. Neither pails nor pans were to be had; and so he cut up the butt of a tree into short blocks which he converted into troughs, of which one served for a milk pail and others for milk pans. In the more thickly settled part at the east branch of Westfield river, two or three miles distant from his house, he succeeded in procuring a large iron spoon which served him for many purposes; with it he skimmed his "pans" of milk and stirred the cream and made it into butter, the iron spoon serving for a churn dasher and for a paddle to work the butter with, and for many other uses. His other appliances for housekeeping were equally rude. But he was as well off as many of his neighbors.

. MINISTER LOT AND THE FIRST MEETING-HOUSE.

Of the lots which were laid out for the first division, No. 18, being centrally located, of good elevation, and overlooking a good deal of the surrounding country, and otherwise well adapted to the purpose, was laid out as the "Minister Lot." It contained 100 acres of land besides the usual allowance for roads, and a plat of "eight acres for a meeting-house place, training field and burying place" was laid out on the south side toward its westerly end.

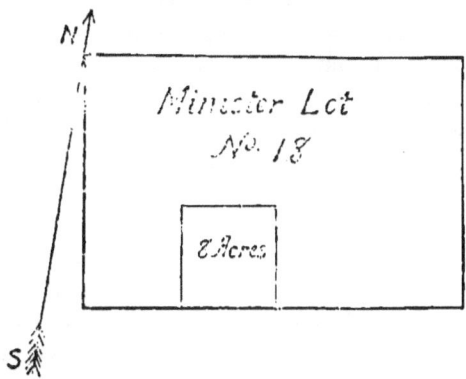

Within the limits of these eight acres is the present meeting-house, schoolhouse, and the cemetery. The first meeting-house was erected, but not completed, in the year 1767, and stood a few rods south of the present one. The foundation, or underpinning, remained to mark the spot and show its size upon the ground until a few years since, when nearly all the underpinning was removed and the stones used for other purposes, leaving merely a ditch to show where the foundation was upon which stood the first meeting-house in the town of Murrayfield. It was forty-five feet long by forty wide and twenty-foot posts. The frame was set up and boarded and shingled, the lower floor laid and the doors made by the original proprietors, Chandler, Murray, and Paine being the proprietors' committee to attend to this duty, which was one of the conditions of their purchase. The house was placed north and south, the front door opening to the north, and there were two smaller doors, one on the east and the other on the west side. Each of the proprietors of the township reserved a pew spot on the lower floor. John Murray's was seven feet long by six feet wide and was located at the right of the front door. Timothy Paine's was of the same dimensions and was located at the left of the front door. John Chandler's was eight feet long by six feet wide and was located at the right of the east door. Abijah Willard's was also eight feet long by six feet wide and was located at the left of the west door. The pew spot of James Otis, who had been admitted one of the proprietors of the township, was at the right of the west door and was six feet square. Several years intervened before this meeting-house was completed. At first the town was not able to finish it, so the work was done little at a time, and the windows were put in one at a time as the town could afford; so several years passed before they were all in. The windows were boarded up during the winter. In this building the town meetings were held. The records of town meetings indicate that sometimes the meeting-house was not sufficiently comfortable for even a town meeting, for the meeting would be opened and a moderator chosen; then immediately it adjourned to a private house and there finished the business of the meeting. This was entirely practicable, for the qualification for voting cut off all whose valuation fell below £20. These adjournments never occurred except in the winter. The religious meetings also were held sometimes at private houses, for there were no means of heating the church. Preaching on the Sabbath was also held at the public inn.

A new generation of men has grown up and passed middle life since the time when all the enrolled militiamen were required to turn out once or twice a year, with the arms and equipments required by law, for drill and inspection. In recent times so many grew to regard this as an unnecessary burden that the law was modified to accommodate this aversion to a duty which our ancestors regarded as absolutely necessary to safety and good government. The disposition to shirk public duties which are attended with personal inconvenience is a sin whose fruits will sooner or later be visited upon our children. At one time two military companies were maintained contemporaneously within the present limits of Chester. The regard for military honors which prevailed in the olden time is well attested by the frequent election to offices of trust and honor, in both church and state, of men who rejoiced in the right to prefix to their names the titles colonel, captain, lieutenant, ensign, and sergeant. Training days were a break in the monotony of rural life, such as cattle-show days are to the modern rural population. This little plat of eight acres was the scene of many stirring events in the early history of the town. To this spot all the town folks came to do and to receive those things which men do and seek for the preservation of society, for the elevation and refinement of social life, and for consolation in those afflictions which are common to all. The church, the schoolhouse, the training field, the cemetery; what a wealth of memory centers here! Upon the headstones you may read the names of men and women who were active in the events which transpired within these eight acres in years long since passed, and who were loved and honored in their day and generation.

The Township named Murrayfield.

The proprietors named this township Murrayfield. They were much disturbed and disappointed by reason of the former grants out of this territory. Their discontent found expression in their memorial to the General Court of the province, in December, 1763, representing the facts of their purchase for £1,500; that they had laid out part of the township into lots and expended large sums of money to bring forward the settlement. They set forth the fact of their disappointment at finding the township so uneven and mountainous, and described it as "divided into three parts by three very rapid, rocky rivers; the banks of which rivers are so steep and rocky that it is almost impossible to pass from one side of said rivers to the other."

Proprietors' Complaint to the General Court.

They complained that about 7,500 acres of the best land had been taken up in former grants and by a pond covering about 500 acres; also, that they found nineteen settlements begun upon the best of the land, and that they had not the power to turn them off, and that if they had the power it would be attended with great trouble and expense, and so they were obliged to give them 100 acres of land each where they had begun to settle; that the only place they could find to lay out the town plat was upon a very high mountain, and that it would always be extremely difficult to get to it, and that they must necessarily expend great sums of money in making roads over mountains and in building expensive bridges over the three rapid rivers. Wherefore they prayed that a part of the sum paid by them for the township be refunded, or else that they be recompensed by the grant of a piece of province land near to or adjoining the township, either in Hampshire or Berkshire counties, "to enable them to make roads and bridges in said township."

THE PROPRIETORS OBTAIN AN ADDITIONAL GRANT OF LAND.

On the 3d of February, 1764, the General Court "ordered that 1,200 acres of the unappropriated lands of the province be granted to the petitioners, and that they present a plan thereof to this court within twelve months from this time for their confirmation, which is in full consideration for the complaint made in the petition." April 26th, 1764, the proprietors presented to the General Court the plan of a tract of land containing 1,200 acres, located in Hampshire county. It was bounded east by No. 4 of the Narragansett grants; north by Huntstown, afterwards incorporated under the name of Ashfield; and west and south by province land. This tract of 1,200 acres is within the present bounds of Cummington. In the "History of the Connecticut Valley," published in 1879, it is erroneously stated that this tract was west of Murrayfield, township No. 4, that was afterwards incorporated under the name of Becket, being mistaken for No. 4 of the Narragansett grants, which were made to the descendents of those who were in the Narragansett fight with the Indians.

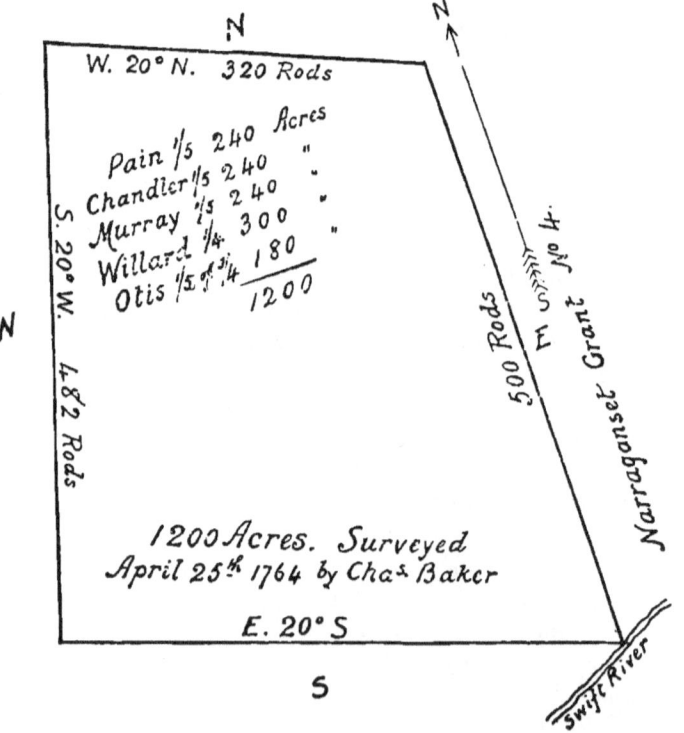

The original proprietors never built any public ways within the limits of Murrayfield, nor any bridge over either of the "three very rapid, rocky rivers" mentioned in their petition. Their conduct in the matter of building roads and bridges can best be told in the language of a memorial to the General Court by the people of Murrayfield and Norwich in January, 1779.

CONDUCT OF THE PROPRIETORS IN THE MATTER OF BRIDGES.

After representing the absolute necessity for a bridge over East Branch at the place where Norwich bridge was afterwards built, the memorial sets forth "That in the year 1764 there was granted by the Honorable General Court of this state unto Timothy Paine, Esq., and others, the proprietors of Murrayfield, 1,200 acres of land adjoining to No. 5, for the extraordinary cost they, the said proprietors of Murrayfield, said they had been at in building bridges across said river and its branches, and in making roads in Murrayfield, as was represented by them in a petition to the General Court which is to be seen on record in the Secretary's office, which cost they, the said proprietors, were never at, neither did they ever build a bridge, nor were they at any cost in building one, or in making roads, either directly or indirectly; as there were no bridges ever built across said river or its branches in Norwich or Murrayfield, and as said petitioners did, soon after they had got the town incorporated, raise the price of their lands to such an extravagant price that it hindered people from buying in said town, and as a number of the proprietors of said Murrayfield have for a number of years past gone off to the enemy, so that people who would have been glad to have purchased their farms in town could not buy because said proprietors could not be found, which has been a great hindrance to the town's settling; and the people that came first into town were many of them low and poor in the world, and always have had a great many roads and of great length to make and maintain in a new and rough country, which in a great measure was occasioned by the proprietors fixing their settling lots in every part of the town, which necessarily made more roads in the town to be made and kept in repair, which has kept the people low and behindhand.

"Therefore we pray your Honors that some method may be devised that a bridge may be built across said river and its branches either by said grant of land which the proprietors got granted to them for services they never did, or out of their estates, or any other way your honors in your wisdom shall see most fit."

Notice of this petition was ordered to be given to Timothy Paine, who appears to have remained loyal to his country. Chandler, Murray and Willard left the country as tories, and were of those who were by law forbidden to return.

In support of the statements made in their memorial, the petitioners obtained and laid before the General Court the affidavits of Stephen Lyman, Gideon Matthews, James Clark, John Smith and William Miller, who were among the first settlers of Murrayfield, who in said affidavit say "that in the year of our Lord 1762 the proprietors of No. 9, known by the name of Murrayfield, proposed to admit sixty settlers to draw for lots in said township of one hundred acres each, including those that had begun on said lands before the purchase. The number of those on the land before the proprietors' purchase were nineteen persons, viz.: Zebulon Fuller, James Clark, John Webber, Thomas Kennedy, William Mann, David Bolton, John Gilmore, Israel Rose, Moses Moss, Ebenezer Meacham, William Miller, David Scott, Ebenezer Webber, Jonathan Hart Webber, William Kennedy, Abraham Flemming, Moses Hale, James Bolton, David Gilmore. Seven of the above men were allowed to hold 100 acres where they had before begun to labor, on the conditions of a bond as the other settlers were under. Six of the nineteen were allowed only to draw lots with the other settlers promiscuously. The other six were not allowed by said proprietors the privilege of drawing lots with the other settlers, nor of holding their lands by their being on before their purchase." After reciting the conditions of the bond, the affidavit proceeds: "The settlers were under no obligations to do anything toward making roads or bridges, neither have said proprietors laid out any cost to make roads or bridges in said town since the settlement of the town. Only thirty-one of the sixty settlers have had lots given them by said proprietors. There is no pond in said township, excepting the pond that is mostly in Green & Walker's grant. According to the best of our judgment the former grants are no better lands than the township is taken together."

Signed by

"STEPHEN LYMAN,
GIDEON MATTHEWS,
JAMES CLARK,
JOHN SMITH,
WILLIAM MILLER.

HAMPSHIRE ss. FEBY 10th, 1779.

Then the within named Stephen Lyman, Gideon Matthews, James Clark, John Smith & William Miller, after being carefully examined & cautioned to testify the truth, made oath that the within deposition according to the best of their knowledge contains the truth and nothing but the truth. Before me,

ABNER MORGAN, Justice of the Peace."

Timothy Paine appeared and made an able effort to defend the proprietors. He claimed that the proprietors had done their part in the matter of making roads and bridges, inasmuch as they had given, at the time they assigned lots to the settlers, the necessary lands for highways. He denied that the proprietors, in their petition to the General Court in 1764, said that they had built a single bridge across said river, or ever made any roads in said town. He then reiterated the substance of their petition, and annexed a copy of it taken from the proprietors' book; and he claimed the extraordinary prosperity of the town was due to the proprietors, and denied the charge that they raised the prices of their land to an extravagant price after the incorporation of the town. He averred "that all the proprietors except one carried on settlements, and some of them had the greatest improvements of any in the place. And their improvements were taxed with other inhabitants in said town and did their part in making bridges and roads."

He claimed that the scattering of the settlers, as the petitioners stated, was for the best interest of the settlers themselves. He also claimed "that the 1,200 acres of land granted the proprietors lay without the lands of any town, and at the time the grant was made was looked upon as of little value, and, according as lands were sold at that time, not worth more than sufficient to recompense the proprietors for the other complaints mentioned in their petition on which said grant was founded, exclusive of making roads and bridges."

He represented lastly: "That by the late law for taxing non-resident proprietors' lands, the proprietors of Murrayfield have been taxed in a greater proportion than any other new town in the neighborhood of Murrayfield; and the inhabitants of said town have had the benefit of said taxes, and they can afford to build bridges and make roads."

The General Court decided in favor of the petitioners by a vote of 31 for to 19 against them ; and passed an act, June 17th, 1779, that the bridge be built at the expense of the original proprietors. The bridge was built, and several lots belonging to Timothy Paine were sold to pay the expense.

JAMES OTIS ADMITTED TO BE A PROPRIETOR.

In June, 1763, James Otis of Barnstable was admitted to a share in township No. 9, as one of its proprietors, by a deed, of which the following is a copy:

"Whereas John Chandler of Worcester, John Murray of Rutland, and Timothy Paine of Worcester, Esqrs. all of the county of Worcester, are interested in three fourths of a tract of land lying in the county of Hampshire, containing about 24,700 acres exclusive of grants & of 250 acres in the possession of John Bolton, said tract being bounded north on New Hingham & to run from the south west corner of New Hingham to the north east corner of No. 4; thence on the line of No. 4, & from thence in the same course to Blandford line; thence to bound south on Blandford & Westfield, & east on Southampton; which tract of land lies in common & undivided, except such part thereof as hath been given away to encourage the settlement of said town. And whereas the tract of land was sold in June last by a committee of the General Court of the Province of Massachusetts Bay to the said John Chandler, John Murray, Timothy Paine, & Abijah Willard of Lancaster, Esqrs. upon conditions of their fulfilling certain conditions of settlement as may appear by the vote of the General Court. Now be it known that the said John Chandler, John Murray, & Timothy Paine in consideration of the sum of £225 lawful money paid unto us by James Otis of Barnstable in the county of Barnstable, Esqr. the receipt whereof is hereby acknowledged, do by these presents so far as in us lies give, grant, demise, & quit unto him, the said James Otis, his heirs & assigns, all our right in & unto one fifth of three fourths of said tract of land as it lies in common & undivided, excepting what hath been given away to encourage settlers as aforesaid, and the public lands in said township reserved for schools, first settled minister, & ministry. The said James Otis performing his proportional part of all duties & obligations of settlement laid on said township with the other proprietors. To have & to hold the hereby quitted & released premises to him, the said James Otis, upon the conditions aforesaid to be by him, his heirs, & assigns held in as full a manner as the said John Chandler, John Murray, & Timothy Paine might have held the same by virtue of the original purchase, in June last.

"In witness whereof the said John Chandler, John Murray, & Timothy Paine have hereunto set their hands & seals this tenth day of June A. D. seventeen hundred & sixty-three.

JOHN CHANDLER, & SEAL.
JOHN MURRAY, & SEAL.
TIMO. PAINE, & SEAL."

CHAPTER THIRD.

THE OLD ROAD FROM EAST BRANCH TO THE MEETING-HOUSE OR CENTER.

A few rods southerly from the point where the highway turns off up the valley of the Middle Branch of Westfield river, a road branches from the main highway and extends westerly to Moose mountain, so-called, and on up the hillside in the valley of a brook to Chester Center. For the distance of about a quarter of a mile from the foot of Moose mountain the road is very steep and more dreaded by teamsters than any other road in the neighborhood for some miles around. At the top of this steep pitch and on the north side of the road is an old cellar-place by the side of which but a few years since stood a Lombardy poplar, a prominent landmark. This tree now lies upon the ground in a state of decay, having fallen several years since; but it is replaced by a younger one which sprouted up from the old root and bids fair to rival its parent if spared by the woodsman's axe. On this spot stood the dwelling house of the David Scott who, January 5th, 1763, drew the lot upon which this house stood. Here is a nearly level tract of fertile land containing several acres, sheltered on the north by a mountain called "Little Moose," and sloping gently toward the east and affording a charming view in the direction of East Branch and beyond down the glen toward Russell, through which Westfield river flows. Near this cellar-place the old road can be traced toward the east until it becomes lost at the edge of the bank of the "dugway," under which lies the present highway. In the other direction the road can be traced winding off in a northwesterly course for half a mile or more through a valley which cuts the ridge of Little Moose, and here is another old cellar-place close by the old roadway. On this spot probably stood the house of Absalom Blair. The only thing in favor of it as a location for a home is that it is sheltered both from winds and from observation, and there is a spring near by. Following this ancient road further on we pass through this valley and come to the northerly side of Little Moose, which descends to Middle Branch, but the road without descending winds westerly on the north side of the ridge of the mountain for the distance of about three-quarters of a mile and passes a spot where another ancient house stood by the roadside and known as the Riley place. It may have been and probably was the old home of James Clark. Passing on by this spot for a quarter of a mile further we come to another cellar-place on a ridge where a good view of the surrounding country challenges the traveler to pause. On the other side of the old road opposite the cellar-place are three ancient elms in a row. The cellar-place is considerably larger than the other ones we passed, which suggests that the house was an inn. There are also two old wells near by. It is altogether probable that here stood the house of Thomas Kennedy, and that he kept an inn. It would seem that this road had been in existence for some time before the township was sold in June, 1762, for Thomas Kennedy was one of the nineteen settlers whom the proprietors found there, and James Clark was another. Their houses had been built before the time of the sale of the township, no one knows how long. Kennedy's house stood upon lot No. 68 of the first division. It is probable that he was permitted to keep the land upon which he had settled.

At this spot a charming view opens to the eye. We are standing near the brow of the glen of Middle Branch upon the southwesterly side and looking toward the east. The foreground is a pasture and we are looking upon out-cropping ledges, bowlders, grass, weeds, brakes, bushes, and scattered trees. No landscape gardener has been here attempting to improve the grade. There is no gently graduated slope; but where the pasture ends abruptly at the distance of a quarter of a mile or less, the surface is considerably lower than at the place where we are standing. At the northwest the pasture is lost at the edge of a forest, over the top of which blue hilltops are seen in the distance. Before us the pasture ends in a sharp outline which suggests a gulf beyond, and the mind is filled with interrogation points. This outline is clear and distinct against the somewhat dim, hazy, and bluish tint of the north side of the glen which is the south slope of Goss Hill. As our field-glass is directed to Goss Hill we almost expect that it will disclose a Rip Van Winkle form slumbering under the southerly face of some ledge. In the sweet and delicious atmosphere at this place one could sleep and dream that sorrow is but a false creation, proceeding from the heat-oppressed brain. Goss Hill stretches toward the north from the confluence of Middle and East Branches, and also forms the west side of the glen of East Branch, which is concealed from our view by the trees along its bank, save a rift where the eye catches the sparkle of water rushing over the stony bed at the foot of Goss Hill; and at the right of this the land rises toward the summit of Norwich Hill. Beyond all these, and dimly outlined, are still higher lands, the whole presenting one grand panorama receding with deepening shades until lost in the distant horizon. If we turn our gaze toward the west we will observe that the surface of the land gradually ascends in a broad plain for the distance of seventy-five to one hundred rods and ends abruptly at the summit of a quite regular ridge, with apparently a gulf beyond, relieved by a strip of the summit of the southerly side of the glen of West Branch and the heights of Blandford beyond that, bluer than the hills on the opposite side and giving a prettier effect. The mental interrogation points are kept in check only by the fact that their gratification is at the price of a somewhat laborious climb to the summit of the ridge. The valley immediately beyond this ridge contains a small brook, and through this valley lies the present road leading to Chester Center.

SECOND MEETING OF THE PROPRIETORS.

The proprietors held their second meeting at the house of Thomas Kennedy, September 29th, 1763. It is probable that their journey to this spot was on horseback. At that season of year when the gorgeously colored foliage is at its best, their journey must have been delightful beyond the power of language to describe. At this meeting they agreed to draw the "blank lots already laid out, so that each proprietor may enjoy his rights therein in severalty." One article in their warrant was: "To agree with some suitable person for building mills in said town, and to see what encouragement shall be given the person that shall undertake the building of said mills," but no formal action was taken touching this subject. After choosing a moderator the meeting adjourned to the 1st of October, at which time they proceeded to divide among themselves the remaining lots of the first divisions.

Abijah Willard drew Nos. 3, 7, 10, 34, 16, 52, 42, 55, 61, 73, 78, 79, 91, 93 and 89. He then exchanged lot. No. 89 with Abraham Flemming for lot No. 53, and lot No. 10 with David Gilmore for lot No. 84, and lot No. 73 with David Scott for lot No. 32.

John Murray drew Nos. 30, 44, 47, 81, 83, 88, 103, 105, 107, 109 and 113, and exchanged lot No. 88 with Nathan Mann for lot No. 92.

James Otis drew Nos. 69, 36, 39, 46, 48, 50, 76, 96 and 115, and exchanged lot No. 69 with Ebenezer Webber for lot No. 33.

Timothy Paine drew Nos. 12, 22, 26, 29, 31, 63, 67, 74, and the "make up" to 77, 62, 99, 101. Lot 77 was in two parts, the "make up" being on Middle Branch. Paine sold it to Abner Smith.

John Chandler drew Nos. 5, 9, 14, 20, 24, 28, 59, 65, 85, 95, 97 and 111, and exchanged lot No. 65 with Jonathan Hart Webber for lot No. 98. This brought the Webbers all into the same neighborhood on the westerly bank of Middle Branch. He exchanged lot No. 24 with John Crawford for lot No. 66.

The proprietors, at this meeting, appointed Thomas Kennedy, John Crawford and Abraham Flemming a committee to lay out highways and make a report to the proprietors for their confirmation. Whatever action the committee took, if any, the proprietors did nothing further touching the laying out of highways in the town.

At this meeting the question of building mills was discussed without any definite result. But it appears that shortly afterwards John Chandler built a sawmill at his own expense; for at a meeting of the proprietors held December 12th, 1764, they voted that "Lot No. 13, originally drawn by Alexander Gordon and granted back to the proprietors, be granted to John Chandler, Esq., his heirs and assigns, in consideration of his having built a sawmill in said township." It was upon the west end of this lot that the sawmill was built, nearly 300 rods southerly from the meeting-house. The west end of lot No. 13, together with the sawmill, subsequently became the property of the Searle family, and was owned by them many years. The mill was built upon "Nooney Brook," which at a lower point is called "Cook Brook." This lot was called Chandler's farm, and was occupied and carried on for him by Robert Smith. Of the highways laid out by the town of Murrayfield in 1769, one is described as laid "From the meeting-house to Col. Chandler's farm where Robert Smith lives; from said Smith's to the sawmill," etc. In 1776 two sawmills had been built, but whether both were built by Chandler is doubtful. John Smith built a sawmill very early, probably as early as 1766. In 1767 the proprietors gave Chandler lot No. 39 in the second division of lots "in consideration of his extraordinary expense in building a sawmill in said town." This lot, No. 39, is within the present bounds of Middlefield.

Third Meeting of Proprietors.

On December 12th, 1764, the proprietors held their third meeting. It was held at Lancaster in the county of Worcester. At this meeting the second division of lots was made among the proprietors as follows: Abijah Willard drew Nos. 2, 8, 11, 13, 16, 19; John Chandler drew

Nos. 1, 23, 24, 26, 27; John Murray drew Nos. 12, 14, 20, 21, 22; Timothy Paine drew Nos. 3, 7, 10, 18, 25; James Otis drew Nos. 4, 9, 17. These were all 200-acre lots and were located between the Middle Branch and the East Branch. The "Connecticut Valley History," published in 1879, makes the inexcusable error of stating that " The settlers upon the tract between the middle and east branches of the Agawam river early in 1764 were, Abijah Willard, John Chandler, John Murray, Timothy Paine and James Otis." None of these proprietors ever resided in the town of Murrayfield. Some of them owned farms in the town, which were cultivated under their directions by agents residing on the farms. They all, with the exception of James Otis whose home was in Barnstable, were residents of Worcester county, and men of prominence in the colony.

At this meeting they also included, in the second division of lots, certain interval lots on the West Branch, in the vicinity of what was for a long time known as Chester Factories. These lots were designated by letters instead of numbers.

Willard drew letters K, L, M.
Chandler drew letters O, P, Q.
Murray drew letters G, H, I.
Paine drew letters A, B, N.
Otis drew letters C, F. Otis attended none of these meetings in person; but John Murray acted for him under a power of attorney.

The larger part of the village of Chester Factories is comprised within lot P. The proprietors reserved a right to lay out a road through these interval lots on the West Branch.

No further action touching the affairs of this township appears to have been taken by the proprietors prior to the incorporation of the town of Murrayfield, except as appears in the following from the Council Records, Vol. XXV, p. 213: "June 2d, 1764, a petition of the proprietors of Murrayfield, praying that the settlers admitted therein may from time to time be impowered to call meetings to agree upon some proper method to settle the Gospel Ministry among them and to transact any other business that may be necessary.

" In council read and ordered that the petitioners have liberty to bring in a bill for the purpose mentioned."

" In House of Representatives read and concurred."

It does not appear that any further action was taken until the following year, when the proprietors procured an act of incorporation of the town of Murrayfield.

First Gristmill.

Either in the year 1764 or early in the year 1765, a gristmill was built on the left bank of the Middle Branch, near the spot where the tannery afterwards stood in Littleville. It was built under the auspices of the original proprietors, and it was probably the first gristmill built in the town. Jonathan Clapp of Northampton was the man who erected it, and he received from the proprietors a deed of the lot upon which it stood, together with the water privilege. It appears that Clapp executed a bond to the proprietors, in which his obligations touching the building of the mill were definitely stated. Some difficulty arose between him and the proprietors touching the conditons of his bond. This bond was executed by Clapp, September 8th, 1764. The penal sum was $500, and the conditions were as follows:

"The condition of the present obligation is such that if the above-named Jonathan Clapp, his heirs, executors, & administrators shall on or before the first day of July next erect a mill-dam on the falls on the Middle Branch of the river called Westfield River, in the new town called Murrayfield in said county of Hampshire, adjoining to the lot of Mr. John Webber, being lot No. 64, & erect a corn-mill thereon & finish the same well & workmanlike & keep the mill & dam to be so erected in good repair for the space of seven years from the first day of May next, & find & provide a good miller to attend to the same during the term aforesaid for the benefit of the inhabitants of said Murrayfield aforesaid to grind their grain (extraordinary casualties excepted), that then this present obligation will be void & of none effect; but in default thereof to abide & remain in full force & virture.
JONATHAN CLAPP & SEAL."

The proprietors brought a suit against him for breach of the conditions of this bond. The writ was dated April 10th, 1767 & returned to the court of common pleas at the following May term. The suit was submitted to referees, & at a meeting of the proprietors in the autumn of 1767 Abijah Willard was appointed "to attend on behalf of the proprietors upon the reference between the proprietors & Mr. Jonathan Clapp relating to the corn-mill in Murrayfield."

The record of the January term of the court, 1768, says: "This action being under reference and no report given in, ordered that the same be continued to next term under the same rule." The case was finished at the August term. The referees found against Clapp and awarded five pounds and fifteen shillings "for damages for not building and finishing the said mill and dam agreeably to the conditions of said bond, and costs of court and reference, the cost of reference being taxed at three pounds and sixteen shillings."

This mill was erected upon lot A of the the third division of lots surveyed October, 1764, located on the left bank of Middle Branch, contained 100 acres, and the proprietors called it the "Mill Lot." On the 30th of October, 1765, Jonathan Clapp, describing himself as of Northampton, gave a deed of this property to Jonathan Wait of Murrayfield and described it as follows:

"Bounded westerly on the Middle Branch of Westfield river, so-called, southerly on Timothy Smith's land; easterly on land belonging to the original proprietors of said Murrayfield; northerly on the Minister Lot, or lands of the original proprietors, together with the grist-mill, dam, & other appurtenances to said mill, standing on said Middle Branch contiguous, on, or adjoining the said tract." This describes the whole of lot A and it was bounded by Timothy Smith's five hundred acre farm on the south; on the east by lot B of the third division, which was granted to Timothy Paine, & by him sold to Gershom Rust. The highway, at first, was on that side of the river, being legally laid out in 1769 & described as "beginning at Worthington line, then southerly by Mr. Wait's mill east side of the Middle Branch, by Timothy Smith's," etc.

Other mills were built shortly after these first ones on the East Branch, both above and below the present location of Norwich bridge.

GENERAL OBSERVATIONS.

The settlers upon the proprietors' settling lots were to some degree under their protection and under their supervision; but with the settlers upon Ingersoll grant and upon Bolton grant, and possibly with those who purchased their lands of the proprietors for a money consideration, it was otherwise. All these settlers were without any organized town government, and without any officers of the law to enforce order, although they were undoubtedly amenable to the laws of the province and were subject to the jurisdiction of the courts within the county of Hampshire. But the remoteness of the officers of the law would naturally lessen their fear of the judicial machinery as a restraining influence upon their conduct, and yet, so far as we can learn, they were an orderly and law-abiding community, as we should have a right to expect from the fact that they were of puritan stock; they were British subjects; they had been educated to respect law and order and religion; wherever they went the common law went with them as their guide and rule of conduct; and they respected whatever was right and hated whatever was wrong. It was because of such people as these that our ancestors were able to establish a republic. These people had that sense of honor which insures respect for the rights of others, and the requisite courage to assert and maintain their own rights.

CHAPTER FOURTH.

INCORPORATION OF MURRAYFIELD.

The incorporation of township No. 9 under the name of Murrayfield took place October 31st, 1765. This is of sufficient importance to justify a full copy of the act, which is as follows: "Whereas the proprietors of the plantation called and known by the name of Murrayfield, have represented to this court that the inhabitants of said plantation labor under many difficulties and inconveniences by reason of their not being incorporated; for the removal thereof, Be it enacted by the Governor, Council, and House of Representatives:

"SECTION 1. That said tract of land bounded and described as follows, viz.: bounded northerly partly on Chesterfield and partly on a new township known by the name of Number Three, and runs from the southwest corner of said Chesterfield to the northeast corner of Becket; thence, on the east line of Becket, to the southeast corner of said Becket; and from thence, the same course, to Blandford line; thence bounded south, partly on said Blandford and partly on Westfield; and east, partly on Southampton and partly on Northampton, be, and hereby is, erected into a town by the name of Murrayfield; and the inhabitants thereof shall have and enjoy all such privileges and immunities as other towns in this province have and do enjoy.

"And be it further enacted:

"SECTION 2. That Eldad Taylor, Esq., of Westfield, be, and hereby is, empowered to issue his warrant to some principal inhabitant of said town of Murrayfield, requiring him in his majesty's name, to warn and notify the said inhabitants qualified to vote in town affairs, to meet together at such time and place in said town, as shall be appointed in said warrant, to choose such officers as the law directs to be chosen annually, in the month of March, and may be necessary to manage the affairs of said town; and the inhabitants, so met, shall be, and hereby are, empowered to choose officers accordingly. Oct. 31st, 1765."

There is no evidence in existence that any valuation list was taken as a basis for determining the qualification of voters. Probably such a list was taken, but it was not preserved.

July 11, 1761, an act was passed for the purpose of providing for calling meetings of the inhabitants of unincorporated plantations for the purposes of taxation by the province or by the county, and for choosing assessors to assess such taxes. Section 2 of the act reads as follows: "The assessors so chosen and sworn shall, thereupon take a list of the rateable polls, and a valuation of the estates and faculties of the inhabitants of such plantation for a rule by which to judge of the qualification of voters in meetings of the said inhabitants thereafter to be holden, until other valuation shall be made." Section 3 provided "that in case the inhabitants of any such plantation shall neglect to assemble, or being assembled shall neglect to choose all such officers as herein before are required, it shall be in the power of the court of general sessions of the peace in the county where such plantation is, and the justices of such court are required to appoint some meet persons, inhabitants of such plantation, to be assessors and collectors of such taxes as aforesaid, who shall be duly sworn to the faithful discharge of their respective trust, and shall conform to the directions and proceed by the rules which assessors and collectors in towns corporate are obliged to observe."

First Town Meeting.

The records of the town of Murrayfield begin with a copy of the act of incorporation; and then immediately the record continues as follows: "Pursuant to said act Eldad Taylor, Esq., issued this warrant under his hand and seal in his majesty's name directed to John Smith of Murrayfield, to notify the inhabitants of said Murrayfield to meet at the house of Malcom Henry in said Murrayfield on Tuesday the eleventh day of March, at ten of the clock in the forenoon, Anno Domini 1766 for the choice of town officers." The record sets forth no copy of the warrant. The inhabitants having met pursuant to the warrant, Eldad Taylor was chosen moderator, and then the following named town officers were chosen and sworn into office:

TOWN CLERK AND TREASURER, Malcom Henry.

SELECTMEN AND ASSESSORS. Timothy Smith, John Smith and Malcom Henry.

SURVEYORS OF HIGHWAYS, Thomas Kennedy, Gideon Matthews, Nathan Mann, William Miller and David Bolton.

TITHINGMEN, Samuel Elder and James Clark.

WARDENS. Israel Rose and William Mann. (Probably Fire Wardens.)

SURVEYORS OF TIMBER AND LUMBER, Abraham Flemming and Isaac Mixer.

FENCE VIEWERS, John McIntyre, Ebenezer Meacham and Ebenezer Webber.

SEALER OF WEIGHTS AND MEASURES, Jonathan Wait.

HOG-REEVES, Ebenezer King and Stephen Lyman, whose duty it was to see that the laws regulating the keeping of swine were observed, and to prosecute all offenders.

DEER-REEVES, Alexander Gordon and Samuel Webb, whose duty it was to enforce the laws which had been passed by the General Court for the preservation of deer. The only vote passed at this meeting other than the election of officers was the following: "Voted that swine shall run at large from the middle of September to the middle of May following." At this time the law required that all swine going at large on the commons from the first of April to the fifteenth of October should be sufficiently yoked or ringed in the nose. No yoke was accounted sufficient which was not the full length of the swine's neck, and half as much below the neck, and the sole or bottom of the yoke three times as long as the breadth or thickness of the swine's neck. If any swine were found unyoked or unringed, their owners were liable to pay sixpence per head, and if also found damage feasant to pay twelvepence per head, over and above double damage to the party injured; and the haywards or field-drivers, or any other person, were authorized to take and impound such swine. Towns, however, were permitted to enlarge the time by so voting at a legal town meeting.

The record shows no action of the town at this time touching the raising and appropriation of money. The reason why no measures were taken at this meeting to raise money was, probably, that the inhabitants, relying upon the expectation that the proprietors were to build the necessary roads and bridges—an expectation which the proprietors had encouraged by their promises—saw no immediate necessity for taxation. They were not then in condition to establish public schools, if, indeed, there was at that time a necessity for schools. Their first necessity was to build suitable houses for shelter, and to clear enough land to provide for the sustenance of themselves and their cattle. The incorporation of the town would have been deferred to a later period had the settlers been left to their own choice. The proprietors urged the incorporation at this time for their own advantage, and it is not improbable that one of their purposes was to escape the burden of road and bridge building. There is reason to believe that many people living within the limits of the township, particularly those living within the Ingersoll grant, were opposed to the incorporation of the town, and felt that it was a scheme to impose taxes upon them for the benefit of the proprietor settlers. Discontent arose on the part of the inhabitants of the east end of the town, which ultimately led to a division of the township.

THE FIRST TOWN CONTROVERSY.

There was enough of the Gaelic and Celtic elements among the settlers of Murrayfield to keep the affairs of the town somewhat lively. It is not at all strange that men of adventurous spirit, and who courted difficulties which would have crushed an effeminate people, should have been at times hot-headed. The spirit of contention appeared early in the town of Murrayfield in an ugly form before the time for holding its second annual town meeting was reached. It was excited to activity in this way: In September, 1766, the selectmen notified the inhabitants of the town to bring in the lists of their rateable estates on or before October 20th of that year. Before that time had expired, Timothy Smith and Malcom Henry, two of the selectmen and assessors, closed and signed a list of valuation. But John Smith, the other assessor, refused to sign it, claiming that they had no right to close the list at that time, and that the list so closed was invalid. Timothy Smith was persuaded to the same view. The two Smiths agreed to give a new notice and re-take the valuation, but Henry refused, claiming that the valuation list just taken was to all intents and purposes a legal list. The Smiths took a new list of valuation and assessed the taxes by the new list. This new list was tendered to Malcom Henry, as town clerk, in order to be lodged with him for the regulation of votes at the March meeting in 1767, but Henry refused to take it. When the inhabitants assembled at the March meeting they at once got into a dispute as to whether the qualification of voters should be determined by the first or by the second valuation list, and the voters thereupon formed into two parties and separated, each party holding a separate town meeting, and two sets of officers were chosen for the town. This led to great confusion and to law suits. The lawyers who were consulted were of opinion that neither set of officers was legally chosen. This state of affairs gave the original proprietors great anxiety; and at a meeting which they held November 4th, 1767, they drafted and sent to the inhabitants of the town the following letter:

"We, the subscribers, the proprietors of Murrayfield, have this day had a meeting; and it is with great concern that we find so many unhappy divisions subsisting in said town to the destruction of the interests of the settlers and proprietors. And after fully considering of your affairs and all circumstances relating thereto do give you our advice in your affairs, and desire your compliance as you value our future favors. First that the lawsuit subsisting between Messrs. Smith and Taggart be dropped, and that each party pay his own costs, and that at present there be an end of lawsuits relating to town affairs. That the town join and petition to the General Court at their next session, and therein set forth the whole transaction of both parties at their last March meeting, and the difficulties subsisting in said town in consequence thereof, and pray for their aid and assistance that all matters may be set right for the future."

An address setting forth the difficulties into which the town had got and praying for relief was presented to the Governor and Council and House of Representatives on behalf of the inhabitants of the town by Timothy Paine and John Murray as their agents, with the following result: "In Council January 23d, 1768, read and ordered, that Abijah Willard, Esq., Eldad Taylor and Capt. Charles Baker, or any two of them, be empowered to take a list of valuation under oath of all the rateable estates real and well and personal in said Murrayfield, they first giving at least ten days notice to said inhabitants before they proceed on said business by posting up a notification in said town, and when they have completed said list make a return thereof to Timothy Smith, John Smith and Malcom Henry, selectmen chosen in said town for the year 1766; and upon receipt thereof the said selectmen be empowered to make out their warrant to some principal inhabitant of said town, requiring him to notify a meeting of said inhabitants qualified to vote in town affairs, to meet and assemble in said town for the choice of town officers for the ensuing year, and that the valuation so taken be the rule for determining the qualification of voters at said meeting, and that Simeon Strong, Esq., be appointed to moderate at said meeting; and that if it should so happen that the said valuation can not be taken in convenient time for holding said meeting in March next, that said meeting be held as soon after as it conveniently may be; and the transactions of said inhabitants at said meeting be valid to all intents and purposes, as if said meeting had been held in the month of March." This order was passed and became a law February 11th, 1768. Abijah Willard and Charles Baker, both non-residents, took the valuation and returned the list to the selectmen named in the order, April 19th, 1768. Unfortunately neither of the former valuation lists were preserved. The list taken by Willard and Baker was as follows:

A HISTORY OF MURRAYFIELD.   57

	Polls	Houses	Oxen	Cows	Sheep	Swine	Money £	Total Personal Estate £ s.	Real Estate £	Total £ s.
Absalom Blair,	1	1	2	2	13	3	0	12	30	42
Robert Blair,	1	0	2	2	0	0	0	7	9	16
David Blair,	1	0	0	0	0	0	0	1-10	6	8
James Brown,	1	0	0	1	0	0	0	1-10	3	4-10
James Black,	1	0	0	0	0	0	0	0- 0	3	3
David Bolton,	1	0	0	2	8	0	0	4- 4	15	19- 4
James Clark,	1	1	0	1	11	1	0	5	38	43
John Crow, Jr.,	1	0	0	1	0	0	0	1-10	0	1-10
James Crow,	1	0	0	0	0	0	0	0- 0	0	0
Thomas Crow,	1	0	0	1	0	0	0	1-10	0	1-10
David Crow,	1	0	0	0	0	0	0	0- 0	0	0
Ebenezer Dowd,	1	0	0	0	0	0	0	0- 0	0	0
Samuel Ellis,	1	0	0	1	4	0	0	2- 2	3	5- 2
Bigott Eggleston,	2	0	0	1	0	0	0	1-10	24	25-10
Jebial Eggleston,	1	0	0	0	0	0	0	0- 0	0	0
Samuel Elder,	3	1	0	2	3	0	0	5- 9	34	39- 9
Caleb Fobes,	1	1	2	3	0	1	0	10-18	49	59-18
William Fobes,	1	1	0	0	0	0	0	2	0	2
Abraham Flemming,	1	1	0	2	0	1	58	8-17	30	38-17
James Fairman,	1	2	4	0	0	0	0	12	10	22
Samuel Firman,	1	0	0	0	0	0	0	0- 0	0	0- 0
Zebul n Fuller,	1	0	0	1	0	2	0	2- 8	19	21- 8
Alexander Gordon,	1	0	0	3	0	0	0	4-10	14	18-10
Malco Hery,	2	1	2	2	4	0	0	9-12	15	24-12
James Hamilton,	1	0	2	1	0	0	0	5-10	12	17-12
James Gilmore,	1	1	0	1	0	3	0	4-14	12	16-14
David Gilmore,	1	0	0	2	0	0	0	4- 0	8	12- 0
John Gilmore,	1	0	0	0	0	0	0	0- 0	0	0- 0
William Campbell,	1	0	0	1	0	0	0	1-10	5	6-10
Matthew Campbell,	1	0	0	0	0	0	0	0- 0	0	0- 0
Thomas Kennedy	2	0	0	2	10	3	0	5-14	17	22-14
William Kennedy,	1	0	0	0	0	0	0	0 0	0	0- 0
John Laccore	2	1	2	2	2	1	0	9-14	30	31-14
Lemuel Laccore,	1	0	0	0	0	0	0	0- 0	0	- -
Stephen Lyman,	1	0	0	1	0	2	5	4-12	22	26-12
Timothy Lyman,	1	0	0	0	0	0	3	0- 3-7	22	23- 3-7
Ebenezer Meacham,	1	1	2	1	8	0	0	8-14	24	32-14
Isaac Mixer,	2	2	0	2	0	1	0	7- 8	52	59- 8
Isaac Mixer Jr.,	1	0	0	1	0	1	0	1-18	6	7-18
William Miller,	1	2	0	1	10	1	0	7- 8	28	35- 8
William Mann,	1	0	0	0	2	0	0	3-10	10	13-10
Ebenezer King,	1	1	2	2	0	0	0			
Nathan Mann,	1	1	2	1	5	1	8			
William Moore,	1	1	0	2	0	0	0	5		
Daniel Meeker,	1	0	0	0	0	0	0	0- 0		
James McKnight,	1	1	2	2	0	0	0	9- 0		
John McIntire,	1	0	2	1	0	0	0	5-10	1	
Gideon Matthews,	1	0	1	1	5	2	0	5- 1	1	
Abner Pease,	1	0	0	2	0	0	0	3	3	6- -
Robert Proctor,	1	0	0	1	0	2	0	2- 6	13	15- 6
Israel Rose,	1	0	2	1	6	0	0	6- 8	16	22- 8
Nathan Rose,	1	0	0	1	6	0	0	2- 8	12	14- 8
Zebulon Rose,	1	0	0	0	3	0	0	0- 9	0	0- 9
Timothy Smith,	1	1	1	2	12	2	0	9 12	26	35-12
Abner Smith,	1	2	2	1	0	2	0	10- 6	16	20- 6
John Smith,	1	1	1	2	0	4	0	8-12	20	28-12
David Scott,	1	1	1	2	3	0	0	11- 5	20	37- 5
Thomas Smith,	1	1	1	3	1	0	0	5-10	16	21-10
Ezekiel Snow,	1	0	0	0	0	0	0	0- 0	0	- -
James Taggart	2	1	2	2	0	7	0	11-16	24	35-16
Daniel Twadwell,	1	0	0	0	3	0	0	0- 9	6	6- 9
Peter Williams,	1	2	4	3	0	0	0	16-10	12	28-10
Samuel Webb	1	0	0	1	0	0	0	1-10	0	1-10
Jonathan Wait,	1	0	0	1	0	0	0	1-10	16	17-10
Jonathan Hart Webber,	1	0	3	1	0	0	2	7-12	24	31-12-4
Ebenezer Webber,	1	2	1	1	5	0	7	8-13-4	30	38-13-4
Reuben Woolworth,	1	1	2	2	0	0	0	9	7	16- -
Thomas Wright	1	0	0	0	0	0	0	0- 0	0	- -
Total.	76	32	50	74	123	40	83			

The old record book in which the foregoing list is recorded has some time been gnawed by mice, so that the record of this list is left imperfect.

WARRANT FOR THE THIRD TOWN MEETING.

Upon receiving the valuation list the selectmen immediately issued a warrant of which the following is a copy:

"Hampshire ss. To Mr. James Fairman, one of the principal inhabitants of the town of Murrayfield. In his majesty's name you are hereby required to notify & warn all the inhabitants of the town of Murrayfield that are qualified to vote in town affairs to meet at the New Public meeting house in said town on Tuesday the fifth day of May next by eleven of the clock in the forenoon then & there to proceed to choose town officers for the ensuing year, viz: town clerk, selectmen, constables, assessors, town treasurer, tything-men, & all other ordinary town officers that are required by law to be chosen in the month of March; & also to grant money to defray the necessary charges of said town. Fail not, but make return hereof with your doings thereon to one of us before the time of meeting. Given under our hands & seals at Murrayfield this nineteenth day of April Anno Domini 1768, & in the 8th year of his majesty's reign.

TIMOTHY SMITH } Selectmen
JOHN SMITH } for Anno
MALCOM HENRY } 1766."

The warrant was duly returned and the meeting held in pursuance thereof. The following town officers were chosen:

For town clerk, John Smith; and he was chosen treasurer also.

For selectmen and assessors, Caleb Fobes, Timothy Smith, and William Miller.

For constables, Stephen Lyman and Ebenezer Webber.

For tithingmen, Israel Rose and Gideon Matthews.

For surveyors of highways, Isaac Mixer, Peter Williams, William Moore, James Fairman, James Clark, Jonathan Hart Webber, and Samuel Ellis.

For fence viewers, Ebenezer Meacham and John Laccore.

For sealer of leather, Isaac Mixer.

For surveyor of timber and lumber, Bigott Eggleston.

For deer-reeves, Ebenezer King and Samuel Fairman.

For hog-reeves, Nathan Rose and Jonathan Hart Webber.

For wardens, John Smith and Reuben Woolworth.

No money appropriations were made at this meeting; but at a meeting held the 28th of June following, £20 were appropriated for preaching, and £40 for ordinary town expenses. These sums were voted in addition to £20 voted in 1766, making in all £80.

John Smith, who was elected town clerk, took his oath of office before Joseph Hawley, a justice of the peace. The certificate of this oath was made by the magistrate in the record book of the town as follows:

"Hampshire ss. May 7th, 1768, John Smith of Murrayfield in said county of Hampshire, appearing to me by the usual written certificate to have been regularly chosen by the inhabitants of said Murrayfield to the office of town clerk for the said town at their meeting held on the fifth of May inst., the said John Smith on the seventh day of May above, took his oath respecting the bills of credit on the neighboring governments by law to be taken by town officers, & also the oath of office in the form prescribed by the law of this province to be taken by persons elected to the office of town clerk. Before me

JOSEPH HAWLEY, Justice of the Peace."

OATH CONCERNING BILLS OF CREDIT.

A law, passed by the general court of this province in December, 1748, required: "That from and after the last day of March, which shall be in the year of our Lord 1750, until the last day of March which shall be in the year 1754, every person who shall be chosen to serve in any office of the towns of this province shall, before his entrance upon said office, take the following oath, to be administered by a justice of the peace, or where no justice of the peace shall be present, by the town clerk, who is hereby impowered to administer the same, viz.: 'You, A. B., do in the presence of God solemnly declare that you have not, since the last day of March, 1750, wittingly or willingly, directly or indirectly, either by yourself or any one for or under you, been concerned in receiving or paying within this government any bill or bills of credit of either of the governments of Connecticut, New Hampshire, or Rhode Island. So help me God.'"

By reënactment this law was in force as late as 1768.

TOWN DEBTS.

The action of the town about this time, touching the payment of its debts, clearly indicates the straitened condition of the people as to money. Towns, like individuals, when under pecuniary embarrassment, will do mean things which they would scorn when in easy circumstances. The treatment of claims presented against the town during these years of its infancy, show either financial distress on the part of the town, or unconscionable meanness on the part of men whom the town continued to honor by reëlecting them to responsible positions. The town was poor.

MARCH MEETING, 1769.

The town meeting in March, 1769, was held at the house of Jonathan Hart Webber. The December meeting in 1768 was called to be held at the new house of Jonathan Hart Webber. As the public meeting-house had been built and some meetings had been held there, it must be presumed that the house was not a comfortable place to hold town meetings in these cold months. But a meeting which was called to be held in April, 1769, was held at the meeting-house. At the April meeting a singular protest was presented to the town and was placed upon the records. Timothy Smith had a son named Thomas whose wife's name was Submit. They had several children— more, indeed, than they could comfortably provide for—in fact, children were the only things of which they had an abundance, and poverty was their lot. The wife and children became objects of public charge. For some reason other than inability Timothy would not help them. The town having been put to expense on their account threatened action against Timothy, which called forth the following protest: " We, the subscribers, do judge the proceedings of the town to be illegal in voting to come into a method to recover the costs of Timothy Smith that hath been made by Thomas Smith's wife and his family, and we do hereby enter our protest against the whole proceedings in that case.

MURRAYFIELD, April 13th, 1769.

John Smith,
Ebenezer Webber,
Samuel Matthews,
Reuben Matthews,
William Miller,
Timothy Smith."

Notwithstanding the protest the town, at the same meeting, voted to take action against Timothy Smith on account of his son's wife and family.

Highways.

At the March meeting in 1769 several roads were accepted as laid out by the selectmen, as follows: One " from Worthington down the left bank of the Middle Branch by Wait's mill, Timothy Smith's and Mr. Fobes' to Hampton line on Westfield Road, road so-called."
One "from Northampton west line at the road, then westerly by John Kirtland's across the river at the ford-way by Mr. Fobes' and to Blandford line east of the West Branch, called Hampton road to Blandford east of Mr. Bolton's."
One beginning at the ford-way west of Timothy Smith's to the meeting-house by Ebenezer Webber's, from the meeting-house westward to James Brown's by McIntere's, Mann's, and Flemming's, and from James Black's to the road above named.
One from Mr. Gordon's by Mr. Laccore's to the meeting-house, from David Blair's to the road above Mr. Hamilton's.
One from William Campbell's to the meeting-house by John and Abner Smith's, from the Worthington road above Mr. Wait's mill northerly to Abner Smith's.
One from Mr. Williams' by Mr. Meacham's by Nathan Rose's by Clerk Henry's to the meeting-house in Webber's road ninety rods.
One from the meeting-house to Col. Chandler's farm where Robert Smith lives, from said Smith's to the sawmill, from said sawmill by David Bolton's to Blandford line where three roads cross, and from Bolton's westwardly east of the West Branch by Proctor's through Capt. Noble's farm, southeasterly from said farm to Blandford line, east side of the branch, from thence to the road that goes from Hampton to Blandford.
One " beginning at Chesterfield line where the road meets the town line; thence southerly by Mr. Miller's to Worthington road east of Ebenezer Webber's." This is probably the road over Goss Hill.
One " from the ford-way at the Middle Branch against Israel Rose's up to the gristmill on the south side of the branch."
One " from Worthington road at the southeast side of Timothy Smith's field across the ford-way a little east of Capt. Geer's." See appendix for particulars of survey.
This same year £50 were raised for the repair of highways, and three shillings per day were allowed for work on the roads.
In 1770 the town voted to lay out £7 in repairing highways, and that four days' work be required of each poll, the work to be done by June 15th, and two shillings eightpence be allowed per day for work

for each poll, to be taken out of the £7. In March, 1772, the town appropriated £20 for repairing highways. In July, the same year, it was voted "to raise half a day's work for each man to work on the county road by Deacon Miller's to Worthington," and that it should be done by the 5th of September. In March, 1773, the town voted to require four days' work on highways for each poll at three shillings per day.

At the town meeting held April 22, 1771, the town voted adversely on propositions to build a bridge at Mr. Wait's mill, at the ford-way west of Timothy Smith's house, and at the ford-way north of Israel Rose's dwelling, all on the Middle Branch. The town also voted adversely to the proposition to "build a boat to carry men and horses over the river near Landlord Mixer's." In January of the same year the question of building a bridge over East Branch, where Norwich bridge now stands, was discussed in town meeting.

Schools.

The first action taken by the town in its corporate capacity touching public schools was at a town meeting held April 13, 1769; it was voted not to raise any money for schools that year. Another subject included in the same vote is significant of the reason why they voted no money for schools, to wit: "Nor to pay any of their debts with specie." But the inhabitants were not indifferent to the importance of public education; for at a meeting held the following May, the town voted to raise four pounds for the support of schools that year, and at a meeting held the following June, eight pounds more were voted for support of schools.

In April, 1770, the town voted £12 for the support of schools that year.

At the March meeting in 1773, £12 were appropriated for the support of schools, and James Hamilton, Jesse Johnson, David Scott, William Carter, and Jonathan Wait, representing different sections of the town, were chosen "a committee to examine and consider the circumstances of the places where they shall think it most convenient for schools to be kept in winter for reading and writing, and in summer for women's schools and make report to the town at the next town meeting, of their judgment."

Newcomers.

The valuation list taken in September, 1769, shows the following new names: John Blair, James Clark, Jr., Timothy Culver, Benjamin

Eggleston, Thomas Elder, Ebenezer Gordon, Ebenezer Geer, Elijah Geer, Samuel Knight, John Kirtland, Jonathan Russell, Nathan Mann, Reuben Matthews, Samuel Matthews. David Palmer, David Palmer, Jr., Samuel Pomeroy, John Rude, Robert Smith, Daniel Williams, Jr., Isaac Williams, Miles Washburn, Nathaniel Weller, Benjamin Whitney, and John Whitney. The valuation list for 1770 shows the following additional names: George Armstrong, John Elder, Samuel Gordon, John Gilmore, John Griswold, Mr. Hubbard, John Harkell, Moses Hale, Daniel Kirtland, James Mulhollan, David Shepard, M.D., Edward Wright, and Edward Wright, Jr. In the meantime the following named persons appear to have left town: Absalom Blair, Robert Blair, James Brown, Abner Pease, John Smith, Samuel Webb, and Thomas Wright.

Qualified Voters, 1770.

Of the persons whose names appear on the list for 1770, only the following persons were by property qualification elegible to vote:

David Bolton, James Clark, Thomas Crow, Samuel Elder, Caleb Fobes, William Fobes, Abraham Flemming, James Fairman, Zebulon Fuller, Ebenezer Gordon, Capt. Ebenezer Geer, James Hamilton, Malcom Henry, Jesse Johnson, John McIntire, Thomas Kennedy, James McKnight, John Kirtland, Ebenezer King, John Laccore, Lemuel Laccore, Stephen Lyman, Timothy Lyman, William Mann, Nathan Mann, Ebenezer Meacham, Isaac Mixer, Samuel Matthews, Gideon Matthews, Jonathan Miller, William Miller, William Moore, David Palmer, Samuel Pomeroy, Robert Proctor, Israel Rose, Nathan Rose, John Rude, Robert Smith, Timothy Smith, David Scott, Abner Smith, James Taggart, Ebenezer Webber, Jonathan Wait, Peter Williams, Reuben Woolworth, Daniel Kirtland, and Edward Wright. These persons were valued at £20 and more. Only eleven were rated as high as £50. The highest was £94.

Dr. Shepard Chosen Town Clerk.

At the annual meeting in 1771, Dr. David Shepard was chosen town clerk; and he was continued in the office for many years. His residence was in the vicinity of the meeting-house; and in extremely cold weather the town meetings, after the choice of moderator, sometimes adjourned to his house and there finished their business. He was the first town clerk of Murrayfield, who was really competent to fill the place.

At this same meeting the town voted to let swine run at large the whole year without yokes or rings.

Between September, 1770, and September, 1771, the following named persons came and settled in the town: William Carter, Asa Carter, William Bell, Samuel Belknap, Archelus Anderson, Solomon Holyday, Solomon Holyday, Jr., Josiah Holyday, Gershom Rust, and Jabez Torry.

The record of the annual meeting in 1771 shows that the selectmen had become liable to suit for failure to make return of the valuation of the town to the Assembly. The town voted "to defend the selectmen from all harm on that account, provided they make it out and deliver the same to one of the proprietors to have them send it in."

It appears that Isaac Mixer, either as constable or tax collector, had got into a suit with Ebenezer Meacham in consequence of having sold Meacham's cart for taxes. From the fact that the town refused to help Mixer, it may be inferred that he had exceeded his authority.

Valuation List, 1772.

The valuation which was taken in September, 1772, shows the following new names: Capt. Zebulon Jones, Samuel Buck, John Tiffany, a Mr. Taylor, and Samuel Wheat.

The total valuation of the town amounted to £2,991 and 4 shillings.

Abner Smith was rated at £111, Caleb Fobes at £115, and Isaac Mixer at £91. They were the wealthiest men in town. Dr. David Shepard appears to have prospered so well that from nothing in 1769 he was rated, in 1772, at £26 and 4 shillings.

At the annual meeting in March, 1773, the last board of selectmen and assessors for the undivided original town of Murrayfield were chosen. They were, Malcom Henry, John Kirtland, Dr. David Shepard, David Scott, and Abner Smith.

Town Lines.

In November, 1768, the line between Blandford and Murrayfield was perambulated; the record of which is as follows: "Blandford, Nov. 7th, A. D., 1768. John Noble and Isaac Gibbs were appointed by the selectmen of Blandford to perambulate between Blandford and Murrayfield. Also Caleb Fobes, selectman of Murrayfield, and Ebenezer Meacham met us the 7th day, and David Bolton went with us two hours the 7th day and all the 8th day. First, we set out at the northeast * corner at Rock House mountain at a yellow pine tree marked with stones about it; from thence west 17° north seven miles to a beech tree with stones about." This line, as run by Edward Taylor and Charles Baker, who surveyed for the original proprietors, was put down as West 20° north. The line as subsequently established by the General Court is given as beginning at a beech tree with stones about it in the northwest corner of Blandford and thence east 17° south to Rock House corner, but the act expressly states that the purpose is not to change the line, but to establish it. The proprietors' surveyors no doubt made an erroneous record.

Action of the Town About Preaching.

The questions which engrossed the attention of the town more than any other one matter of public concern were those pertaining to providing for preaching, but especially as to the places of meeting for religious worship. This subject was to some extent provided for, as we have already seen, in the conditions of settlement, and, before that, in the conditions of purchase imposed by the government upon the proprietors themselves. No action appears to have been taken by the town until the year 1768, after it was reorganized. At the first meeting called by the newly elected board of selectmen to be holden at the public meeting-house on the 28th day of June, the third article was, "For the town to vote, if they think it proper, a suitable sum of money for them to pay for preaching, and also to choose a minister for supplying the pulpit." Another article was, "To see if the town will vote a place or places for to meet at for public worship."

At this meeting the town voted to raise £20 for preaching that year; and chose Isaac Mixer, Abner Smith and Stephen Lyman a committee to "supply the town with preaching this present year." A vote was taken "that the preaching this year should not be all at the meeting-house," which vote was immediately reconsidered, and a vote then taken "that the preaching this year shall be all at the public meeting-house," and then the town voted "that the committee for preaching should apply themselves to the Revd. Mr. Tud, Mr. Hooker at South and Northampton, and the Revd. Mr. Ballentine of Westfield for advice."

In a warrant for a meeting to be holden October 14, 1768, there was an article "to see if the town will vote to give Mr. Asahel Hart a call

---
* Northeast corner of Blandford.

to settle in the gospel ministry in said town; also to see if the town will appoint a place or places to meet at for public worship." No action appears to have been taken with reference to giving Mr. Hart a call; but the town voted "that the preaching for the winter shall be one-half of the time at Mr. Reuben Woolworth's, or Jonathan Webber's;" and "that the other half of the preaching for the winter ensuing shall be at Mr. John Laccore's." Jonathan Hart Webber's house was on Middle Branch.

FIXING UPON PLACES WHERE PREACHING SHOULD BE HELD.

At a town meeting held December 14th, 1768, "at the new house of Jonathan Hart Webber," the town voted "that the vote passed the fourteenth day of October last, to have preaching one-half of the time at Mr. John Laccore's and the other half at Mr. Jonathan Hart Webber's shall be revoked or disannulled." The town then voted "that the first six Sabbaths of preaching in Murrayfield shall ! at the dwelling house of Israel Rose; and that there shall be three Sabbaths of preaching at the dwelling house of Israel Rose out of seven for and through the year ensuing."

£3 and 12 shillings were voted to be paid to Mr. Simeon Miller, it being the sum due him for preaching.

At a town meeting held April 13th, 1769, £25 were appropriated for preaching during the year, and James Hamilton, Jesse Johnson, and Gideon Matthews were chosen "a committee to supply the town with preaching according to the agreement drawn from Mr. Baldwin's advice on the 6th of March, 1769."

At a meeting held in May it was voted "that one-half of the preaching during the present year should be at Ebenezer Webber's barn, and the other half at the meeting-house."

ARBITRATION AGREED TO.

At a town meeting held in June of the same year, which was called to be held, and was held, at the house of Reuben Woolworth, " to see if the town will vote to submit the difference subsisting between the people at the river and the people on the hill, so-called, to the judgment of indifferent men of any other town or towns to judge and determine how big a part of the preaching shall be at the meeting-house, and how big a part at some place to be by them appointed for the benefit of the people at the river."

Another subject named in the warrant was stated in language following : " To see if the town will discover how they approve of the performances of Mr. Bascom while he has been in town." The record states that the town " voted that they like the performances of Mr. Bascom well."

REPORT OF THE ARBITRATORS.

The town voted " To submit the difference about the place where the preaching shall be held to indifferent men." The men selected were, Capt. Nathan Leonard of Worthington, Lieut. Nathaniel Kingsley of Becket, and Deacon Benjamin Tupper of Chesterfield. And it was voted that preaching should be held at the places so designated by the arbitration, for the next three years. The report of these referees was as follows :

" We, the subscribers, being appointed a committee by the inhabitants of Murrayfield to settle the dispute subsisting among the inhabitants of said town respecting the place or places for meeting for public worship for three years next ensuing, & having viewed the different parts of said town, have agreed to report as follows, viz.: Two-thirds of the time at the meeting-house in said town, & one-third of the time at Mr. Isaac Mixer's in said town; that is to say, two Sabbaths at the meeting-house & one Sabbath at said Mixer's successively for three years next ensuing the date hereof. Dated at Murrayfield this 9th day of July, 1769.

NATHAN LEONARD.
NATHANIEL KINGSLEY.
BENJA. TUPPER."

THE REV. AARON BASCOM CALLED.

This arrangement was carried out for the time agreed upon.

At a town meeting held July 17th, the town passed the following vote : " Voted to give Mr. Aaron Bascom a call to settle amongst us in the work of the ministry, and "according to the agreement drawn by Mr. Baldwin on the 29th of April, 1768." The offer was "to give Mr. Aaron Bascom for a settlement seventy pounds, one half to be paid in money and the other half to be paid in work." To give him "forty pounds salary for three years, and then raise five pounds per year to sixty pounds; and then sixty pounds per year whilst he is our minister."

Jesse Johnson, Stephen Lyman, and John Kirtland were chosen to be a committee " to make report to Mr. Bascom what the town hath done for his encouragement, and to make report of his answer to the town at their next meeting." Apparently Mr. Bascom's answer was not given until after he had carefully considered the offer and negotiated somewhat with the "committee concerning his salary; and that it resulted in calling a town meeting which was held at Mixer's Inn, September 13th, 1769, when the town voted to give Mr. Bascom his firewood during his ministry. At the same meeting James Hamilton and Jesse Johnson were chosen "a committee to send to the Presbytery to see if the Presbytery will grant that platform that was voted by this town of Murrayfield the 17th of July, 1769, for church discipline for Murrayfield." The town then voted to raise 10 pounds for preaching.

On the 7th of October, 1769, Abner Smith and John Hamilton, two of the selectmen, issued a warrant for a town meeting to be held at the public meeting-house on the 12th, "to see if the town will choose a committee to send for such ministers as Mr. Bascom and the town shall agree upon in order to assist in embodying a church and ordaining Mr. Bascom." It also proposed the 8th of November as the time. The meeting was held; but adjourned to November 2d; at which time it was voted not to act upon the foregoing article. On the 6th of November, another meeting was called to be held on the 14th, at Mixer's Inn, and it was voted to reconsider the vote passed July 17th, to settle Mr. Bascom according to the agreement drawn by Mr. Baldwin. Another meeting was called November 9th, to be holden November 25th, at the public meeting-house; at which time it was "voted to give Mr. Aaron Bascom a call to settle in the work of ministry among us according to an agreement made and consented to by the inhabitants of Murrayfield on the 14th inst." The town also voted to give him "the same encouragement that we did before: that is to say, to give him £70 for settlement, one half to be paid in money and the other half in work; and to give him £40 salary for three years; and then raise £5 a year to £60, and then pay him £60 while he shall remain, also his firewood." The ordination was fixed to take place December 20th, and Jesse Johnson, John Kirtland, David Palmer and Samuel Matthews were chosen a committee to arrange for the ordination.

Mr. Bascom's acceptance of the call was worded as follows:

"To the inhabitants of the town of Murrayfield. Whereas you have invited me to settle with you in the work of the Gospel Ministry, & voted to give me seventy pounds as a settlement, and forty pounds for a salary per year during three years, then raise five pounds per year till it comes to sixty pounds, then to continue at sixty pounds per year so long as I shall be your minister, & also to provide me with firewood annually for the time above mentioned, I, having fully considered the matter & taken advice of my friends & of my Rev. fathers in the ministry, am inclined to think it my duty & hereby express my sincere willingness to settle with you in the work of the Gospel.

AARON BASCOM."

Towns Required to Support Preaching.

At this point it may be well to explain that it was a law of the province "that the inhabitants of each town within this province shall take due care, from time to time, to be constantly provided of an able, learned, orthodox minister or ministers of good conversation, to dispense the word of God to them, which minister or ministers shall be suitably encouraged and sufficiently supported and maintained by the inhabitants of such town." It was made the duty of the court of quarter sessions to compel towns to comply with this law; and the court was empowered to make such necessary orders as would insure maintenance of the preaching of the Gospel in every town. Churches were permitted to choose their own ministers, but were required to submit their choice for the approval or disapproval of the inhabitants of the town; and if the town, by a majority of its votes, denied its approbation, the church could call in the help of a council consisting of the elders and messengers of three or five neighboring churches, which council had power to hear, examine and consider the exceptions and allegations made against the church's election; and if the council also disapproved, then the church had to make a new election, but if the council sustained the election of the church, their elected minister, upon accepting and settling with them, should be the minister of the town, and be supported and maintained the same as though he had been chosen by the town.

Organization of the Church.

After the town of Murrayfield had elected to call Mr. Bascom according to the agreement drawn by Mr. Ballentine, then came the question of organizing the church. The Scotch element in town was quite large, and they probably preferred the Presbyterian form of church government; but the English element most likely preferred the Congregational form. At any rate it is certain that there was disagreement in the town upon this subject, which was compromised by an agreement entered into on the 14th of November, 1769, as follows:

"Articles of agreement made and concluded by the inhabitants of Murrayfield.

Whereas there is a difference of opinion among the inhabitants of Murrayfield with respect to the mode of church discipline, which difference seems to be an impediment to our settling a minister among us and enjoying the ordinances of the Gospel: we, the subscribers, under a solemn sense of the importance of peace and union among churches, and with an earnest desire to remove every obstruction in the way of our enjoying gospel ordinances, do agree and consent to the following articles, viz.:

1. That there shall be a church incorporated in this place according to the usual method in the neighboring churches, that is to say, by a church covenant & a confession of faith, which confession shall be agreeable to the Westminster confession, so-called.

2. That all persons who shall desire to join themselves to this church after its incorporation shall be examined by its pastor & elders chosen to assist the pastor (as hereinafter mentioned) & shall be propounded to the church that any one may have opportunity to offer his objections against him if any there be, & shall be admitted by the recommendation of the pastor & elders & the vote of the brethren, & members of other churches who shall desire stated communion with this church shall bring letters of recommendation from the churches to which they stand related.

3. That there shall be a number of elders not exceeding seven chosen by the brethren of the church to join with & assist the pastor in ruling & governing the church according to the word of God, & particularly in such matters as are hereinafter mentioned, & that any two of the elders with the pastor, in case more shall see fit not to attend, shall be a session.

4. In all cases of offence where such private dealing as the gospel prescribes fails of bringing the matter to a peaceable issue the person or persons dissatisfied shall lodge with the pastor a written complaint, clearly & explicitly setting forth the matter of the offence & naming the witnesses who are to be cited in support of said complaint.

5. When any complaint as aforesaid is lodged with the pastor he shall notify the party accused thereof & give him, if required, a copy of said complaint & a list of the witnesses' names fourteen days before he is required to make his defence, & in case the complainant shall, after he has exhibited his complaint, with a list of his witnesses to the pastor, give notice of other witnesses to be cited, the party accused shall be allowed further time to prepare for his defence if he shall desire it.

6. That the pastor with the ruling elders have full power to hear such complaint & judge & pass sentence thereupon.

7. That if either party shall think himself aggrieved with the judgment of

the session, he shall have liberty of an appeal to the church who shall have power to revise or confirm the judgment of the session as to them shall seem right, & that the concurrence of the pastor with a major part of the brethren present (they having been duly notified to attend) shall in all cases be deemed a valid act of the church.

8. In case either party shall be aggrieved with the judgment of the church there shall be liberty of an appeal to an evangelical council.

9. That whenever there shall be occasion for an evangelical council, it shall be called by letters missive from the pastor in the name & by the vote of the church; & said council shall if the church or any party concerned so request, consist of an equal number of Congregational & Presbyterian churches; provided, nevertheless, that in case any of the churches shall fail of attending, so that there shall not be an equality of Presbyterian & Congregational churches actually present, such inequality shall be no bar to said council's proceeding & judging in the case to be referred, whose judgment shall be final & decisive.

10. That in case any special difficulty shall arise between the pastor & the church or any particular members of the church or other fixed inhabitants of the town attending his ministry, which shall require the presence of a council, in such case a council shall be called in manner & form as above mentioned, to hear & judge the same, & their judgment shall be decisive.

11. That in case the pastor shall refuse to join the church in calling a council in any case in which he is especially concerned, then the ruling elders or a majority of them, if they see fit, shall desire two or more neighboring churches to come & look into the matter; & if these churches find occasion for a council, they shall advise the pastor to join with the church in calling one—but in case he still obstinately refuses, then these churches so present shall have power to call an ecclesiastical council of such churches as they judge proper, after consulting the pastor & brethren thereupon; which council so called shall have full power to act to all intents & purposes as if it had been called by the pastor & brethren.

12. And when the council is to be called the parties concerned shall have liberty to nominate the churches which are to form the council, & may proceed in the nomination till they name such as shall be agreeable to the church.

13. That such persons as the pastor & elders shall approve, upon their consenting to the confession of faith adopted by the church & to a covenant drawn up for them, shall, according to the Presbyterian method, have right to offer their children to baptism, though they do not see fit to join in full communion; & that all such persons as well as those in full communion, they being under no scandal, shall be allowed at all times to bring their children to baptism.

14. That previous to the communion of the Lord's table the pastor shall set apart a suitable portion of time to prepare for that ordinance & that during the administration thereof he shall discourse upon the nature of the ordinance, & shall give suitable exhortation to the communicants as is practiced in Presbyterian churches.

15. That it will be agreeable to our minds that the pastor should visit his flock & caution the members thereof as often as he judges convenient & the duties of his office & other circumstances will allow."

Signed by "Aaron Bascom, David Palmer, Abner Smith, Stephen Lyman, Timothy Smith, Samuel Pomeroy, John Kirtland, Samuel Matthews, Jonathan Hart Webber, Gideon Matthews, Timothy Lyman, William Miller, James Hambleton, Samuel Elder, Malcom Henry, William Moore, Jesse Johnson, Daniel Williams, Alexander Gordon, Ebenezer Webber, Jonathan Wait, James Clark."

The Confession of Faith.

The confession of faith was as follows:

"We believe that there is one & but one only living & true God who is infinite in his being & perfection, power, wisdom, justice, holiness, goodness & truth, who is the creator, governor & disposer of all things, & we believe in the unity of the godhead there are three persons of one substance, power & eternity—Father, Son, & Holy Ghost, & we believed that God created man male & female after his own image in knowledge, righteousness & true holiness & entered into a covenant of life with him upon condition of perfect obedience, forbidding him to eat of the tree of knowledge of good & evil upon the pain of death, & that our first parents being left to themselves sinned by eating the forbidden fruit & thereby brought themselves & their ordinary posterity into a state of sin & misery; & that God might have justly left them in that state; but in His infinite wisdom & goodness sent his son to take upon him the human nature, who suffered & died & arose again the third day & appeared & sitteth at the right hand of the father, continually making intercession for us, & will come to judge the world in righteousness at the last day, & by his perfect obedience & sacrifice of himself hath fully satisfied divine justice & the law that whomsoever believeth in him shall have everlasting life; & we believe that God has elected a certain number to everlasting life, whom he will effectually call, justify & sanctify in time & will secure against apostasy; which is accomplished by the special influence of the blessed spirit, & that not the works of men but the righteousness of Christ imputed to believers is the sole ground of their justification before God, & that holiness of heart & life flow from that faith that unites the soul to Christ, and we believe that the scriptures of the Old & New Testament are the word of God, & are a perfect rule of faith & practice. We believe in the great doctrines of the resurrection of the dead & future judgment & the eternal happiness of those that believe & obey the gospel, & the eternal misery of the unbelievers & disobedient."

The names signed, as subscribing to this confession of faith, as they appear upon the church record such as was kept at different times, are as follows:

Aaron Bascom & wife, S'ephen Lyman, Timothy Lyman, John Laccore & wife, Timothy Smith & wife, Samuel Pomeroy & wife, Samuel Matthews & wife, Jesse Johnson & wife, Jonathan Wait & wife, Gideon Matthews & wife, David Palmer & wife, John Kirtland & wife, Abner Smith & wife, Wm. Miller & wife, James Hamilton & wife, Edward Wright & wife, James Clark & wife, Reuben Woolworth & wife, Widow Webber, Samuel Wright & wife, Gershom Rust & wife, Samuel Elder & wife.

The church was duly organized on the 20th of December, 1769. Only three elders were chosen at that time, to wit: Samuel Mattnews, John Kirtland, William Miller.

ORDINATION OF MR. BASCOM.

On the same day the ordination of Mr. Bascom took place. This was a great event for Murrayfield, and great preparations were made for the entertainment of the ministers and delegates from other churches whose presence was required for the occasion. The committee appointed by the town to take charge of the arrangements were, Jesse Johnson, James Hamilton, John Kirtland, David Palmer, and Samuel Matthews. Some of the items of expense look queer to us, but they were in keeping with the views of people at that time, and are a part of the history of the town. Some of the items, which came before the town at the town meeting next following and were voted to be paid, are as follows: Three pounds and two pence half penny to Stephen Lyman for keeping the council and their horses and for going after rum and wine. Eleven shillings and three pence to Isaac Mixer for keeping the council: Five shillings and nine pence to Caleb Fobes for keeping ministers, to wit: Mr. Judd, Mr. Lathrop, and Mr. Ballentine. Eight shillings to James Hamilton for going to Brookfield and to Weston after ministers. Six shillings and five pence to Malcom Henry for keeping the Rev. Mr. Judd and Rev. Mr. Baldwin. One of the articles, inserted in the warrant for the March meeting, 1770, was, "To see if the town will give Stephen Lyman three shillings and two pence more for that wine that he borrowed for the ordination." The town voted to give it.

FIREWOOD FOR MR. BASCOM.

At the December town meetings the town always took action about procuring Mr. Bascom's annual supply of firewood. The following vote was passed at the December meeting, 1770: "Voted to give Mr.

John McIntire two pounds and two shillings for to get the Rev. Mr. Bascom's firewood for the year to come, that is to say, a year from this date, and the wood to be cut eight feet long and piled up handsomely at his door."

Church Discipline.

There were frequent cases of church discipline, as appears by the church record. A few specimens may not be uninteresting. June 21st, 1771, a meeting of pastor and elders was held to hear a complaint made by Jonathan Wait, who was the miller, at what was afterwards known as Littleville, against Reuben Woolworth and his wife. The nature of the complaint does not appear by the record, which simply shows that a hearing was had and resulted in a dismissal of the complaint with a statement that Woolworth was guilty of only a human infirmity. But the Waits were not to be silenced in this way; and Mr. Wait and his wife jointly preferred another complaint against Mr. Woolworth and his wife which was heard July 17th, 1771, and it appears to have been concerning a scandalous report that both Wait and his wife had taken undue toll at their gristmill. It was ordered that Mr. Woolworth make a private confession to Mrs. Wait and ask her forgiveness. But Woolworth afterwards complained that Mrs. Wait would not forgive him, and brought it again before the pastor and elders; and upon a hearing Mrs. Wait was adjudged innocent, which appears to have set the matter at rest so far as the church was concerned. In December, 1772, Abraham Flemming was summoned before the pastor and elders on a complaint made against him for fighting. He was found guilty; but he refused to admit his fault. Subsequently the matter was taken up again and he confessed; whereupon he was restored to good and regular standing. January 26th, 1773, Abner Smith preferred a complaint against his brother, Timothy Smith, for profane swearing. Timothy was found guilty but refused to acknowledge his fault; and continuing obstinate and incorrigible he was excommunicated with solemn formality and declared to be as one of the heathen. At some time in 1774, however, Timothy, finding the odium of excommunication too much to bear, repented of his obstinacy and confessed his fault; whereupon he was taken back into good and regular standing in the church. The records show that Abraham Flemming was also dealt with for profane swearing; as was also Mr. Crawford and Caleb Bascom. Caleb was also dealt with for the excessive use of intoxicating liquors.

Action of the Town as to where Preaching shall be Done.

In July, 1772, the agreement fixed by the arbitration to have preaching part of the time for three years from July, 1769, at Isaac Mixer's Inn, had expired. The town then passed the following vote: "That Mr. Bascom shall not preach any more at the River on the Sabbath." Right here began a difficulty which resulted in a division of the town. On the same day a protest was presented, which was entered upon the records of the town of Murrayfield, as follows:

"Murrayfield, July 24th. 1772. A protest of a number of the inhabitants of said town against a vote passed at a meeting of said town wherein it voted that no part of the preaching be at the River the present year. We, the subscribers, look upon it that we are unjustly injured by said vote, & shall declare against paying any part of the salary to the minister the ensuing year. Ebenezer Geer, John Kirtland, David Scott, Miles Washburn, Peter Williams, Elijah Geer, Isaac Mixer, Jr., Isaac Mixer, Caleb Fobes, Thomas Crow, David Palmer."

John Kirtland.

On the part of the people in the east end of the town, John Kirtland—or more properly Kirkland—was the leading man. He came from Norwich, Conn., and purchased a tract of land in the southwest corner of the Williams grant. He took up his residence in Murrayfield sometime between September, 1769, and September, 1770. The record shows that he conveyed about 50 acres of his land to James Clark, June 20, 1768. This was not the James Clark who was among the first settlers of the town, but was James Clark of Norwich, Conn., who came to reside in town at a date later than his purchase of Kirtland. At a town meeting held December 14th, 1772, in view of the fact that the people in the east part of the town felt aggrieved by the action which had been taken touching the question of holding religious meeting with preaching at the River, the town voted to "consent and agree that, Col. John Murray, Col. John Chandler, Timothy Paine, Esq., and Col. Abijah Willard shall be a committee to view and examine into the circumstances and situation of the town of Murrayfield respecting the town's being divided, and if they judge it best for the town to be divided, the town agrees to their fixing a line and establishing it for the division line, the east end of the town paying the cost of the committee."

The Question of Dividing the Town Referred to the Original Proprietors.

The proprietors took the subject into consideration and sent to the town the following response:

"January 6th, 1773. To the inhabitants of Murrayfield, in the County of Hampshire, whereas the said town at a meeting held on the 14th day of December, 1772, among other things consented & agreed that we, the subscribers, be a committee to view and examine into the circumstances & situation of said town respecting said town's being divided, & to agree, in case we think best to have a division, to fix the limit of division. We this day met upon the affair, & heard Deacon John Kirtland & Mr. Timothy Smith, a Committee chosen by said town, & having maturely considered of the affair of dividing said town and the circumstances of the Eastern and Western parts of said town, are very sensible that the situation of the town is such that a division in some future time will be necessary; but as the town is now in its infancy & many of the inhabitants under low circumstances, not able at present to support the changes & build up another parish, therefore advise that the town continue together for the present, & look upon it reasonable that preaching be divided as has been usual between the East & West parts of the town. But in case a division is insisted upon by the inhabitants & peace cannot continue in the town without, we advise to the following division line, viz: Beginning at the southwest corner of the Ingersol grant & from thence extending on the west line of said grant till it comes to the second division lot No. 1. owned by John Chandler, Esq., & from thence a straight line to the southeast corner of lot No. 16; & from thence running on the east lines of lots Nos. 15, 28, & 29 to Chesterfield southwest corner. And as the proprietors have been to great expense in settling said town, in case of division, the east part of said town must not expect any assistance from the proprietors, as we look upon it that a division at present will not serve the interest of said proprietors. Wishing you prosperity in all your affairs we subscribe your humble servants.

John Chandler.
Timo. Paine.
Abijah Willard.
John Murray."

Memorial to the General Court.

At a town meeting held January 13th, 1773, it was voted that the town be divided upon the line recommended by the proprietors.

The next measure taken in this business was the following memorial to the General Court:

" Province of Massachusetts Bay.
To his Excellency Thomas Hutchinson, Esq., Captain General & Governor in Chief of the province aforesaid. The Honorable his Majesty's Council & Hon. House of Representatives in General Court assembled at Boston, June, 1773.
The memorial of John Kirtland of Murrayfield, in the county of Hampshire, as agent for & in behalf of such of the inhabitants of said Murrayfield as live in the easterly part thereof, humbly shows : That in the year 1762 this Great & General Court sold at public vendue to the Hon. John Chandler, Esq., & others all the lands of said Murrayfield (excepting what was before granted out to particular persons) for a certain price & on certain conditions of settlement as by the records of this Honorable Court appears; that there was then about 7500 acres, part of said town granted out to particular persons, all lying eastward of a mountain, called Moose Hill, that runs north & south through said township. That said Col. Chandler & others, the purchasers of the unappropriated lands there, had on their said lands (under contract of performing settlement duties) about forty persons, all of which excepting one were west of the line that said purchasers made the divisional line of said town. That in the year 1765, on the application of said purchasers of said unappropriated lands to this Honorable Court, & not by the inhabitants or any of them, the said lands including said grants & the inhabitants thereon were incorporated & erected into a town with the power and immunities of other towns in the province. That in the year 1767 a house of public worship was set up by said purchasers in said town on the west side of said Moose Mountain merely to accommodate their settlers, the inhabitants of that part of the town & where all the settlers under said purchasers, excepting one, then dwelt.
That in the year 1765 eight or nine families were settled on the grants aforesaid, & the number of them now settled on said grants is increased to thirty-five.
That since the year 1767, the said town has laid out considerable monies toward furnishing the meeting house set up as aforesaid; that in 1770 the said town settled a minister & gave him seventy-five pounds for a settlement & engaged to give him sixty pounds per annum salary. That there are to this day but six families in said town settled east of said divisional line, under the said purchasers; all the rest being on the old grants aforesaid. That the building of said meeting house & settling said minister answer for said purchasers toward a fulfilment in part of the conditions of their grant from the province, & to the settlers under them it answers for a performance in part of their settling contract with said original proprietors, but answers no purpose of advantage whatever to any of the people settled on the east side of said mountain, as they cannot without insupportable expense & labor attend public worship among them, they all of them living from five to eight miles distant from said place of public worship beyond said mountain. That by the kind application of the original purchasers (in favor of their tenants or under purchasers) to this Honorable Court & procuring the incorporation aforesaid they

have brought the settlers on the grants aforesaid (as they are the minor part of said town) subject to a proportion of the expense of fulfilling their duty in part to the province in regard to their lands in which these settlers have no interest & with whom most of them never consented to be any way concerned, & in the year 1768 when the first tax of eighty pounds was made for town charges, many of the settlers under the purchasers being turned off their lands, two-fifths of the burden of said tax actually fell upon the settlers on the grants.

That these memorialists under the circumstances soliciting the town that as they paid their proportion of these expenses of settling a minister, & pay their proportion of his yearly salary, that they might have a proportionable part of the preaching on their side of the mountain where they could enjoy it, which the town granted them for the space of three years; but since July last have wholly denied to do for the future. Your memorialists beg leave to observe to your Excellency & Honors that as the tract of land sold to these gentlemen was very large, much more than an ordinary township, they have been at a loss for the reason that induced your Excellency & Honors to make those grants (without the knowledge and consent of the proprietors and settlers) part of the same town with the Western part of said purchase, though they were never at a loss for the reason that induces said purchasers to apply for it.

That this act of incorporation so extended has not only thus unequally burdened the present settlers of said grants in the respect before mentioned, but also in this respect: that it is a great discouragement to the further sale or settlement of such of said lands as yet remain unsold.

The said memorialists, the inhabitants on the east side of said mountain, in said Murrayfield, under these difficulties are constrained humbly to implore your Excellency & Honors that there may be a division of the said town of Murrayfield by the following line, viz: Beginning at the southwest corner of Ingersole grant, so called, thence extending on the west line of said grant till it comes to the second division lot No. 1, owned by John Chandler, Esq.; from thence a straight line to the southeast corner of lot No. 16 ; and from thence running on the east line of lots Nos. 15, 28, & 29 to Chesterfield southwest corner, & that the inhabitants & lands in said township east of said line may be erected into a separate town or district with the powers & privileges that other towns in this province enjoy.

And as in duty bound shall ever pray, &c,

JOHN KIRTLAND, Agent for the memorialists."

NORWICH INCORPORATED.

This petition was presented to the General Court, June 12th, 1773. and the petitioners were ordered to notify the proprietors of Murrayfield. But no opposition appears to have been made. June 29, 1773, an act was passed incorporating the territory lying east of the division line named in the memorial, as a separate district under the name of Norwich—or rather, in the language of the act, it was "erected into a separate district."

It was "invested with all the powers, privileges, and immunities that towns in this province do, or by law ought to, enjoy; that of sending a representative to the General Assembly only excepted, and that the inhabitants of said district shall have full power, from time to time, to join with said town of Murrayfield in the choice of representative or representatives, which representative or representatives may be chosen indifferently either from said town or district, and the selectmen of said town of Murrayfield, as often as they shall call a meeting for the purpose of making choice of a representative or representatives, shall give seasonable notice to the clerk of said district for the time being, of the time and place of said meeting, to the end that the said district may join them therein; and the clerk of said district shall set up in some convenient public place in said district, a notification thereof accordingly, or shall notify the district in such other way as said district may hereafter determine upon, and the pay and allowance of said representative or representatives to be borne by said town and district to their respective proportion of the province tax." The district was to pay its proportion of taxes; it was to enjoy its share of the ministerial lands; it was to have its proportion of the public money; it was to contribute its share towards the relief of the poor in Murrayfield, and to pay one-third of the taxes until a new valuation. Joseph Hawley, Esq., was empowered to issue his warrant to call the first meeting. It is not at all probable that this district of Norwich ever enjoyed representation conjointly with Murrayfield in any other way than to submit to representation by a Murrayfield man.

The memorial of John Kirtland on behalf of the inhabitants of the east part of Murrayfield, asking to be formed into a separate district, could not have been written by him, for, although he was a leading man, if not the leading man, among these people, subsequent records of Norwich, made by him as town clerk, clearly show that he was not equal to the framing of such a document.

The first valuation list of Norwich was taken September 1, 1773, by John Kirtland, Caleb Fobes, and David Scott. The names contained therein are important as showing who were the tax paying inhabitants of the new town.

THE TAXPAYERS IN THE NEW TOWN.

They were as follows:

Christian Angell, Solomon Blair, Thomas Crow, James Crow, David Crow, John Crow, Wm. Carter, Asa Carter, Caleb Fobes, Wm. Fobes, Elijah Fobes, Zebulon Fuller, James Fairman, Samuel Fairman, Wm. French, John Griswold, James Gilmore, David Halberd, Jabez Homes, Nathaniel Bennett, John Barnard, Solomon Holaday, Daniel Dana, John Crossett, Ebenezer Freeman, Solomon Holaday, Patrick Crekle, John Kirtland, Ebenezer King, Samuel Knight, Daniel Kirtland, Isaac Mixer, Isaac Mixer, Jr., Ebenezer Meacham, Wm. Miller, David Palmer, John D. Palmer, David Palmer, Jr., Capt. E. B. Geer, Elijah Geer, Mace Cook, Zebulon Rose, John Rude, David Scott, Joseph Stanton, John Fiffany, Miles Washburn, Peter Williams, Daniel Williams, Charles Williams, Jabez Story, James Clark, Jehial Eggleston, Jonathan Ware, and B. G. Peter Bunda.

The assessors of Murrayfield also took their valuation list in September, 1773. The following is a full copy of the list and the valuations:

THE TAXPAYERS LEFT IN THE OLD TOWN.

	Polls	Real Estate			Personal			Total		
		£	s.	d.	£	s.	d.	£	s.	d.
Archilus Anderson	1	05	08	—	02	16	—	08	04	—
Geo. Armstrong	1	01	10	—	01	18	—	03	08	—
John Bolton	0	07	10	—	—	—	—	07	10	—
David Bolton	3	57	—	—	13	04	—	70	04	—
David Blair	1	33	—	—	06	14	—	39	14	—
James Black, Jr	1	23	—	—	05	08	—	28	08	—
John Blair	1	27	—	—	09	16	—	36	16	—
Wm. Bell	1	39	—	—	09	12	—	48	12	—
James Black	1	—	—	—	02	—	—	02	—	—
Caleb Bascom	1	—	—	—	04	17	—	04	17	—
Geo. Black	1	01	16	—	02	03	—	03	19	—
James Clark	1	60	—	—	12	14	—	72	14	—
Wm. Campbell	1	26	10	—	12	14	—	39	04	—
Saml. Elder	1	70	—	—	13	07	—	83	07	—
Thos. Elder	1	10	—	—	03	16	—	13	16	—
John Elder	1	—	—	—	—	—	—	—	—	—
Saml. Ellis	1	20	10	—	04	10	—	25	—	—
Bigott Eggleston	2	27	—	—	01	—	—	28	—	—
Benja. Eggleston	1	10	16	—	02	—	—	12	16	—
Abraham Fleming	1	58	06	—	03	08	—	61	14	—
James Gilmore	0	25	—	—	—	—	—	25	—	—
John Gilmore	1	06	—	—	—	—	—	06	—	—
Alexander Gordon	1	49	—	—	12	14	—	61	14	—
Silby Geer	1	30	12	—	09	14	—	40	06	—
James Geer	1	27	—	—	02	06	—	29	06	—
James Hamilton	1	30	12	—	13	05	—	43	17	—
Lieut Mellenry	1	66	—	—	15	09	—	81	09	—
William Henry	1	24	—	—	03	19	—	27	19	—
Andrew Henry	1	—	—	—	—	—	—	—	—	—
Jesse Johnson	1	15	16	—	07	10	—	23	06	—
Zebulon Jones	2	—	—	—	01	10	—	01	10	—
John Laccore	1	33	18	—	09	—	—	42	18	—
Lemuel Laccore	1	21	12	—	03	13	—	25	05	—
John Laccore, Jr	1	—	—	—	—	—	—	—	—	—
Stephen Lyman	1	64	—	—	09	09	—	73	09	—
Timothy Lyman	1	50	—	—	10	12	—	60	12	—
John McIntire	1	46	10	—	07	18	—	54	08	—
Daniel Meeker	1	19	10	—	01	18	—	21	08	—
Samuel Matthews	2	15	12	—	05	09	—	21	01	—
Gideon Matthews	1	31	10	—	08	17	—	40	07	—
William Moore	1	40	04	—	08	15	—	48	19	—
James Mulhallan	1	25	—	—	04	03	—	29	03	—
Wid. Jane Mann	0	18	—	—	01	18	—	19	18	—
William Mann	0	08	—	—	08	—	—	16	—	—
Robert Proctor	1	24	—	—	07	17	—	31	17	—
Gershom Rust	1	24	04	—	07	10	—	31	14	—
Timothy Smith	1	14	08	—	09	—	—	23	08	—
David Shepard	1	21	12	—	19	—	—	40	12	—
Robert Smith	2	19	10	—	01	18	—	21	08	—
Abner Smith	1	105	08	—	21	17	—	127	05	—
David Scott	0	10	10	—	—	—	—	10	10	—
Thos. Smith	1	—	—	—	—	—	—	—	—	—
Abner Smith, Jr	1	—	—	—	01	10	—	01	10	—
Joel Seward	1	63	—	—	09	02	—	72	02	—
Ezekiel Snow	1	—	—	—	—	—	—	—	—	—
John Thompson	1	—	—	—	02	—	—	02	—	—
John Thompson, Jr	1	—	—	—	05	10	—	05	10	—
John Taylor	2	—	—	—	01	18	—	01	18	—
Edward Wright	3	42	—	—	06	15	—	48	15	—
Edward Wright, Jr	1	13	10	—	01	10	—	15	—	—
Nathan Wright	1	40	—	—	09	—	—	49	—	—
Bazella Wright	1	—	—	—	—	—	—	—	—	—
Reuben Woolworth	1	40	—	—	05	—	—	45	—	—
Jonathan Hart Webber	1	40	16	—	05	10	—	46	06	—
Jonathan Wait	2	24	—	—	07	04	—	31	04	—
Isaac Williams	2	35	16	—	06	11	—	42	07	—
Enoch Shepard	0	30	—	—	—	—	—	30	—	—
Thaddeus Newton	1	75	12	—	15	15	—	91	07	—
Obidiah Newton	1	—	—	—	—	—	—	—	—	—
Robert Field	1	—	—	—	—	—	—	—	—	—
Daniel Twadwell	1	05	—	—	—	08	—	05	08	—
George Napping	1	—	—	—	—	—	—	—	—	—
John Wade	1	—	—	—	01	10	—	01	10	—
Joseph Henry	1	—	—	—	—	—	—	—	—	—

The total valuation in Murrayfield in 1773, after Norwich was set off, amounted to 2,178 pounds and 19 shillings.

FIRST TOWN MEETING AFTER THE DIVISION.

On the 7th of August, 1773, the selectmen of Murrayfield issued a warrant for a town meeting to be held the 16th. An exact copy of the warrant and of the record of the meeting will convey more information upon several points than any description, or statement of facts, that can be written within the same space, so I propose to give them in full:

"HAMPSHIRE, ss. To Mr. William Henry, Constable of Murrayfield, greeting : In his majesty's name, you are hereby required forthwith to warn & give notice to all & every one of the freeholders & other inhabitants of the town of Murrayfield that are qualified according to law to act in town affairs to assemble & meet at the meeting house in said town on Monday the 16th day of August, inst., at one of the clock in the afternoon, then & there to act on the articles as follows, namely :

1st To choose a moderator to preside in said meeting.

2d To choose town officers that are set off in Norwich District, to supply their places.

3d To see if the town will choose a committee of correspond to consult upon the letters that are sent from Boston concerning the Governor & to write back an answer to the committee of correspond at Boston their result of the same & for the town to give the committee their instructions what they would have done.

4th To see if the town will choose a committee to reckon with the town Treasurer that was in last year.

5th To see if the town will allow Isaac Mixer anything for the use of his house the three years that one-third of the preaching was there.

6th To see if the town will do anything further in order to get the old warrants sealed and made good.

7th To see if the town will do anything about seating the meeting house this summer ; & if they should, to see what method the town will come into respecting the same, & to pass such votes as they shall judge best & most proper respecting the same.

8th To see if the town will choose a committee to join with a committee from Norwich District in order to look into the town affairs that has been transacted whilst we were all together, & likewise to look into the bill of incorporation respecting the money that the town has to pay back to the district, & to make report of their doings to the town the next town meeting.

9th To see if the town will choose a committee to settle with Abner Smith & to look over his rate bills & see if there is not a mistake made in the footing or carrying out, & to make report of their doings to the town the next town meeting.

10th To see if the town will alter the sum of the school money that was voted last March meeting, & to pass such vote as the town shall judge best.

11th To see if the town will allow David Scott & Lieut. Clark particular men's rates they cannot collect.

12th To see if the town will vote to have the assessors go round to every man to take the valuation this year.

13th To see if the town will vote any more highway work to be done soon on the county road that goes to Worthington & pass such votes as the town thinks best respecting the same.

14th To see if the town will allow Samuel Elder six shillings that he paid to the town when he was constable that he could not collect.

15th To hear the report of the committee that is appointed to settle the places where men's and women's schools shall be kept, & to pass such vote as the town shall judge best.

Hereof fail not & make return of this warrant with your doings thereon to some one of the Selectmen before the meeting as you will answer the law in that case made and provided. Given under our hands & seals this seventh day of August & in the thirteenth year of his majesty's reign, Anno Domini, 1773.

DAVID SHEPARD, } Selectmen
ABNER SMITH,   } of Murrayfield."

"Additional article.

16th To see if the town will do anything respecting the road that goes through David Scott's land down Moose Hill."

"The foregoing is a true copy of the warrant, examined & recorded by me David Shepard, town clerk."

"HAMPSHIRE, SS. By virtue of this warrant I have warned the inhabitants of the town of Murrayfield to meet according to the time and place mentioned.

WILLIAM HENRY, Constable of Murrayfield."

"Murrayfield, August 16th, 1773. At a legal meeting of the freeholders & other inhabitants of the town of Murrayfield regularly assembled at the meeting house the following things was acted upon & voted, viz.:

1. Chose Mr. Timothy Smith moderator for said meeting.

2. Voted to choose town officers that are set off in Norwich. Chose William Campbell Assessor and sworn. Chose Caleb Bascom Sealer of Weights & Measures. Chose Bigott Eggleston Sealer of timber & lumber & sworn.

3. Voted not to choose a committee of correspond.

4. Voted Timothy Smith, Jesse Johnson, & James Hamilton to settle with Malcom Henry, town treasurer.

5. Voted not to allow Isaac Mixer anything for the use of his house.

6. Voted not to do anything respecting the getting the old warrants sealed at present.

7. Voted to seat the meeting house floor.

8. Voted to have two fore-seats in the body, two on each side.

9. Voted that those that are highest in valuation shall have the highest pews, and voted that Deac. Samuel Matthews, Lieut. Malcom Henry, & Ensign Stephen Lyman be a committee to dignify the pew ground.

10. Voted that those that draw the pews shall build the fore-seats & their pews by the first of July next or lose their right in the pews.

11. Voted that the committee lay out the pew ground by the 25th of this month.

12. Voted that the same committee that is to reckon with the treasurer shall be a committee to meet the Norwich committee & look over the town affairs whilst together, & look up their bill of incorporation to see what money we must pay back to them.

13. Voted Ensign Stephen Lyman, Doct. David Shepard, & James Hamilton to be a committee to look over Abner Smith's rate bill & see if there is not a mistake in footing as it now stands.

14. Voted to abate four pounds of the school money.

15. Voted to assist Mr. David Scott to get a committee from the court to view the road down Moose Hill if they will come without our paying of them.

16. Voted to give Lieut. Clark Moses Haile's rate till he can get it, & Mr. Scott Moses Haile's rate & Holyday's.

17. Voted that the assessors take the valuation without going round to them.

18. Voted to cut out Worthington road so as the surveyors shall think it will do, & they to have the same price they had before.

The foregoing are the votes passed in the meeting. Test per me Timothy Smith.

MODERATOR."

SEATING THE MEETING-HOUSE.

The next action of the town was to seat the meeting-house. A town meeting for that purpose was held August 25th, 1773.

Samuel Matthews was chosen moderator, and the following votes were then passed:

"Voted to reconsider those votes that was passed at the last meeting respecting the seating of the meeting house."

"Voted to have two seats, one on each side of the Broad Alley."

"Voted that Jonathan Wait, Timothy Smith, Samuel Elder, John Laccore, & Capt. Zebulon Jones shall have the fore-seat, on their building one of them, during their life or residence in town."

"Voted that Abner Smith & wife shall have the privilege of sitting in the fore-seat on his building one of them."

"Voted that Abner Smith & David Shepard shall have the pew next to the fore-seat on the right of the Broad Alley to them and their heirs so long as the meeting house stands."

"Voted that Deac. Samuel Matthews, Deac. Jesse Johnson, & Deac. James Hamilton & their wifes shall have the next pew to the pulpit as long as the meeting house stands."

"Voted that Benj. Eggleston, John Laccore, Jr., John Elder, Thos. Smith, Nathan Wright, Bazaliel Wright, George Black, Abner Smith, Jr., Andrew Henry, & John Smith shall have the fore-seat in the front gallery upon their raising the gallery stairs & building the seat."

"Voted that what the committee did with respect to seating the meeting house & dignifying the pew ground shall stand."

"Voted that the persons that possess the pews shall have them to them & their heirs so long as the meeting house stands."

"Voted that those persons that draw the pew ground shall have them established to them on the consideration of their building the gallery stairs & that those pews & stairs shall be built by the last of May next, & if any persons refuses to join with his partner in building said pew he shall forfeit his title to said pew to his partner that builds it."

"Voted that the young men that are seated in the front gallery shall build the seat through the front & make a division in the middle, one half for them & the other half for the girls."

"Voted that the people that possess the pews shall pay the cost of the building the gallery stairs equally on the poll."

"Voted that every man that is set down in the plan of the meeting house shall possess the pews according to the number."

"Voted that Gershom Rust & his wife shall sit with Mr. Jonathan Wait & Edward Wright, Jr., upon their giving consent."

The town took some action touching Mr. Bascom's supply of firewood, from which it appears that wood was worth four shillings per cord at that time in Murrayfield.

PLAN OF THE LOWER FLOOR OF THE FIRST CHURCH IN
MURRAYFIELD, IN 1773.

Dig 2 N°4 Dav⁴ Blair Rob¹ Smith Wm Jane Mann	Dig.1 N°1	Rev. Mr. Bascom	Pulpit Stairs	Pulpit		Jos Hamilton S. Matthews & Jesse Johnson	Dig.1 N°2 Jas Clark Dav Bolton Joel Seward	D.2 — 3 E Wright R Woolworth Sam¹ Elder
Willard & Ward		Five Seats.				Five Seats		Col. Willard
D4 - 3 Tim° Smith A. Anderson		D.2. N°1 Wm Bell Alex Gordon	Dig 1 N°3 J.H. Webber Mrs Webber during widowhood	Steph Lyman		Dig.1 N°4 Dr Shepard Abner Smith	Dig.2. N°2 Tim° Lyman Wm Moore	Dig.4 - 4. John Taylor John Thompson
E. Door		D3 - 3 Tho⁵ Elder Enoch Shepard	D3 - 1 Jon^a Elder G Matthews		Broad Alley	D3 - 2 Sam¹ Laccore Ab Fleming	D3 - 4 John McIntire John Blair	W Door
		D4 - 1 John Laccore B Eggleston	D3 - 5 Jos Black Wm Campbell			D3 - 6 W^m. Henry Sam¹ Ellis	D4 - 2 Gershom Rast with their wives Ed Wright Jr. Jon. Waite	Col. Otis
John Chandler	Gallery Stairs	D4 - 5 Caleb Bascom Sibel Geer Eben Snow	Tim° Paine			John Murray	D4. 6 Jos. Geer Jos. Gilmore	Gallery Stairs

Front Door

CHAPTER FIFTH.

CARING FOR THE MEETING-HOUSE.

It is not my purpose to write anything of the history of the church as an ecclesiastical entity. But this history would be incomplete and unsatisfactory if the history of the meeting-house and the ministry, so far as it touches the town in its corporate capacity, were left out; for the care of the meeting-house and the maintenance of the gospel ministry were matters of public concern, and were of the duties required of towns by law. It is also interesting as an exhibition of how these things were done in the good old days of our rigidly pious ancestors. The care of the meeting-house, provided for by the town at its annual town meeting as a part of the regular business of the town, is worthy our attention. In March, 1774, the town voted to employ John McIntire, who lived near by, to sweep the meeting-house and lock and unlock the doors for one year; and his compensation was fixed at three shillings for the year. This was not so small a sum for the service when we take unto account that the making and care of fires was no part of the duty, and that there was no church bell to ring. Then again, McIntire would attend church every Sunday any way, so that the matter of unlocking the doors before service and of locking them again after service imposed upon him no burden except a little earlier and a little later attendance. The sweeping was not frequent. At the March meeting in 1777, the town voted "to sweep the meeting-house twelve times a year;"—so says the record. The sweeping was done, of course, by proxy, and John McIntire was the proxy. In 1779, McIntire, who was in the militia, had been promoted—it was a sergeant's warrant. At the March meeting the town voted " to pay Sergeant John McIntire eleven dollars to sweep the meeting-house for the ensuing year." But in 1782, John McIntire had been promoted again—it was a lieutenant's commission this time. So far as the records show he never again swept the meeting-house. Sergeants, however, were still available, and the job of sweeping the meeting-house twelve times a year was given, by vote of the town, to Sergeant Draper at a salary of five shillings for the year. In 1780, the town voted " to give Deac. Matthews five shillings to sweep the meeting-house twelve times the ensuing year, at the rate of two shillings per bushel for Indian corn."

The unfinished condition of the meeting-house is attested by the votes passed in town meeting from time to time. At the March meeting, 1774, the town voted that "Mr. Aaron Bell and Mr. Matthew Campbell may build one pew on the south side of the west door, and sit there during the town's pleasure, and if the town dispossess them, to pay them their cost of building." The following article appeared in the warrant for the December meeting, 1775: "To see if the town will vote to board up the windows in the meeting house and pass such vote as they think proper."

At a meeting held May 20, 1777, it was voted "that the town will build all the pews on the lower floor at the cost of the town for the use of those that are destitute of pews," and Lieut. William Moore, Deacon Jesse Johnson, and Capt. Henry were chosen a committee to attend to the building of them. The town also voted "that Lieut. Williams and wife, John Abbott and wife, and Abiel Abbott should sit in Ward and Willard's pew until pews are built." This pew was one of those reserved by the proprietors when they gave the meeting-house to the town. Its owners were non-residents.

At the March meeting, 1782, the town voted "to put in studds and raves for the present in the side of the gallery, and rough-board them, and make a seat convenient for the people to sit in." This was estimated to require five hundred feet of boards. Deacon Johnson, Gideon Matthews, and David Shepard were chosen a committee to do the work, and were required to have it done by the last of May. In August, 1782, William Foot and William Stone were appointed a committee "to board the meeting house windows up tight to keep out the rain." It was also voted "that Edward Wright, Jr., come and view the glass windows of the meeting house and fix them up as well as he can, and the town will pay him."

At the meeting in May it was voted that, pending the building of the pews on the lower floor, "Ebenezer Dowd and wife, William McIntire, John Thompson and wife, and Samuel Gould and wife are seated in Col. Willard's pew for the present;" and it also recorded in the town records of that meeting that "Lieut. William Moore and Timothy Lyman give leave if the pew is full, they may sit in their pew;" also that "Abner Smith, Jr., and wife sit in Deacon Matthews' pew until the pews are built."

Manner of Seating Worshippers.

The matter of adjusting people with regard to their proper dignity was by no means free from difficulty. It must have been as delicate a piece of social engineering as seating the singers of a volunteer chorus choir. As we have seen, this was arranged according to the rating of individuals in the town valuation list. We arrange it on the same principle now—the wealthiest hire the best pews,—but there was somewhat more formality in the manner of arranging this question by our ancestors. The pews were arranged with strict regard to the dignity of location. It is not to be presumed that every one was satisfied, although injured pride was not always spread upon the town records. Indeed, few people care to expose to the public gaze, the bandages with which they bind up their hurt feelings. But David Bolton was not to be suppressed by any such delicacy. In 1774, he complained to the town, and brought his complaint before the town meeting, "that he did not have his right in the meeting house according to his valuation." But the town wisely refused to do anything about it. Over sensitive people seldom receive any comfort at the hands of public assemblies. In public assemblies there is usually a disposition to be fair and just; and this was exhibited toward Timothy Smith, who, in 1778, represented to the town that as he lived in the east part of the town he preferred to attend public worship with the people of Norwich, and asked to be relieved from the minister tax in Murrayfield. His request was granted.

The following queer vote was passed at a meeting in 1774 : "That Robert Proctor and Jonas Henry shall have the pew spot between Caleb Bascom's pew and the stairs as other people have theirs."

Mr. Bascom's Firewood.

There was always a town meeting held in November or in December, at which it was one of the regular items of business to vote a supply of firewood for the Rev. Mr. Bascom, in accordance with the terms of his settlement. At first there was, probably, little or no difficulty in obtaining a suitable supply; but in December, 1775, the vote of the town indicates that the duty had been thrown upon the individual citizen to furnish each his share of this supply of wood for the parsonage. The town voted that "Lieut. Enoch Shepard, Mr. Wm. Moore, Mr. Reuben Woolworth, and Mr. John McIntire be a committee to desire the people in their quarter to get said wood on days they shall appoint, and that if any person neglect his duty as to getting wood, said committee make return of their names and neglect to be read in open town meeting." It is to be presumed that this threat had the desired effect; for no names were reported. This was undoubtedly a burdensome way of furnishing the wood, and very likely it fell unequally upon the people in proportion to their distance from the parsonage. The roads were poor and difficult for traveling, and often so drifted with snow as to be nearly or quite impassable for loaded teams. Perhaps this would explain the action of the town in November, 1777, in choosing a committee consisting of Deacon James Hamilton, Gideon Matthews, and Sergeant John McIntire to wait upon and "try to hire Rev. Aaron Bascom to get his firewood, and report to the meeting in half an hour." The committee soon returned and reported an arrangement with Mr. Bascom to the effect that he would accept from the town the sum of thirty dollars and get his own firewood." The town voted to accept the arrangement. This, of course, meant a money tax upon each one ; and this, too, was burdensome. People living near, or who could easily reach the parsonage with loaded teams, preferred to pay the tax in wood. So in November, 1778, the town voted Mr. Bascom thirty dollars for his firewood, but with the provision that "if any man gets his share of the firewood by the middle of December next, he shall have at the rate of ten shillings per load 3 feet high, 4 feet wide, and 8 feet long." But at the November meeting, 1779, with a list of about one hundred tax payers, the town voted to pay John McIntire seventy-five pounds to get Mr. Bascom's firewood for the year ensuing, and that every man who brings one-half cord by the 1st of January shall be allowed fifteen shillings out of his town rate, and that the same shall be deducted from the seventy-five pounds." After this it does not appear that there was any difficulty in getting the parson's firewood. At a meeting held in October, 1780, the town voted "to pay John Hamilton four pounds and eight shillings in the old way to get Rev. Mr. Bascom's firewood the year ensuing, he allowing each man to get his proportion of wood by the 15th of December, next, and to be allowed two shillings and six pence per cord the old way." In November, 1781, under an article in the warrant "To let out the getting wood for our Rev. Pastor the year ensuing," it was by vote let out to Lieut. John McIntire for three pounds and eight shillings. In November, 1782, the town voted sixty pounds for Mr. Bascom's salary and three pounds to get his firewood.

Mr. Bascom's Salary.

As the currency depreciated during the War of the Revolution, Mr. Bascom found his salary insufficient, and on Thanksgiving Day, 1778, he laid the matter before the congregation in a letter read from the pulpit, which led to the calling of a town meeting to be held December 16th, "to give answer to Rev. Mr. Bascom's letter, which he read last Thanksgiving Day, and to see if the town will vote to raise any money or specie for the use of Rev. Mr. Bascom on account of the deficiency of our paper currency." After the meeting was opened a request was sent to Mr. Bascom to attend the meeting and have his letter read. The result of this meeting was a vote "to pay Mr. Bascom for his support for the year ensuing forty pounds in specie or labor, as labor and specie went amongst us in the year 1774, or money enough to buy so much specie at the year's end, or by 20th of next December."

Depreciated Currency.

In 1779, Congress issued $140,000,000 currency, worth in coin only $7,000,000. It depreciated more rapidly than it was issued. In March, 1780, Congress decided to resume in silver at the rate of one dollar in silver to forty in paper. No wonder Mr. Bascom complained when his salary was paid in the depreciated continental currency.

Cemetery.

The clearing of the land about the meeting house and in the cemetery was limited to what was absolutely necessary; and no wonder, for these people had enough to do in clearing their own farms. At the March meeting in 1774, the town voted "to clear the grave yard and around the meeting house." But time passed on and little or no improvement was made, as would appear from the following article in the warrant for a town meeting to be held in April, 1776 : "To see if the town will vote to do any work this summer on the burying yard to make it decent." That its condition was bad and that some of the people of the town were a good deal in earnest about it may fairly be inferred from the following vote : "That all the polls in this town shall work one day on the grave yard by the 20th of June next, or pay four shillings, and that the selectmen shall notify the people what work to do." At this time there were nearly one hundred polls in the town ; which would indicate that a good deal of work was needed to put the cemetery in decent condition.

In May, 1777, the town voted "to get a funeral cloth."

Schools.

The inhabitants of Murrayfield were never indifferent to the subject of education, but poverty often prevented them from appropriating money for schools. In the warrant for the December meeting, 1775, there was an article "to see if the town will vote any school money and how much, and when to pay it into the treasury." But the town voted to raise no money. In March, 1777, the town voted "to raise no money either for schools or highways this year." The vote in 1778 was to raise no money for schools. But at the March meeting, 1779, the town voted "to raise some school money this present year, and to have it divided according as the committee shall divide the districts." Deacon James Hamilton, Doctor David Shepard, Samuel Jones, Lieut. James Clark, and Samuel Ellis were chosen a committee to divide the town into school districts; and it was "voted to raise one penny half penny on the pound and as much on the poll in proportion as other taxes are laid for the support of schools this year." In May of the same year the town voted to do something with the school lands; and Lieut. Newton Parmenter, Capt. Smith, and Capt. Enoch Shepard were chosen a committee to view the school lands, and make report to the next town meeting.

In April, 1780, the question of building school houses was brought before the town. The vote was that the town build none this year, but that permission be given to each school district to build one not exceeding the dimensions of twenty feet long, by eighteen feet wide, and one story high; and also that the districts be permitted to choose their own committees to build the houses. It was further voted not to raise any more money for schools the present year. But in June of the same year the town voted to raise four hundred pounds for the support of schools. In May, 1781, the town voted to raise for schools "thirty pounds in hard cash or paper currency equivalent," to be paid in by November 1st. In the warrant for the meeting in November, 1781, was an article "to see if the town will choose committees in their several districts to see that their school money is expended according to law." The town voted such committees in the several districts as follows: Ensign Stephen Lyman for the Middle District, Deacon James Hamilton for the North End District, Samuel Jones for the Eggleston District, Aaron Bell for the Abbott District, Gershom Rust for the East District, Jabez Tracy for the South District, and Robert Proctor for the West Branch.

Leasing School Lands.

In February, 1783, the town passed the following vote: "That the Selectmen and their successors in said office be a committee to hunt up the school lands lying in, and belonging to, the township of Murrayfield; and they are hereby directed to appraise said school lands for its real value per acre cash in hand, and to lease out said lands to any person or persons by the lot or part of a lot for any term of time not exceeding nine hundred and ninety-nine years ; the person or persons to pay the lawful interest annually on the sums which said lands shall amount to; the lease to be so framed that in case the interest shall not be paid annually, the selectmen are hereby empowered to sue said lease or leases in such manner as the law directs ; and said lands to return to the town again to dispose of."

A specimen copy of the leases drafted under this vote will not be uninteresting.

"This agreement made this twenty-seventh day of February in the year of our Lord 1783 between William Campbell & John Blair selectmen of Murrayfield & Enoch Shepard of Murrayfield, all in the County of Hampshire, gentlemen, witnesseth: that agreeably to a vote of the freeholders & other inhabitants of the town of Murrayfield, assembled in a legal town meeting on the third day of February, inst., & passed a vote to lease out their school lands, & that the selectmen and their successors in said office should be a committee for said purpose; in conformity to said vote, we, by these presents, have agreed to lease out one lot of said school land to said Enoch Shepard for the term of nine hundred and ninety-nine years from the date above. Said lot is called a fifty acre lot in the Third Division on the West Branch, be the same more or less. Bounded as follows, viz., by letter P northeasterly, by No. 7 southeasterly, by No. 5 southwesterly, by No. Nought northwesterly. The above described lot is leased out to said Enoch Shepard, his heirs & assigns for the above term of nine hundred & ninety-nine years on the following terms: Said school lot as above described is valued by our appraisment at twenty-five pounds lawful money. The interest of twenty-five pounds lawful money at six per cent. is to be paid annually by Enoch Shepard his heirs & assigns into the hands of the Selectmen of Murrayfield. And in case the interest is not paid agreeably to the above terms the Selectmen of said town of Murrayfield are to ask & demand of said Enoch Shepard his heirs & assigns the interest as above; & if the interest is not paid within sixty days after such demand is made, the Selectmen then in being are to inform said Enoch Shepard, his heirs & assigns that this lease with all its privileges is forfeited & to be considered as nul & void & is to be at the disposal of the town again unless in extraordinary case, viz: if said Enoch Shepard, his heirs or assigns should be absent or should be delerious or in case of decease, in such cases said Enoch Shepard, his heirs & assigns, are to make good all interest that may be due with all reasonable damages for any neglect longer than the term of eighteen months, when such extraordinaries may happen, & if such neglect exceeds the term of eighteen months then the above demand of the Selectmen to be in force. By virtue of the power & authority to us given by said vote of the third day of February, inst., & by these presents, to have & to hold the said premises together with all their appurtenances to him the said Enoch Shepard, his heirs & assigns as an absolute estate of inheritance for the term of time as above.

"And we, the said William Campbell & John Blair, do in our said capacity & in the name & behalf of the town, covenant & engage that said demised premises to him, the said Enoch Shepard, his heirs and assigns, against the lawful claims & demands of all persons whatsoever hereafter for the term of time as above to warrant, secure, & defend by these presents.

"In witness whereof we, the said William & John, in our said capacity & in behalf of said town, have hereunto set our hands and seals this seventeenth day of February, A. D. 1783.

```
Signed, sealed, & delivered ⎫    ENOCH SHEPARD & Seal.
in presence of               ⎬
    DAVID SHEPARD,           ⎪    JOHN BLAIR & Seal,       ⎫ Selectmen of
    LUCINDA SHEPARD.         ⎭    WILLIAM CAMPBELL & Seal. ⎬ Murrayfield."
```

This lease was recorded in the record book of the town of Murrayfield.

Similar leases were given of other tracts of school land after the name of the town was changed from Murrayfield to Chester.

SCHOOLHOUSES.

At a town meeting held April 7th, 1783, the town "voted that the Middle School District have liberty to set a school house on the town's land the west side of the highway west of the burying yard." This was the west side of the road leading to the East Branch, and on the spot where the present schoolhouse stands at Chester Center, and is within the eight acres laid out for a meeting-house place, and burial place, and a training field in 1763.

TOWN POUND.

At the annual town meeting, 1774, the town voted for the first time to build a pound, and appropriated for this purpose the sum of twelve pounds. This was equal to the sum which the undivided town appropriated for schools the previous year.

In July, 1778, the town voted "that the rams must be shut up from September 20th to November 20th on penalty of forfeiture of the ram to the person finding it." In March, 1782, the town voted "that hogs should not run at large during any part of the year."

The progress attained in cattle raising, as late as 1776, may be judged by an article which was in a town meeting called in June, 1776:

"To see if the town will vote to hire a bull for the service of the town." The town voted against the article.

WOLVES.

At a meeting held as late as 1781, one item of business was, "To see if the town will vote to give a bounty for wolves' heads," and the town voted "to give twelve shillings for a wolf head if it is killed by any of the inhabitants of this town in this or in the neighboring towns." This was the first action taken by the town in any town meeting upon this subject; and down to the spring of 1783 no action appears to have been taken by the town touching wolves, other than the vote above named.

FIRST JUSTICE OF THE PEACE.

In the warrant calling the December town meeting in 1775, was the following article: "To see if the town will vote to have a justice of the peace in this town and also nominate one." The vote taken under this article is recorded as follows: "Voted that it is the mind of the town if there is established to confess judgment for debts it is best to have a justice of the peace in town, also nominated Lieut. Enoch Shepard."

FORM OF CAPTION OF TOWN WARRANTS.

Prior to 1775 town meetings were called by warrants issued "in his majesty's name;" but in this year the warrants were directed to the constable, requiring him, "in the name and by the direction of the Continental Provincial Congress," to warn, etc.

TOWN POOR.

The question of supporting the poor in the town came up in town meeting for the first time in June, 1778, in the form of a proposition "to see if the town would choose a committee to take care of the poor in town." The town refused to choose a committee. It does not appear whether the town had in any way provided for the poor; neither does it appear that there had been poor persons in the town needing public charity, except as it may be inferred from the fact of bringing the question before the town.

SMALL-POX AND INOCULATION.

The action of the town at a town meeting held in April, 1778, touching inoculation as a protection against small-pox is interesting as giving some idea of how this was managed before the world was in possession of Jenner's discovery, which was made about this time. At this meeting the town voted that "Capt. Shepard may have his family inoculated in his house if he will give good obligations for his good behavior," and that he "may let others of this town as long as the first day of May and no longer, if there is room for them." In May following the town voted "that any person may have liberty to have the small-pox by inoculation in the fall at proper places as the town shall judge best." The process of inoculation was as follows: "If the matter of a variolous (or small-pox) pustule, taken after the commencement of the eighth day, be inserted in or beneath the skin of a person who has not previously suffered from small-pox, the following phenomena are induced: 1. Local inflammation is set up; 2. At the end of six days there is fever similar to that of small-pox; and 3. After the lapse of three more days, there is a more or less abundant eruption of pustules. This process is termed inoculation, and the disease thus produced is denominated inoculated small-pox. The disease produced in this artificial manner is much simpler and less dangerous than ordinary small-pox; and as this was an almost certain means of preventing a subsequent attack of the ordinary disease, inoculation was much practiced until the discovery (about 1796) of the anti-variolous power of vaccination." See Chamber's Encyclopædia.

In the spring of 1720 small-pox broke out again in Massachusetts after an interval of about twenty years, and "out of five thousand eight hundred and eighty-nine persons who were attacked in Boston," says Barry, "eight hundred and forty-four died." In view of this fact it is strange that any intelligent person should question the importance of vaccination, or the wisdom of the law requiring it. Barry adds: "The practice of inoculation had been recently introduced into Europe, and Cotton Mather, one of the ministers of Boston, having read in the Transactions of the Royal Society of England, of which he was a member, letters from Constantinople and Smyrna giving an account of its practice and its success, interested himself to introduce it into America; but his application to the physicians of the town was at first unsuccessful." For a time it met with bitter opposition, based upon all sorts of grounds, moral, religious and political; and violence was indulged in, both by words and acts.

HIGHWAYS.

As we have already seen, building and repairing of highways were always important items of expense to the town. The roads over the highlands were not only difficult to travel, but often difficult to make and keep in repair in places where the grade is steep, rendering them liable to be washed badly by heavy rains, and in the spring by the rapid thawing of snow. But in places where the grade is light or the ground level, the roads when once made need but little attention to keep them in reasonably good condition. This would be the fact on all the roads along the river banks, except in places—and they are numerous—where the interval lands are but little elevated above the river in high water, exposing them to the gradual encroachment of the river which tends to crowd toward one side or the other of the valley, often washing away several feet in times of great freshets, and often overflowing the roadbed and washing out the material of which it is made, so that between this kind of damage and the maintaining of bridges, the river roads—so called—are far more expensive than those upon the higher lands. In March, 1774, the town voted to raise eighty pounds for the repair of highways, twelve shillings on the poll and the remainder on the estates, and voted to allow three shillings per day for work on the highway. At this meeting the town voted to build a "highway from William Henry's down to the dugway at David Scott's land," and at the same time it was voted not to discontinue the "old road from Lieut. James Clark's house down Moose Hill to dugway in David Scott's land." From a point near the old cellar-place which marks the spot where Absolom Blair's house stood, is an old road leading off from the older road in the direction of the house formerly known as the "Raymond place," but better known to-day as the "Woodruff place." This road would have let both Clark and Blair out into the new road from "Henry's down to the dugway," but it would have been less convenient for them. Many new roads were laid out from time to time as necessity required, and their locations were fully described in the records of the town. In 1777 ninety pounds were raised for repair of highways that year, and at the same meeting the town voted that "the selectmen lay out a road, if they judge best, with the consent of Deac. Johnson and the Wrights that own the land, across from Deac. Johnson's, kitter-cornering across Wright's land into the old road near the corner of said Wright's lot, or across the corner of Major Taylor's." At the March meeting in 1778 the town appropriated one hundred pounds for the repair of highways, and voted to pay nine shillings per day until the last of June for work on the highways." There was pressing need for bridges. An article "To see if the town will assist Norwich in building a bridge across the river near Mr. Way's mill"—that is to say, near where Norwich bridge now stands—

was inserted in the warrant for the November meeting in 1778, but the town voted no. But when the proposition took the form of asking the General Court to require the original proprietors to build the bridge, the town, at a meeting held February 8th, 1779, voted "to bear its proportional cost with Norwich to procure the building of a bridge near Way's mill." The joint action of the town of Norwich and Murrayfield resulted, as has been related before, in the building of the bridge at the expense of the proprietors, and in the sale of lands belonging to Timothy Paine to pay the expense.

In March, 1779, the town voted to lay a road "from Landlord Taylor's for Partridgefield"—now Middlefield. Five dollars was allowed this year per day for work on the highways, and the town voted "to raise four hundred pounds for the repair of highways the present year."

It sometimes happens that heavy rains come in the latter part of summer, causing freshets, which do great damage to the roads. That this happened in 1779 would appear from the fact that a town meeting was held August 18th, at which the town passed the following vote: "If any man will do a good, faithful day's work on the highways this summer or fall, it shall be allowed in the next year's highway rate." In May, 1781, the town voted to raise sixty pounds in hard cash to repair highways, and that four shillings in hard cash should be paid for a day's work. In 1780 it was voted "to give twenty dollars per day for highway work." In April, 1782, the town voted to raise sixty pounds for the repair of highways, and to allow three shillings for a day's work. And in March, 1783, eighty pounds were appropriated to the repair of highways, and three shillings allowed for a day's work.

REPRESENTATIVES TO THE GENERAL COURT.

When the east part of Murrayfield was set off into a separate district, it was invested with all the privileges of other towns, with the exception that it was not permitted to choose a separate representative to the General Court; but for that purpose it was still to act with Murrayfield. In July, 1775, Murrayfield "voted to send one representative to the General Court." And it was also "voted that the representative be paid in work or grain for his own time and horses." Lieut. Enoch Shepard was the first representative chosen by the town of Murrayfield to the General Court. The town also "chose for a committee to give instructions to the representative, Deac. John Kirtland, Lieut. David Scott, Ensign Stephen Lyman, Deac. Samuel Matthews, and Capt. Abner Smith." One of the articles in the warrant for the December meeting was "To see if the town will reconsider the vote respecting paying the representative, and pass such votes as the town shall judge best respecting the same." The vote under this article, as recorded is: "Voted to reconsider the vote respecting paying the representative." It would seem that Shepard was continued in the office of representative for several years; for in May, 1779, the town passed the following vote: "Voted that the town will be obliged to pay Capt. Enoch Shepard his expenses for his travel and attendance on the General Court, he giving his time and allowing the town his fees." In May, 1780, Timothy Lyman was chosen representative to the General Court, and Capt. John Kelso, Capt. Enoch Shepard, Deac. James Hamilton, Alexander Gordon, and Timothy Smith were chosen a committee "to instruct the representative and order him when to go to Boston." In May, 1782, Deac. Johnson was chosen representative, and the town passed the following vote: "Voted to choose a committee of five to give Deac. Johnson instructions how to conduct at Boston with regard to the business of the town and when to go, and not to tarry upon other public business. Chose Dr. David Shepard, Capt. Enoch Shepard, Deac. Matthews, and Capt. Abner Smith committee."

RELATIONS WITH NORWICH.

At the March meeting in 1774, the claim of Norwich to its share of the seals and measures came up for action; the justice of which was conceded, and the constable instructed to procure such other measures as should be necessary.

The following petition to the selectmen was duly brought before the town at a meeting held July 5th, 1779:

"To the Honorable Selectmen of the town of Murrayfield, namely, Timothy Lyman & John Blair: We, who are undernamed, do humbly desire you would warn a town meeting in order to set us off from the town of Murrayfield to the town of Norwich, that we may know the minds of the town & have their vote for being set off. Our grievances are so heavy that we can not lie still under them; which grievances we shall declare to the meeting when the meeting is, we looking to ourselves to be the humble servants at so far a distance that we can not enjoy the privileges of the town which causes us to make this address to select gentlemen of the town; & in hopes of your granting our weak request we take the boldness, with love & pleasure to subscribe ourselves your well-meaning, though aggrieved friends & very humble servants so long as we are. Dated at Murrayfield, May 13th, 1779.

ABEL PARTRIDGE,
ALLYN GREEN,
EBENEZER FREEMAN,
EUNICE GEER,
JOHN MORSE,
EMANUEL NORTHROP,
JOSEPH NORTHROP,
DAVID TWADWELL."

The article in the warrant was as follows: "To see if the town will vote off the east part of this town to Norwich about as far as the house where Silsbury Geer formerly lived." But the town rejected the proposition. This, however, did not settle the question, as we see by the action of the town in May, 1780, in choosing Dr. David Shepard, Mr. Timothy Lyman and Mr. Timothy Smith, "a committee to meet the court's committee appointed to straighten the line between Murrayfield and Norwich," and the committee was instructed to "object against Norwich having a straight line." This subject came before the town again at a meeting held December 25th, 1780. That the inhabitants of Murrayfield were a good deal excited about the question may fairly be inferred from the following votes: "Voted to choose a committee of five to wait on the court's committee appointed to view the situation and circumstances of straightening the line between the towns of Murrayfield and Norwich, and chose Dr. David Shepard, Mr. Timothy Smith, Mr. Timothy Lyman, Capt. Abner Smith, Ensign Stephen Lyman. Also voted that the committee use their utmost influence to hinder the town of Norwich from obtaining one inch more than the line already fixed." Also voted "that if the court's committee should think best to straighten the line between Murrayfield and Norwich that the town will petition the General Court to incorporate both towns together."

At a town meeting held in January, 1781, the town voted "that Timothy Lyman shall take a plan of the town and go to Major Taylor's on account of the land that Norwich has taken off of this town to straighten the line."

On the 8th of May, 1781, the General Court passed the following:

"An act to set off a part of the town of Murrayfield & annex it to the town of Norwich.

Whereas, It appears that Abel Partridge and others, living in the easterly part of Murrayfield, would be greatly accommodated by being set off from said town of Murrayfield & annexed to the town of Norwich.

§ 1. Be it, therefore, enacted by the Senate and House of Representatives in General Court assembled, & by the authority of the same, that all that part of the town of Murrayfield that lies easterly of a direct line from the south west corner of Ingersole Grant, so called, to the south west corner of Chesterfield, with the inhabitants thereon, shall forever hereafter be considered as belonging to the town of Norwich.

§ 2. *Provided nevertheless*, that the said inhabitants shall pay their proportionable part of all the taxes, & of men to be raised for the Continental army, which are already ordered by the General Court on said town of Murrayfield, anything in this act to the contrary notwithstanding.

§ 3. Provided also, & be it further enacted by the authority aforesaid, that the amount of the estate contained on & in said tract of land, & the polls thereon returned by the assessors of the town of Murrayfield, be deducted from the return made by the assessors of the town of Norwich."

MIDDLEFIELD.

The inhabitants of the northwest part of the town thought they would be better off if annexed to the town of Middlefield, and signified their wish by a petition as follows:

"MURRAYFIELD, February 18th, 1779. Whereas we, the inhabitants of the north west part of the town of Murrayfield being convened together with the inhabitants of the north east part of Becket & south west part of Worthington unanimously think it best to be set off as a town; wherefore we request & desire to be set off from this town & adjoin those forementioned inhabitants; our living so remote from the Middle of the town makes it very tedious attending any town business, especially the preaching of the Gospel; therefore we, whose names are underwritten, do humbly petition to this town to set us off near as far as Thomas Elder's.

"To the select men of Murrayfield: The above writing to be put into the warrant for the March meeting or immediately to call a meeting on the same account.
SAMUEL JONES,
JOHN TAYLOR,
JOHN THOMPSON,
JOHN JONES,
BENJAMIN EGGLESTON,
BIGOTT EGGLESTON,
LEBANON ISHAM."

It was put into the warrant for the March meeting, but the town refused to grant the request of the petitioners. But the petitioners went to the General Court and obtained their desire.

VALUATION LISTS.

The aggregate valuation of the town in 1775 was sixteen hundred and five pounds and six shillings.

In 1776, Capt. Abner Smith was rated at one hundred and nineteen pounds and fifteen shillings; Joel Seward was rated at seventy-one pounds and four shillings; Capt. Enoch Shepard was rated at sixty-six pounds and four shillings; James Clark was rated at sixty-four pounds; Thaddeus Newton was rated at sixty-three pounds and sixteen shillings, and Malcom Henry was rated at sixty-eight pounds and fourteen shillings. Abner Smith was for several years the richest man in town.

In 1777 the aggregate valuation of the town was thirty-eight thousand eight hundred and nineteen pounds and sixteen shillings. The same year Abner Smith was rated at twelve hundred and seventy-three pounds. This same year the Rev. Mr. Bascom's name appeared for the first time on the valuation list, and he was rated at one hundred and ninety pounds; but no poll tax was assessed to him. The rating of non-resident tax-payers in 1777 was as follows:

Abijah Willard,	rated at	£3000
John Murray,	"	4000
John Chandler,	"	5600
Timothy Paine,	"	4400
James Otis,	"	516
Col. James Otis,	"	400
Col. Samuel Ward,	"	1400
Brig. Joseph Otis,	"	487
Capt. Beaumont,	"	118

In May, 1780, the town's valuation had shrunk to four thousand nine hundred and fifteen pounds, and Abner Smith's rating was one hundred and thirty-nine pounds, he being the only resident tax-payer who was rated as high as one hundred pounds. In October the aggregate valuation of the town was four thousand seven hundred and thirty-eight pounds, and Abner Smith's rating was one hundred and thirty-seven pounds.

In July, 1781, the aggregate valuation of the town was four thousand nine hundred and twenty-four pounds; and in November it was three thousand and six pounds; at which time Abner Smith, still the richest man in town, was rated at only thirty-one pounds and six shillings. But this same year the valuation of Timothy Paine, non-resident, was twelve hundred pounds. The valuation list showed that the property of the other non-resident tax-payers did not shrink proportionately with that of resident tax-payers.

The last valuation list taken by the assessors of the town under the name of Murrayfield, was dated November 15, 1782, a copy of which is given:

	Poll.	Real. £. s. d.	Personal. £. s. d.	Total. £. s. d.
Joseph Abbott,	1	0 4 9	0 13 8	0 18 5
Abial Abbott,	1	0 15 0	1 13 5	2 8 5
John Abbott,	1	2 5 0	2 13 11	4 18 11
Ebenezer Abbott,	1	0 11 0	0 7 0	0 18 0
David Allen,	0	0 6 0	0 0 0	0 6 0
William Bell,	2	2 18 0	2 7 5	5 5 5
Aaron Bell,	1	1 6 5	1 14 10	3 1 3
Samuel Bell,	1	1 8 7	1 10 5	2 19 0

A HISTORY OF MURRAYFIELD.

	Poll.	Real. £. s. d.	Personal. £. s. d.	Total. £. s. d.
John Bell,	1	2 6 5	1 19 5	4 5 10
Ebenezer Babcock,	2	1 13 2	1 13 3	3 6 5
Daniel Babcock,	1	0 4 0	0 3 7	0 7 7
Rodolphus Babcock,	1	0 0 0	0 0 0	0 0 0
James Campbell,	1	1 4 11	1 4 5	2 9 4
Matthew Campbell,	1	0 12 11	1 7 1	2 0 0
Lieut. Wm. Campbell,	1	1 10 6	1 10 6	3 1 0
Robert Campbell,	1	0 0 0	0 8 0	0 8 0
William Crossman,	1	1 4 0	0 10 6	1 14 6
Samuel Kellogg,	0	0 12 0	0 0 0	0 12 0
Ebenezer Collins,	0	0 11 6	0 0 0	0 11 6
Edward Crafts,	1	2 8 0	0 0 0	2 8 0
Robert Crawford,	1	0 16 0	0 8 10	1 4 10
Ebenezer Dowd,	1	0 4 0	0 5 9	0 9 9
Joshua Draper,	1	0 14 3	0 9 4	1 3 7
Samuel Elder,	1	1 10 0	1 10 0	3 0 0
Thomas Elder,	1	1 1 9	1 5 8	2 7 5
John Elder,	1	1 10 2	1 6 9	2 16 11
William Elder,	1	1 10 0	1 16 1	3 6 1
Benjamin Eggleston,	1	1 11 1	1 14 6	3 5 7
Abraham Fleming,	1	3 5 11	2 15 0	6 0 11
William Foot,	1	1 12 4	1 9 0	3 1 4
Jacob Fowle,	1	0 17 1	0 9 0	1 6 1
Thomas Flint,	1	0 8 8	0 0 0	0 8 8
Alexander Gordon,	1	2 16 8	2 7 7	5 4 3
David Gleason,	1	3 2 11	1 13 2	4 16 1
Capt. Grout,	1	0 0 0	0 10 6	0 10 6
James Hamilton,	3	2 5 0	2 13 3	4 18 3
James Mulhollon,	3	2 11 2	1 13 0	4 4 2
Simeon E. Mulhollon,	1	0 0 0	0 13 2	0 19 2
William Hill,	1	0 9 5	0 2 5	0 11 10
Zebulon Isham,	1	0 12 6	0 14 1	1 6 7
Jesse Johnson,	2	1 2 2	2 4 9	3 6 11
Samuel Jones,	1	2 1 2	1 8 9	3 9 11
John Jones,	1	1 16 4	0 19 2	2 15 6
Stephen Lyman,	1	4 12 5	3 4 0	7 16 5
Timothy Lyman,	1	4 1 0	3 10 15	7 11 5
John Laccore,	0	0 4 9	0 2 5	0 7 2
John Laccore, Jr.,	1	0 12 2	0 15 11	1 8 1

	Poll.	Real. £. s. d.	Personal. £. s. d.	Faculty. £. s. d.	Total. £. s. d.
William Moore,	1	2 18 7	2 6 8	0 0 0	5 5 3
John Moore,	0	1 7 1	1 1 0	0 0 0	2 8 1
James Moore,	1	1 1 3	0 18 7	0 0 0	1 19 10
Widow Jane Mann,	1	0 19 6	1 4 2	0 0 0	2 3 8
Samuel Matthews,	1	1 1 4	1 3 7	0 0 0	2 4 11
Gideon Matthews,	2	2 0 8	2 2 6	0 0 0	4 3 2
Ebenezer Prior,	0	1 0 0	0 7 2	0 0 0	1 7 2
William Prior,	1	0 0 0	0 0 0	0 0 0	0 0 0
David Mathar,	1	0 0 0	0 0 0	0 0 0	0 0 0
John McIntire,	2	3 2 9	2 6 4	0 0 0	5 9 1
Amasa Pomeroy,	1	0 13 1	0 8 0	0 0 0	1 1 1
John N. Parmenter,	1	1 7 4	1 10 0	0 0 0	2 17 4

A HISTORY OF MURRAYFIELD.

	Poll.	Real. £. s. d.	Personal. £. s. d.	Faculty. £. s. d.	Total. £. s. d.
Solomon Root,	1	1 4 9	2 3 11	0 0 0	3 8 8
Abner Smith,	2	8 0 0	5 9 11	0 0 0	13 9 11
Abner Smith, Jr.,	1	4 3 6	4 7 7	0 0 0	8 11 1
Timothy Smith,	1	2 10 0	1 8 4	0 0 0	3 18 4
Thomas Smith,	1	1 0 7	0 14 9	0 0 0	1 15 4
Joab Smith,	1	3 4 8	1 4 4	0 0 0	4 9 0
Daniel Smith,	0	0 12 1	0 7 3	0 0 0	0 19 4
Enoch Shepard,	2	4 14 1	1 12 4	0 0 0	6 6 5
David Shepard,	1	2 17 6	2 14 1	0 16 0	6 7 7
Widow Thompson,	1	1 0 10	0 15 10	0 0 0	1 16 8
Ebenezer Tillotson,	0	0 6 0	0 0 0	0 0 0	0 6 0
Edward Wright,	1	4 3 2	3 9 6	0 0 0	7 12 8
Edward Wright, Jr.,	1	2 1 11	1 13 7	0 19 2	4 14 8
Bazalel Wright,	1	0 3 0	0 8 7	0 4 0	0 15 7
Jude Wright,	1	0 0 0	0 12 0	0 0 0	0 12 0
Jesse Wright,	1	0 0 0	0 0 0	0 0 0	0 0 0
Elijah White,	1	0 9 0	0 3 7	0 0 0	0 12 7
John Williams,	1	0 0 0	0 0 0	0 0 0	0 0 0
Widow Ann Williams,	0	0 13 7	0 0 0	0 0 0	0 13 7
John Ward,	0	1 12 4	0 6 5	0 0 0	1 18 1
Ebenezer Webber,	0	1 4 0	0 0 0	0 0 0	1 4 0
Zadreus Farnsworth,	1	1 0 0	0 0 0	0 0 0	1 0 0
James Nooney,	1	1 3 0	0 14 4	0 0 0	1 17 4
John Taylor.	0	0 0 0	0 12 2	0 0 0	0 12 2
Ephraim Shelden,	1	1 11 7	0 5 0	0 0 0	1 16 7
Zadock Ingall,	0	0 18 4	0 5 3	0 0 0	1 3 7
Daniel Stone,	0	0 4 3	0 1 3	0 0 0	0 5 6
Elijah Stanton,	0	1 0 0	0 0 0	0 0 0	1 0 0
Thomas Armes.	1	1 0 0	0 3 7	0 0 0	1 3 7
William Rhoades,	1	1 0 0	0 6 0	0 0 0	1 6 0
Isaac Rhoades,	1	0 0 0	0 4 0	0 0 0	0 4 0
Noadiah Seward,	2	1 4 4	1 3 9	0 0 0	2 8 1
Widow Smith,	1	1 0 0	0 11 5	0 0 0	1 11 5
Samuel Morse,	0	1 8 0	0 0 0	0 0 0	1 8 0
Lieut. McIntire (wild land),	0	1 1 4	0 0 0	0 0 0	1 1 4
John Hamilton,	1	0 0 0	0 0 0	0 0 0	0 0 0
Ebenezer Smith,	1	0 0 0	1 1 7	0 0 0	1 1 7
Widow Sarah Anderson,	0	1 5 0	0 19 0	0 0 0	2 4 0
James Black,	1	1 7 10	2 9 1	0 4 0	4 0 11
William Russell,	1	0 0 0	0 0 0	0 0 0	0 0 0
John Blair,	1	0 12 0	1 7 0	0 0 0	1 19 0
Abial Baldwin,	0	1 0 0	0 0 0	0 0 0	1 0 0
Isaac Bissell,	1	0 0 0	1 15 2	0 0 0	1 15 2
Jonathan Miller,	1	0 10 0	0 10 0	0 0 0	1 0 0
James Clark,	2	2 15 4	2 7 9	0 0 0	5 3 9
John Crow,	1	0 0 0	0 0 0	0 0 0	0 0 0
Benjamin Converse,	2	3 14 9	1 13 7	0 0 0	5 8 4
James Cores,	1	0 16 0	0 11 4	0 0 0	1 7 4
Eliakim Cooley,	0	0 10 0	1 0 4	0 0 0	1 10 4
John Clark,	1	0 0 0	0 12 4	0 0 0	0 12 4
Isaac Dowd,	1	0 12 0	0 14 1	0 0 0	1 6 1
Samuel Ellis,	2	1 2 1	1 6 0	0 0 0	2 8 1
Silas Freeman,	2	0 10 0	0 10 2	0 0 0	1 0 2
James Gilmore,	0	1 10 0	0 0 0	0 0 0	1 10 0

A HISTORY OF MURRAYFIELD.

	Poll.	Real. £. s. d.	Personal. £. s. d.	Faculty. £. s. d.	Total. £. s. d.
Andrew Henry,	1	0 16 0	1 12 0	0 0 0	2 8 0
Joseph Henry,	1	2 11 10	1 13 4	0 0 0	4 5 2
John Kelso,	1	4 14 0	3 6 0	0 3 0	8 3 0
Hugh Kelso,	1	0 0 0	0 0 0	0 0 0	0 0 0
Noah Kingsbury,	0	0 5 0	0 4 9	0 0 0	0 9 9
Robert Moore,	1	0 15 4	0 7 9	0 0 0	1 3 1
Samuel Moore,	1	3 18 0	3 9 5	0 0 0	7 7 5
Thaddeus Newton,	1	1 0 0	1 5 8	0 0 0	2 5 8
Joseph Northrop,	0	0 4 0	0 3 7	0 0 0	0 7 7
Ebenezer Freeman,	1	0 9 10	0 9 6	0 0 0	0 19 4
Gershom Rust,	1	1 6 8	0 16 0	0 0 0	2 2 4
Ebenezer Stowe,	1	2 14 0	1 19 5	0 0 0	4 13 5
John Smith,	1	1 0 0	0 14 6	0 0 0	1 14 6
William Smith,	1	0 0 0	0 8 9	0 0 0	0 8 9
David Scott,	0	0 19 2	0 0 0	0 0 0	0 19 2

	Poll.	Real. £. s. d.	Personal. £. s. d.	Total. £. s. d.
Joel Seward,	1	7 0 0	3 19 7	10 19 7
Daniel Twadwell,	0	0 13 0	0 0 0	0 13 0
Jabez Tracey,	1	4 8 0	2 2 0	6 10 0
John Smith, 2d.	1	0 0 0	0 0 0	0 0 0
Reuben Woolworth,	2	2 15 0	1 19 0	4 14 0
Eli Woolworth,	1	0 0 0	1 0 0	1 0 0
Jonathan Webber,	1	2 9 4	2 2 1	4 11 3
Jonathan Wait,	1	0 19 7	0 19 11	1 19 6
Joseph Stebbins,	0	1 0 0	0 0 0	1 0 0
Joseph Stebbins, Jr.,	0	0 16 0	0 0 0	0 16 0
Daniel Smith, Jr.,	1	2 5 9	1 12 9	3 18 6
Richard Falley,	0	0 0 0	0 0 0	0 0 0
Samuel French,	2	0 16 11	1 0 0	1 16 11
Gershom Flagg,	1	0 6 0	0 3 9	0 9 9
David Hedges,	0	0 10 0	0 0 0	0 10 0
Capt. Alexander,	1	0 6 0	1 12 0	1 18 0
Ebenezer Meacham,	0	0 6 0	0 0 0	0 6 0
Joseph Pomeroy,	0	0 12 0	0 0 0	0 12 0
Robert Smith,	2	1 12 3	2 4 0	3 16 3
Oliver Hitchcock,	0	1 10 0	0 0 0	1 10 0
Robert Proctor,	2	1 14 0	1 0 9	2 14 9
John Bolton,	0	1 0 7	0 0 0	1 0 7
William Stone,	1	1 9 0	1 5 4	2 14 4
John Carlisle,	1	0 10 0	0 8 1	0 8 1
Solomon Cooley,	1	0 0 0	0 3 10	0 3 10
Job Clark,	0	1 0 0	0 0 0	1 0 0
Sylvester Sanderson,	0	0 10 0	0 0 0	0 10 0
William Hunt,	0	0 10 0	0 0 0	0 10 0
Zophar Searle,	0	2 0 0	0 0 0	2 0 0
John Griswold,	0	0 10 0	0 0 0	0 10 0
Timothy Culver,	0	1 13 0	0 0 0	1 13 0
Bildad Fowler,	0	1 0 0	0 0 0	1 0 0
Lieut. Simeon Fobes,	0	1 9 3	0 3 0	1 12 3
George Cooley,	0	0 10 0	0 0 0	0 10 0
Sylvester Judd,	0	1 0 0	0 0 0	1 0 0

A HISTORY OF MURRAYFIELD.

	Poll.	Real. £. s. d.	Faculty. £. s. d.	Total. £. s. d.
Davenport Williams,	1	0 3 0	0 3 0	0 6 0
Ward & Willard, heirs,	0	8 6 5	0 0 0	8 6 5
Samuel Ward,	0	5 5 0	0 0 0	5 5 0
Joshua Brocket,	0	4 1 0	0 0 0	4 1 0
James Otis,	0	4 4 0	0 0 0	4 4 0
Samuel Chandler,	0	3 12 0	0 0 0 Personal.	3 12 0
William Sizer,	0	3 11 7	0 0 0	3 11 7
Elijah Blackman,	0	3 11 7	0 0 0	3 11 7
Abner Witt,	1	0 16 0	0 0 0	0 16 0
Ebenezer Stowe,	0	1 0 0	0 0 0	1 0 0
Capt. Black, undiv'd lands	0	0 10 2	0 0 0	0 10 2
Richard Falley & Wood & Company,	0	4 10 0	0 0 0	4 10 0
Timothy Paine, Esq.,	0	12 0 0	0 0 0	12 0 0

ACCESSIONS TO THE VALUATION LIST.

The valuation list taken in September, 1774, showed the following new names among the resident tax-payers: Aaron Bell, Russell Dewey, Asa Gould, William Brown, John Jones, William Lunnon, Samuel Moore, James Moore, Abel Partridge, Larkin Williams, George Williams, and Rodman Williams. Between September, 1774, and September, 1777, the following named persons became citizens of the town of Murrayfield: Samuel Bell, Benjamin Babcock, Daniel Stone, John N. Parmenter, Calvin Torry, Joshua Draper, Nathan White, William Foot, Samuel French, Allyn Geer, Samuel Gould, William McIntire, Ebenezer Stowe, John Morse, James Bentley, Samuel Converse, Matthew Campbell, and Moses Orcutt. The list of 1778 showed the following new resident tax-payers: Aaron Crawford, Thomas Judd, Jethro Kenney, Thomas Kenney, Silas Freeman, Noah Kingsbury, Manuel Northrop, Robert Campbell, Moses Hale, Zebulon Isham, Joseph Wilter, Abraham Bell, and Elijah White.

The new resident tax-payers upon the list of 1779 were, Henry Lamberton, John Carlisle, and Jacob Fowle. The valuation list taken November, 1781, shows new names of resident tax-payers, as follows: Ebenezer Abbott, John Bell, Daniel Babcock, Job Belknap, Samuel Baldwin, Job Clark, Calvin Dunham, Maj. Edward Crafts, Othiel Pratt, Joab Smith, Simeon E. Mulhollon, Thomas Flint, Joseph Pomeroy, Capt. Nathaniel Alexander, Eli Woolworth, John Smith, 3d, Jabez Tracy, and Gershom Flagg.

DIFFICULTY OF COLLECTING TAXES DURING THE REVOLUTIONARY WAR.

At a town meeting called and held at six o'clock in the afternoon of June 25, 1776, the town passed the following vote: "Voted that those persons that do not pay their rates to Mr. Woolworth and Capt. Smith by next Monday shall pay interest till they do pay them." And the selectmen were appointed "a committee to take security of those which do not pay their rates by the time appointed. Also voted that those that will not comply with these votes shall be obliged to pay their rates as soon as the constables can collect them in the usual manner, unless the committees of the neighboring towns do advise otherwise; that this committee shall examine the treasurer and constables and see if they have not got some money in their hands; and if they have the town money, that they shall pay interest for it from this time till paid. Also voted that the committee shall meet next Monday to do this business, and those that do not come there, that have not paid their rates shall be viewed as persons that don't intend to comply with the votes of the town, unless they can give this committee satisfaction for their not coming. Also voted that this committee shall examine the list of those that have not paid their rates, and if they find that there is any that in their judgment ought not to pay their interest, to make report of that and all their other proceedings at the next town meeting."

At the November meeting, 1778, the town voted "that the assessors, in making the rates, where a man's rate in the pence column is above six pence to set it down one shilling, and where it is under six pence to set it down naught."

TOWN FINED FOR NOT FILLING ITS QUOTA OF MEN FOR THE WAR.

At a meeting held in May, 1779, one article in the warrant was: "To see what the town will do concerning the fine that is laid on us for want of three continental men." The town voted "not to have the assessors assess the fine at present," and also "voted to choose a committee of three to get things ready to get the fine off." The committee were Dr. David Shepard, Capt. Enoch Shepard, and Lieut. John Newton Parmenter. The town also voted "to give Mr. Stowe (who was constable) his part of the fine if the town is obliged to assess it." Touching this fine the town sent to the General Court a memorial as follows:

"To the Honorable Council & House of Representatives of the State of Massachusetts Bay, now sitting at Boston: We, your humble petitioners, beg leave to represent to your Honors the true state of affairs relative to the town of Murrayfield's raising their quota of men in the present war, & their willingness always to obey all orders & resolves of the General Court of this State

& the Honorable Continental Congress. Pursuant to which in the year 1777 the Honorable General Court of this State resolved that every town in this State should raise for the Continental service every seventh man; which in this town amounted to fourteen men. Accordingly the town by a large hire immediately procured the men; some for three years & some engaged during the war; soon after which, upon the Continental Army's not being filled up, there came a resolve from the Honorable Continental Congress that if any two men would hire a man for the Continental service more than their proportional part of every seventh man they should be freed from further draughts. Upon this encouragement from Congress that we should be favored in future draughts, a number of the inhabitants of this town, though unable to spare the money, joined together and hired five men more than our quota into the Continental service, supposing they would answer for the town when called upon afterwards. Accordingly in the year 1778 this town was called upon by the Honorable General Court of this State for two men to go for eight months & three for nine months to join the Continental Army to have it completed. The town being called together to get the men agreeably to orders from the General Court, they judged it no more than reasonable that we should have some allowance made us for those men that we had in the Continental service more than our proportion, & had given them a larger hire; therefore, relying on the justice of the cause of the town, thought it no more than honest & right not to draught any men for the nine months' service to join the Continental Army, but to make return of three of those men that we had already in the Continental service more than our quota; not doubting but that the Honorable General Court would, as soon as they saw the return, allow the men to stand good & answer for the town; though to our disappointment we find the town of Murrayfield fined three hundred pounds for the neglect of those three men which we viewed were in actual service for the town, & for no other, & are still in the service. Therefore your humble petitioners pray that the Honorable Council & House of Representatives would take into their wise consideration the poverty of the town, the services we have done in the war more than our proportion, especially in the Continental service, as we have in a great measure exhausted ourselves of money to hire so many men into the service. Therefore we pray that your honors would take these things into your wise consideration, & be pleased to take off our fine as your Honors in your wisdom shall judge best, & as in duty bound your petitioners shall ever pray.

Signed, by order of the Selectmen, in behalf of the town.

DAVID SHEPARD, Town Clerk of Murrayfield.
Murrayfield, April 13th, 1779."

At a meeting held in October, the town voted "to impower Capt. Enoch Shepard to borrow three hundred pounds to pay the fine laid on the town for want of three Continental soldiers." Also "that the three hundred pound fine or any part of which must be paid shall be assessed in the great State rate."

But when the facts were laid before the General Court and fully investigated, justice was done to the town, as appears by the following copy of the action of the General Court:

"State of Massachusetts Bay. In the House of Representatives, November 25th, 1779. On the petition of the inhabitants of the town of Murrayfield praying for abatement of a fine laid on said town by the tax bill in February last, in being deficient in raising two men for nine months and one for eight months. And whereas it appears to this Court, that said town had two men inlisted for three years more than their quota of the seventh part of the inhabitants of said town,

"Resolved, that the fine of three hundred pounds laid on said town be remitted. And that there be allowed & paid out of the treasury of this State to the town of Murrayfield, the aforesaid sum of three hundred pounds for the fines above mentioned."

A meeting was called to be held October 1st, 1782, "To see what measures the town will take with regard to the uneasiness of the non-resident proprietors about the taxes laid upon them last year."

The proprietors claimed that their lands were "taxed in a greater proportion than any other new town in the neighborhood of Murrayfield." But the town was inexorable, and voted "to have the rates that are set to the absentees settled as the selectmen and agents agreed, and that the selectmen be a committee to see this done." The assessment to the non-residents stood as follows:

				£.	s.	d.
Bildad Fowler,	100	acres of land;	tax	2	10	0
Job Clark,	100	" "	"	2	10	0
Silvanus Sanderson,	50	" "	"	1	5	0
William Hunt,	50	" "	"	1	5	0
Brigdr. Warham Parks,	777	" "	"	17	10	0
Capt. Ward,	1230	" "	"	27	10	0
Willard's Heirs,	680	" "	"	15	10	0
Samuel Chandler,	600	" "	"	13	10	0
Israel Bissel,	260	" "	"	7	0	0
Luther Loomis,	260	" "	"	7	0	0
Abel Baldwin,	100	" "	"	2	10	0
Timothy Paine, Esq.,	1200	" "	"	25	0	0
Allen Otis,	400	" "	"	10	0	0

CHAPTER SIXTH.

THE REVOLUTIONARY WAR.

The General Court of the Province of Massachusetts Bay had for some time been held at Cambridge. In 1772 by order of the governor it was adjourned to meet at Boston. The House, learning that the governor had accepted a salary from the King, voted 85 to 19 that "the making provision for the support of the governor of the province, independent of the acts and grants of the General Assembly, is an infraction upon the rights granted to the inhabitants by the royal charter, and in derogation of the constitution." And the court refused to repair the Province House occupied by the governor as his residence.

In a letter to Hillsborough, the governor recommended that severe measures be taken to put down "this new doctrine of independence." It was soon after announced that the King, " with the entire concurrence of Lord North, had made provision for the support of his law servants in the Massachusetts Bay." This excited the inhabitants of Boston to call a town meeting. John Hancock was chosen moderator; and an address to the governor was prepared requesting information as to the truth of the report that "stipends had been fixed to the offices of the judges." The governor refused this request. A new petition was immediately drafted and sent to him with a request that the subject be referred to the General Court. This request he also refused, and in response said : "If, in compliance with your petition, I should alter my determination, and meet the Assembly, contrary to my own judgment, at such time as you judge necessary, I should, in effect, yield to you the exercise of that part of my prerogative, and should be unable to justify my conduct to the King. There would, moreover, be danger of encouraging the inhabitants of the other towns in the province to assemble from time to time in order to consider the necessity or expediency of a session of the General Assembly, or to debate and transact other matters which the law that authorizes towns to assemble does not make the business of town meetings."

"This reply," says Barry, " which invaded the rights of the little republics of New England, was communicated to the meeting, and read several times; after which it was unanimously voted that the inhabitants of Boston 'have ever had, and ought to have, a right to petition the King for the redress of such grievances as they feel, or for the prevention of such as they have reason to apprehend, and to communicate their sentiments to other towns.' Then followed the step 'which included the whole revolution,' and Samuel Adams, the master spirit of the times, who had matured his plans by consulting the oldest men in the province, moved 'that a committee of correspondence be appointed, to consist of twenty-one persons, to state the rights of the colonists, and of this province in particular, as men and christians, and as subjects ; and to communicate and publish the same to the several towns and to the world, as the sense of this town, with the infringements and violations thereof that have been or from time to time may be made.' This motion was carried without a division, the vote in favor being nearly unanimous." Otis was the chairman of this committee. Its first meeting was held the following day in the representatives' chamber, and William Cooper was elected its clerk. The members of the committee pledged their honor "not to divulge any part of the conversation at any of the meetings to any person whatsoever, excepting what the committee itself should make known." This pledge was faithfully kept.*

The General Court stood prorogued to the 12th of January, 1774, when the governor again prorogued it to the 26th. In his opening address he particularly alluded to " his majesty's disapprobation of the appointment of committees of correspondence." The House replied to this that " while the common rights of the American subjects continued to be attacked at times when the general assemblies were not sitting, it was highly necessary that they should correspond with each other, in order to unite in the most effectual means for the obtaining a redress of their grievances," and that "as it had been the practice for years past for the governor and lieutenant governor of this province, and other officers of the crown, at all times, to correspond with the ministers of state and persons of distinction and influence in the nation, in order to concert and carry on such measures of the British administration as have been deemed by the colonists to be grievous to them, it cannot be thought unreasonable or improper for the colonists to correspond with their agents, as well as with each other, to the end that their grievances may be so explained to his majesty as that, in his justice, he may afford them necessary relief."

While affairs were in this attitude in America there was hardly less activity in England, and in Parliament the policy toward the colonists

* See Barry's Hist. of Mass., 2d period, pp. 445-449.

was discussed with great spirit; but the councils of the wiser statesmen were unheeded, and the colonists were threatened with coercion and further oppression. The insolence of British troops stationed in Boston, and the "Boston Massacre" maddened the colony still more; and added to this was the landing of additional British troops in Boston. In the meantime the colonists were not idle. Military discipline received due attention and encouragement; old guns were repaired; soldiers' accoutrements were anxiously provided for in anticipation of their probable need; and the towns began to provide themselves with ammunition. Such was the attitude affairs had reached in 1774. On the 25th of July in that year a town meeting was held in Murrayfield, the objects of which were "to see if the town would take into their serious consideration the covenant letters that the committee of correspondence have sent to us from Boston, and to sign the same, or pass any vote respecting the same, as the town shall judge best," and "to see what measures the town will come into with respect to getting or collecting the money that the General Assembly have desired us to collect in order for the support of the General Congress, and to pass any vote respecting the same, as the town shall think best." At this meeting the town voted unanimously not to "purchase, buy, or consume any goods or wares that shall be imported from Great Britain after the last of August next ensuing, until the meeting of the General Congress at Philadelphia." Also that "we will comply with what measures the General Congress shall agree upon at their meeting in Philadelphia in September next." A vote was also passed "to choose a committee of correspondence to transmit these votes to the committee of correspondence at Boston, and to correspond with said committee for this year." And the town appropriated twelve shillings and fourpence toward the support of the Congress.

The persons chosen to act on behalf of the town as a committee of correspondence for the ensuing year were, Capt. David Shepard, Deac. Jesse Johnson, Lieut. Malcom Henry, Deac. Samuel Matthews, and Lieut. James Clark. These persons all lived at or near the center of the town, excepting, perhaps, James Clark.

In the spring of 1774, Governor Hutchinson was superceded by Thomas Gage, whose activity in setting on foot measures for bringing the colonists to submission is a part of the history of Massachusetts.

"Writs were issued early in September convening the General Court at Salem on the fifth of October; but before that time arrived, a proclamation from the governor dissolved the assembly. For this step the patriots of the province were prepared; and, pursuant to the course which had been already agreed upon, after meeting on the appointed day, they resolved themselves into a PROVISIONAL CONGRESS.

The first session of this body, so memorable in our annals, was held at Salem on Friday, the seventh of October; the meeting was temporarily organized by choosing John Hancock chairman and Benjamin Lincoln clerk, and was adjourned to the following Tuesday, then to meet at the court house in Concord. Finding the court house too small for their purpose, however, the meeting-house was procured; the Congress was permanently organized by choosing John Hancock president and Benjamin Lincoln clerk; and provisions were made for opening the session each day with prayer. A committee on the state of the province was next appointed; and an address to his excellency the governor was reported, which was ordered to be printed in the Boston newspapers; the several constables and collectors throughout the province, having moneys in their hands payable to the order of Harrison Gray, Esq., were advised to retain the same, subject to the advice of a constitutional assembly; and the convention was adjourned to the town of Cambridge." (*See Barry's Hist. of Mass., Second Period, p. 495.*) The business of the Congress was transacted for several days with closed doors, and everything was done that could be to prepare for the crisis that was approaching. The several towns and districts in the province were advised to "see that each of the *minute men* not already provided therewith should be immediately equipped with an efficient fire arm, bayonet, pouch, knapsack, and thirty rounds of cartridge and balls, and be disciplined three times a week and oftener as opportunity may offer;" and that whenever there was any deficiency in arms and accouterments, the selectmen supply the same "out of the town stock; and in case of a deficiency there, to apply to such inhabitants as can best spare their arms and accouterments, and to borrow or purchase the same for the use of the inhabitants so enlisting."

At a meeting of the inhabitants of the town of Murrayfield, held December 26th, 1774, " To see if the town will take into their serious consideration the resolves of the Continental and Provincial Congress and come into some measures in the town to see that the same be put in execution or kept, and pass such votes in the town respecting the same as the town shall judge best." Also, "to see if the town will adopt any measures in order that the town may be provided with a stock of ammunition, and to pass such votes respecting the same as the town shall think best and most prudent." The town voted that " Capt. Abner Smith, Mr. Timothy Smith, Lieut. James Clark, Lieut. Malcom Henry, Mr. Archelus Anderson, Ensign George Williams,

Ensign Stephen Lyman, Mr. James Black, and Capt. David Shepard be a committee of inspection." And also voted that the town would stand by this committee in the execution of their office.

It was the duty of constables, who were also collectors of taxes, to collect the province tax upon the towns, and to pay it directly into the provincial treasury. At this meeting the town passed the following vote: "That the town will indemnify the constables if they will pay the province money they have in their hands into the town treasury to procure ammunition for a stock; and that the selectmen lay out said monies, when they get it, for a stock of ammunition." At its March meeting, 1775, the town voted that eight pounds be paid out of the treasury to provide a stock of powder and lead. Another meeting was held 24th April, 1775, and Malcom Henry was chosen a delegate to the Provincial Congress.

Although the town records do not show how many men were sent to the army, it is certain that several men had been sent; for at a meeting held May 4th, the town voted that the selectmen provide a supply of blankets and clothing "for our men now at Cambridge."

The Provincial Congress had addressed letters to the towns, urging the raising of troops and entreating them to " hasten and encourage by all possible means the enlistment of men to form an army."

By a vote of the committee of safety the Provincial Congress reassembled, after they had adjourned to May, in the town of Concord, and adjourned from that place to Watertown, and immediately, about April 20th, entered upon measures " indispensable for the salvation of the country."

The town of Murrayfield, at a meeting held June 19th, 1775, voted " that the committee shall attend to the orders of Congress respecting tory goods."

REPRESENTATIVES TO THE GENERAL COURT.

A meeting was held July 11th, 1775, " To see if the town will choose one or more representatives to attend and represent the town of Murrayfield in a great and general court or assembly to be convened at the meeting house in Watertown upon Wednesday the nineteenth day of July inst." Ensign Stephen Lyman was moderator. Lieut. Enoch Shepard was chosen representative; and the committee to instruct the representative was composed of the following persons: John Kirtland, David Scott, Stephen Lyman, Samuel Matthews, and Abner Smith.

The British troops evacuated Boston in March, 1776. In April the

General Court passed a resolve to alter the style of writs and other legal processes, substituting "The People and Government of Massachusetts" for George III, and in dating them using only "in the year of our Lord" instead of giving also the year of "his majesty's reign." In May the General Court passed an order advising the people in the several towns to instruct their representatives on the subject of independence.

Vote in Favor of a Declaration of Independence.

The selectmen of Murrayfield called a meeting to be held June 17th, 1776, "To see if the inhabitants will sign an agreement or oath that the General Court have sent out to see who are friends to liberty and their country and who are not;" also "to see if the town as a body are willing to have the thirteen united colonies declared an independent State from Great Britain if the Continental and General Courts shall judge best, and to pass any vote respecting the same as the town shall judge best and most prudent." The following votes were passed: "Voted to sign an agreement or oath sent out from the General Court;" also "voted that it is the mind of this town that the Continental Congress declare independence from Great Britain, to a man, in a full meeting."

Money for Soldiers.

September 19th, 1776, the town voted "to hire a sum of money for the use of the soldiers in their march to Horse Neck;" also " to hire a sum of money for the town to provide a drum and fife." A committee of inspection was chosen consisting of the following persons: "Deac. Jesse Johnson, Lieut. Samuel Matthews, Mr. Joel Seaward, Lieut. James Clark, and Ensign Stephen Lyman." Another town meeting was held October 17th, at which, under the article, "To see if the town are willing that the present House of Representatives, together with the Council of this State, should form a charter and make laws for the present and future generations, and to pass such votes respecting the same as the town shall judge best," and also under the article "To see whether the town choose that the laws that are made by this House should be sent through the State to every town before they are ratified, for the perusal of the people," the town voted "yes."

War Charges.

During the year 1777 the records of the town do not show much activity on the part of the town touching the war; probably much was done that does not appear. At the November meeting the town voted "to do something toward bringing the charges of the war equally on the town," and chose a committee to accomplish it. The town also "voted that it will pay for all the Continental clothing that the town is required to get or provide for the soldiers at the rates clothing goes for now among us." It was also voted "to allow Sergeant John McIntire the interest of the money that he shall borrow in order to pay the province rates of those soldiers that are gone into the Continental Army from the time that he borrows it till he gets it back of them or somewhere else." The stirring events and excitements of the war did not come within the limits of Massachusetts in the form of battles, after the British troops departed from Boston. But Massachusetts men were no small factor of the Continental army. The State of Massachusetts was represented at the posts of danger. She shirked no duty—the cause was her cause—her weal or woe hung in the same balance with the other States.

So far as towns like Murrayfield were concerned, their duty lay in furnishing each its quota of men and supplies for the Continental army; and they were faithful to the demands of the hour. At the March meeting, 1778, Deac. Jesse Johnson, Lieut. James Clark, Lieut. William Campbell, Lieut. Larkin Williams, and Gideon Matthews were chosen as the committee of inspection and safety. The records of subsequent town meetings held this year show the action of the town touching the new constitution which the General Court, acting as a convention by the consent of the towns in the state, framed as a form of government and sent to the several towns in the state for their approval, February 28th, 1778. A copy of the Resolve which the General Court sent out to each town, with a copy of the proposed constitution, will enable the reader to better understand the votes passed by the town of Murrayfield:

"A Constitution & Form of Government for the State of Massachusetts Bay, agreed upon by the Convention of this State, February 28th, 1778—to be laid before the several towns and plantations in said State, for their approbation or disapprobation.

STATE OF MASSACHUSETTS BAY,
IN CONVENTION, February 28, 1778.

Whereas, Upon the Declaration of Independence, made by the Representatives of the United States, in Congress assembled, by which all connections between the said States & Great Britain were dissolved, the General Assembly of this State thought it expedient, that a new Constitution of Government for this State should be formed; &, apprehending that they were not invested with sufficient authority to deliberate and determine upon so interesting a subject, did, on the fifth day of May, 1777, for effecting this valuable purpose, pass the following resolve:

'Resolved, That it be, & hereby is recommended to the several towns & places in this State, empowered by the laws thereof to send members to the General Assembly, that, at their next election of a member or members to represent them, they make choice of men in whose integrity and ability they can place the greatest confidence; &, in addition to the common & ordinary powers of representation, instruct them with full powers, in one body with the Council, to form such a Constitution of Government as they shall judge best calculated to promote the happiness of this State; &, when completed, to cause the same to be printed in all the Boston newspapers, and also in hand bills, one of which to be transmitted to the Selectmen of each town, or the committee of each plantation, to be by them laid before their respective towns or plantations, at a regular meeting of the inhabitants thereof, to be called for that purpose, in order to its being, by each town & plantation, duly considered, & a return of their approbation or disapprobation to be made into the Secretary's office of this State, at a reasonable time, to be fixed by the General Court; specifying the numbers present at such meeting voting for, & those voting against the same; &, if upon a fair examination of said returns by the General Court, or such a committee as they shall appoint for the purpose, it shall appear, that the said Form of Government is approved by at least two thirds of those who are free, & twenty-one years of age, belonging to this State, & present in the several meetings, then the General Court shall be empowered to establish the same as the Constitution & Form of Government of the State of Massachusetts Bay; according to which the inhabitants thereof shall be governed in all succeeding generations, unless the same shall be altered by their express direction, or at least of two-thirds of them. And it is further recommended to the Selectmen of the several towns, in the return of their precepts for the choice of Representatives, to signify their having considered this resolve, & their doings therein.'

And whereas the good people of this State in pursuance of said resolution, & reposing special trust & confidence in the Council & in their Representatives, have appointed, authorized and instructed their Representatives, in one body with the Council, to form such a Constitution of Government as they shall judge best calculated to promote the happiness of this State, & when completed, to cause the same to be published for their inspection & consideration.

We, therefore, the Council & Representatives of the People of the State of Massachusetts Bay, in convention assembled by virtue of the power delegated to us, & acknowledging our dependence upon the all wise Governor of the Universe for direction, do agree upon the following Form of a Constitution of Government for this State, to be sent out to the People, that they may act thereon, agreeably to the aforesaid resolves."

The Form of Constitution proposed and sent out with the aforesaid resolve, for the people to act upon, was as follows:

I.—There shall be convened, held & kept, a General Court, upon the last Wednesday in the month of May of every year, & as many other times as the said General Court shall order & appoint. Which General Court shall consist of a Senate & House of Representatives, to be elected as this Constitution hereafter directs.

II.—There shall be elected annually a Governor & Lieutenant Governor, who shall each have, by virtue of such election, a seat & voice in the Senate; & the style & title of the Governor shall be His Excellency; & the style & title of the Lieutenant Governor shall be His Honor.

III.—No person shall be considered as qualified to serve as Governor, Lieutenant Governor, Senator, or Representative, unless qualified respectively at the time of their several elections, as follows, viz.: The Governor & Lieutenant Governor shall have been inhabitants of this State five years immediately preceding the time of their respective election; the Governor shall be possessed, in his own right, of an estate of the value of one thousand pounds, whereof five hundred pounds value, at the least, shall be in real estate within this State; the Lieutenant Governor shall be possessed, in his own right, of an estate of the value of five hundred pounds, two hundred and fifty pounds thereof, at the least, to be in real estate, within this State; a Senator shall be possessed, in his own right, of an estate to the value of four hundred pounds, two hundred pounds thereof, at the least, to be in real estate, lying in the district for which he shall be elected. A Representative shall be possessed, in his own right, of an estate of the value of two hundred pounds, one hundred pounds thereof, at the least, to be in real estate lying in the town, for which he shall be elected. Senators & Representatives shall have been inhabitants of the districts & towns, for which they shall be respectively elected, one full year immediately preceding such election; provided, that when two or more towns join in the choice of a Representative, they may choose an inhabitant of either of said towns, being otherwise qualified as this article directs.

IV.—The Judges of the Superior Court, Secretary, Treasurer General, Commissary General, & settled Ministers of the Gospel, while in office; also all Military Officers, while in the pay of this or of the United States, shall be considered as disqualified for holding a seat in the General Court; & the Judges & Registers of Probate, for holding a seat in the Senate.

V.—Every male inhabitant of any town in this State, being free and twenty-one years of age, excepting negroes, Indians & mulattoes, shall be entitled to vote for a Representative or Representatives, as the case may be, in the town where he is resident; provided he has paid taxes in said town (unless by law excused from taxes) & been resident therein one full year, immediately preceding such voting, or that such town has been his known & usual place of abode for that time, or that he is considered as an inhabitant thereof; & every such inhabitant qualified as above, & worth sixty pounds, clear of all charges thereon, shall be entitled to put in his vote for Governor, Lieutenant Governor, & Senators; and all such voting for Governor, Lieutenant Governor, Senators or Representatives, shall be by ballot, & not otherwise.

VI.—Every incorporated town within this State shall be entitled to send one Representative to the General Court; any town having three hundred voters may send two; having five hundred & twenty voters may send three; having seven hundred & sixty may send four; & so on, making the increasing number necessary for another member, twenty more than the last immediately preceding increasing number, till the whole number of voters in any town are reckoned. And each town shall pay the expense of its own Representative or Representatives; & the inhabitants of any two or more towns, who do not incline to send a Representative for each town, may join in the choice of one, if they shall so agree.

VII.—The Selectmen of each town shall, some time in the month of April, annually, issue their warrant or warrants, under their hands and seals, directed to some constable or constables, within their towns respectively, requiring him or them to notify the inhabitants qualified to vote for a Representative, to assemble in some convenient place in such town, for the choice of some person or persons, as the case may be, to represent them in the General Court the ensuing year; the time & place of meeting to be mentioned in the warrant or warrants for calling such meeting. And the Selectmen of each town respectively, or the major part of them, shall make return of the name or names of the person or persons elected by the major part of the voters present, & voting in such meeting to represent said town in the General Court the ensuing year, into the Secretary's office, on or before the last Wednesday of May then next ensuing; & when two or more towns shall agree to join for such choice, the major part of the Selectmen of those towns shall, in the manner above directed, warn a meeting to be held in either of the said towns, as they shall judge most convenient for that purpose, & shall make return as aforesaid, of the person chosen at such meeting.

VIII.—The number of Senators shall be *twenty-eight;* (Exclusive of the Governor & Lieutenant Governor) their election shall be annual, & from certain districts, into which the State shall be divided as follows, viz.: The middle district to contain the Counties of Suffolk, Essex, & Middlesex, within which ten Senators shall be elected; the southern district to contain the Counties of Plymouth, Barnstable, Bristol, Duke's County, & Nantucket, within which six Senators shall be elected; the western district to contain the Counties of Hampshire, Worcester, & Berkshire, within which eight Senators shall be elected; the northern district to contain the Counties of York & Cumberland, within which three shall be elected; the eastern district to contain the County of Lincoln, within which one shall be elected. And as the number of inhabitants in the several districts may vary, from time to time, the General Court shall, in the way they shall judge best, some time in the year one thousand seven hundred & ninety, & once in twenty years ever after, order the number of the inhabitants of the several districts to be taken, that the Senators may be apportioned anew to the several districts, according to the number of the inhabitants therein. And the General Court may, at such new apportionment, increase the number of Senators to be chosen as they may see fit; provided that the whole number shall never exceed *thirty-six*, exclusive of the Governor & Lieutenant Governor.

IX.—The inhabitants of the several towns in this State, qualified as this Constitution directs, shall, on the first Wednesday in the month of November, annually, give in their votes in their respective towns, at a meeting, which the Selectmen shall call for that purpose, for Senators for the year ensuing the last Wednesday in May then next. The votes shall be given in for the members of each district separately, according to the foregoing apportionment, or such as shall be hereafter ordered ; & the Selectmen & town Clerk of each town shall sort & count the votes, &, by the third Wednesday in December then next, transmit to the Secretary's office a list, certified by the town Clerk, of all the persons, who had votes as Senators for each district at such meeting, & the number each person had affixed to his name. The list, so sent in shall be examined by the General Court at their next sitting, & a list for each district of those voted for, to the amount of double the number assigned to such district (if so many shall have votes) taking those who had the highest numbers, shall be made out and sent by the first of March, then next after, to the several towns of this State, as a nomination list, from which said towns shall, at their meeting for the choice of Governor in the month of May, vote for the Senators assigned the respective districts ; which votes shall be counted & sorted & lists certified as before directed, made out & sent in to the Secretary's office, by ten o'clock in the forenoon of the last Wednesday in said May, & not afterwards ; which lists shall be examined by the House of Representatives for the first time of the election of Senators, & ever afterwards by the Senate & House of Representatives on said last Wednesday of May, or as soon after as may be ; and those persons in each district, equal to the number assigned such district, who have the greatest number of votes, shall be Senators for the ensuing year, unless it shall appear to the Senate that any member or members thereof were unduly elected or not legally qualified ; of which the Senate shall be the judges. And the Senate, when so constituted, shall continue in being till another Senate is chosen, & the members thereof gone through all the steps necessary to qualify them to enter on the business assigned them by this Constitution.

X.—There shall forever hereafter, on the first Wednesday in the month of May annually, be held, in each town in this State, a meeting of the inhabitants of such towns respectively, to give or put in their votes for Governor, Lieutenant Governor, & Senators, which meeting the Selectmen shall cause to be notified in the manner before directed for the meeting for the choice of Representatives ; & the town Clerk shall return into the Secretary's office by ten o'clock in the morning of the last Wednesday of said May, & not afterwards, an attested copy of all the persons, who had votes for Governor & Lieutenant Governor respectively, certifying the number of votes each person so voted for had ; which list shall be, on said last Wednesday of May, or as soon after as may be, examined by the Senate & House of Representatives; & the persons, who, on such examination, shall appear to have the greatest number of votes for those offices respectively, provided it be a majority of the whole number, shall be by the two Houses declared Governor & Lieutenant Governor, & entitled to act as such the ensuing year; & if no person shall have such majority for Governor & for Lieutenant Governor, the Senate & House of Representatives shall, as soon as may be, after examining said lists, proceed by joint ballot to elect a Governor or Lieutenant Governor, or both, as the case may require, confining themselves to one of those three, who had the greatest number of votes collected in the several towns for the office to be filled.

XI.—If any person chosen Governor, Lieutenant Governor, Senator, or Representative, whose qualification shall be questioned by any one member of the Senate or House of Representatives, within twenty-four days after his appearing to enter upon the execution of his office, shall not make oath before a Senator, the Speaker of the House of Representatives, or some Justice of the Peace, that he is qualified as required by this constitution, and lodge a certificate thereof in the Secretary's office, within ten days after notice given him of such questioning by the Secretary, whose duty it shall be to give such notice, his election shall be void; & any person claiming privilege of voting for Governor, Lieutenant Governor, Senators, or Representatives, & whose qualification shall be questioned in town meeting, shall by the Selectmen be prevented from voting, unless he shall make oath that he is qualified as this Constitution requires; said oath to be administered by a Justice of the Peace, or the town clerk, who is hereby empowered to administer the same, when no Justice is present.

XII.—Whenever any person, who may be chosen a member of the Senate, shall decline the office, to which he is elected, or shall resign his place, or die, or remove out of the State, or be any way disqualified, the House of Representatives may, if they see fit, by ballot, fill up any vacancy occasioned thereby, confining themselves in the choice to the nomination list for the district, to which such member belongs, whose place is to be supplied, if a sufficient number is thereon for the purpose; otherwise the choice may be made at large in said district.

· XIII.—The General Court shall be the supreme legislative authority of this State, and shall accordingly have full power & authority to erect & constitute judicatories and courts of record, or other courts; and, from time to time, to make and establish all manner of wholesome and reasonable orders, laws and statutes; and also, for the necessary support and defence of this government, they shall have full power and authority to levy proportionable and reasonable assessments, rates and taxes; and to do all and every thing they shall judge to be for the good and welfare of the state, and for the government and ordering thereof; provided nevertheless, they shall not have any power to add to, alter, abolish, or infringe any part of this constitution. And the enacting style in making laws shall be by the Senate and House of Representatives in General Court assembled and by the authority of the same.

XIV.—The Senate and House of Representatives shall be two separate and distinct bodies, each to appoint its own officers, and settle its own rules of proceedings, and each shall have an equal right to originate or reject any bill, resolve or order, or to propose amendments to the same, excepting bill and resolves levying and granting money or other property of the State, which shall originate in the House of Representatives only, and be concurred or nonconcurred in whole by the Senate.

XV.—Not less than sixty members shall constitute or make a quorum of the House of Representatives; and not less than nine shall make a quorum of the Senate.

XVI.—The Senate and House of Representatives shall have power to adjourn themselves respectively; provided such adjournment shall not exceed two days at any one time.

XVII.—The Governor shall be president of the Senate. He shall be General and Commander in Chief of the Militia, and Admiral of the Navy of this State; and empowered to embody the militia and cause them to be marched to any part of the State for the public safety, when he shall think necessary; and in the recess of the General Court, to march the militia, by advice of the Senate, out of the State, for the defence of this or any other of the United States; provided always, that the Governor shall exercise the power given by this constitution, over the militia and navy of the State, according to the laws thereof, or the resolves of the General Court. He shall, with the advice of the Senate, in the recess of the General Court, have power to prorogue the same from time to time, not exceeding forty days in any one recess of said Court; and, in the sitting of said Court, to adjourn or prorogue the said Court to any time they shall desire, or to dissolve the same at their request, or to call said Court together sooner than the time to which it may be adjourned or prorogued, if the welfare of the State should require the same. He shall have power, at his discretion, to grant reprieves to condemned criminals for a term or terms of time, not exceeding six months. It shall be the duty of the Governor to inform the legislature, at every session of the General Court, of the condition of the State; and, from time to time, to recommend such matters to their consideration, as shall appear to him to concern its good government, welfare and prosperity.

XVIII.—Whenever the person, who may be chosen Governor, shall decline the trust to which he is thereby elected, or shall resign or die, or remove out of the State, or be otherwise disqualified, the Lieutenant Governor shall have the like power during the vacancy in the office of Governor, as the Governor is by this Constitution vested with; and, in case of a vacancy in the office of Governor and Lieutenant Governor, the major part of the Senate shall have authority to exercise all the powers of a Governor during such vacancy; and, in case both the Governor and the Lieutenant Governor be absent from the Senate, the senior or first Senator then present shall preside.

XIX.—All civil officers annually chosen, with salaries annually granted for their services, shall be appointed by the General Court by ballot; each branch to have a right to originate or negative the choice. All other civil officers, and also all general, field and staff officers, both of the militia and of the troops which may be raised by, and be in the pay of this State, shall be appointed by the Governor and Senate; captains and subalterns of troops raised by, and in the pay of the State, to be also appointed by the Governor and Senate.

XX.—The Governor and Senate shall be a Court for the trial of all impeachments of any officers of this State, provided, that if any impeachment shall be prosecuted against the Governor, Lieutenant Governor, or any one of the Senate; in such case the person impeached shall not continue one of the Court for that trial. Previous to the trial of any impeachment, the members of the court shall be respectively sworn, truly and impartially to try and determine the charge in question, according to evidence; which oath shall be administered to the members by the President, and to him by any one of the Senate. And no judgment of said Court shall be valid, unless it be assented to by two-third of the members of said Court present at such trial; nor shall judgment extend further than to removal of the person tried from office, and disqualification to hold or enjoy any place of honor, trust or profit under the State: the party so convicted shall nevertheless be liable and subject to indictment, trial, judgment, and punishment, according to the laws of the State; and the power of impeaching all officers of the State for mal-conduct in their respective offices shall be vested in the House of Representatives.

XXI.—The Governor may with the advice of the Senate, in the recess of the General Court, lay an Embargo, or prohibit the exportation of any commodity for any term of time, not exceeding forty days in any one recess of said Court.

XXII.—The Governor shall have no negative, as Governor, in any matter pointed out by this Constitution to be done by the Governor and Senate, but shall have an equal voice with any Senator on any question before them; provided that the Governor, or, in his absence out of the State, the Lieutenant Governor, shall be present in Senate to enable them to proceed on the business assigned them by this constitution, as Governor and Senate.

XXIII.—The power of granting pardons shall be vested in the Governor, Lieutenant Governor, and Speaker of the House of Representatives, for the time being, or in either two of them.

XXIV.—The Justices of the Superior Court, the Justices of the Inferior Courts of Common Pleas, Judges of Probate of Wills, Judges of the Maritime Courts, and Justices of the Peace, shall hold their respective places during good behavior.

XXV.—The Secretary, Treasurer-General, Commissary-General, shall be appointed annually.

XXVI.—The Attorney-General, Sheriffs, Registers of the Courts of Probate, Coroners, Notaries Public, and Naval Officers, shall be appointed and hold their offices during pleasure.

XXVII.—The Justices of the Superior Court, Justices of the Inferior Courts, Courts of the General Sessions of the Peace, and Judges of the Maritime Courts, shall appoint their respective clerks.

XXVIII.—The Delegates for this State to the Continental Congress shall be chosen annually by joint ballot of the Senate and House of Representatives, and may be superseded, in the mean time, in the same manner. If any person holding the office of Governor, Lieutenant Governor, Senator, Judge of the Superior Court, Secretary, Attorney-General, Treasurer-General, or Commissary-General, shall be chosen a member of Congress, and accept the trust, the place, which he so held as aforesaid, shall be considered as vacated thereby, and some other person chosen to succeed him therein. And if any person, serving for this State at said Congress, shall be appointed to either of the aforesaid offices, and accept thereof, he shall be considered as resigning his seat in Congress, and some other person shall be chosen in his stead.

XXIX.—No persons unless of the Protestant Religion shall be Governor, Lieutenant Governor, a member of the Senate, or of the House of Representatives, or hold any judiciary employment within this State.

XXX.—All commissions shall run in the name of the State of Massachusetts Bay, bear test and be signed by the Governor or Commander-in-Chief of the State, for the time being, and have the seal of the state thereunto affixed, and be attested by the Secretary or his Deputy.

XXXI.—All writs issuing out of the clerk's office of any of the courts of law within this State shall be in the name of the State of Massachusetts Bay, under the seal of the Court from which they issue, bear test of the Chief Justice, or senior or first Justice of the Court, where such writ is returnable, and be signed by the Clerk of such Court. Indictments shall conclude 'against the peace and dignity of the State.'

XXXII.—All the statute laws of this State, the common law, and all such parts of the English and British statute laws, as have been adopted and usually practiced in the Courts of Law in this State, shall still remain and be in full force until altered or repealed by a future law or laws of the legislature; and shall be accordingly observed and obeyed by the people of this State; such parts only excepted as are repugnant to the rights and privileges contained in this Constitution; and all parts of such laws as refer to and mention the council shall be construed to extend to the Senate. And the inestimable right of trial by jury shall remain confirmed as part of this Constitution forever.

XXXIII.—All monies shall be issued out of the Treasury of this State, and disposed of by warrants under the hand of the Governor for the time being, with the advice and consent of the Senate, for the necessary defence and support of the government, and the protection and preservation of the inhabitants thereof, agreeably to the acts and resolves of the General Court.

XXXIV.—The free exercise and enjoyment of religious profession and worship shall forever be allowed to every denomination of Protestants within this State.

XXXV.—The following oath shall be taken by every person appointed to any office in this State, before his entering on the execution of his office; viz. *I, A. B., do swear (or affirm as the case may be) that I will bear faith and true allegiance to the State of Massachusetts; and that I will faithfully execute the business of the office of   agreeably to the laws of this State, according to my best skill and judgment without fear, favor, affection, or partiality.*

XXXVI.—And whereas it may not be practicable to conform to this Constitution in the election of Governor, Lieutenant Governor, Senators, and Representatives for the first year; therefore, The present Convention, if in being, or the next General Assembly, which shall be chosen upon the present Constitution, shall determine the time and manner, in which the people shall choose said officers for the first year, and upon said choice the General Assembly then in being shall be dissolved and give place to the free execution of this Constitution.

By order of the Convention,
JEREMIAH POWELL,
President.

Attest. SAMUEL FREEMAN, Clerk."

The foregoing draft of "Form of a Constitution of Government," was rejected by the people of the state. The town of Murrayfield held its town meeting April 7, at which forty-four voted against and ten for the proposed constitution.

Another meeting was held June 1st, 1778, at three o'clock in the afternoon, "to elect some person or persons to serve & represent the town in the Great & General Court of this state this present year;" also "to see if the town will give their particular reasons they have against the constitution sent to us from the Court;" and the town passed the following vote: "Voted that something be done further upon the article respecting the constitution." The meeting then adjourned to June 8th, to further consider the matter; at which time the town voted "not to do anything upon the article respecting the constitution; also "that this article shall never in the world be brought into question without special order from the General Court."

CLOTHING FOR SOLDIERS.

One article in the warrant for the April meeting was "To see what method the town will come into to provide their quota of clothing for the Continental Army, agreeable to a late handbill received from the Court in pressing terms requiring us to complete our quota of clothing." Under this article the town voted "to raise five shillings on the poll & one farthing on the pound to pay for this clothing." Touching this subject another town meeting was held July 21st, and it was voted that the town give six dollars apiece for shirts, four dollars and fifty cents a pair for stockings, and forty shillings a pair for shoes. These were required to be provided by September 20th. At the same meeting the town chose "Ensign Lyman, Sergeant John McIntire, & Edward Wright, Jr., a committee to take care of the soldiers' families."

At the November meeting the town voted to petition the General Court "to have the tory lands in this town sold at private sale," and David Shepard, Timothy Lyman, and John Blair were chosen to be a committee to draft the petition. One hundred pounds was then voted "for the support of soldiers' families till next March."

The General Court passed an act October 16th, 1778, forbidding the return of certain persons who had gone over to the enemy; and among the persons named in said act were three of the original proprietors of Murrayfield: John Chandler, Abijah Willard, and John Murray.

The following act was passed by the General Court June 28th, 1781:

"Whereas, Thaddeus Newton of Murrayfield in the county of Hampshire, in the year 1773, was entitled to a good and lawful deed of one hundred acres of land in said Murrayfield, from Col. John Chandler of Worcester, on certain conditions, which conditions said Newton has fulfilled on his part, but said John Chandler hath taken refuge with the enemies of these United States, & hath not complied with his said agreement; by which means the said Newton will sustain great damage unless he is relieved by this Commonwealth.

"Therefore, Be it enacted by the Senate & House of Representatives in General Court assembled, & by the authority of the same, that lot No. 9, in the First Division in said Murrayfield, laid out to John Chandler, Esq., an absentee, be, & hereby is, granted & confirmed to him the said Thaddeus Newton, his heirs and assigns as an absolute estate of inheritance, in fee simple, forever."

State of Affairs 1779.

"At the opening of the new year" (1779) says Barry, "The situation of affairs was discouraging and gloomy. The country was heavily burdened with debt; soldiers and their families were subjected to incredible hardships and sufferings; with the depreciation in the currency, the salaries of the clergy, which remained as before the war, were reduced to a mere pittance, utterly inadequate to their comfortable support, and their parishioners were unable, & in some cases unwilling, to afford them relief; lukewarm patriots were murmuring & complaining; symptoms of insubordination were manifested in various quarters; & the utmost vigilance & prudence were required to steer the ship of state successfully through the breakers which threatened its destruction, & bring it safe to the desired haven."

Depreciation of the Currency.

The depreciation of the continental bills were such that they would not pass for more than one-tenth or one-twentieth of their nominal value; "and, as the state had promised the soldiers a *bona fide* compensation, their families were provided for by the selectmen of the towns, & clothing was furnished the soldiers themselves." To remedy these evils conventions were held at Concord in July and in October, 1779, at which prices were fixed for all the products of the country, and measures taken for the purpose and in the hope of preventing further depreciation of the currency. A general convention was held in Hartford to devise plans for checking extortions and speculations.

In these patriotic measures Murrayfield was true always to the public cause. A meeting was called for July 5th, 1779, "To see what method the town will take in order to procure clothing for the army, agreeable to a late resolve of the General Court." Also "To see if the town will send a man to Concord for to meet with a convention of committees of this state in order to adopt some measure for to prevent the further depreciation of our paper currency." It does not appear that the town sent a "man to Concord;" but at a meeting held August 18th, the town "voted unanimously to approve the doings of the Concord convention of July 14th, and that the town will carry the resolves of the convention into execution to the utmost of its power."

A committee, consisting of eleven: Samuel Matthews, William Moore, David Shepard, Stephen Lyman, William Campbell, John Blair, James Hamilton, Timothy Lyman, Jesse Johnson, Enoch Shepard, and James Clark, was chosen to state the prices of things in this town. It was also voted "that this committee make a return of this vote to the committee at Boston, concerning the regulation of prices;" and also, "that this committee take up & secure any person that breaks over the resolves of the convention at Concord;" and further "that this committee make a report to the town at some future day of the prices they set to labor and other things in the town."

Facts Exhibited by the Valuation Lists.

The valuation lists of Murrayfield from the year 1773 to the year 1781, show facts not uninteresting to the political economist. During this period there was no unusual growth in the number of taxpayers. The valuation taken in 1773, showed the aggregate taxable property in town to be twenty-one hundred and seventy-eight pounds and nineteen shillings. Abner Smith, who was and had been for a long time the wealthiest man in town, and continued such during the period of time above named, was rated at one hundred and twenty-seven pounds and five shillings. No other man in the town was that year rated as high as one hundred pounds. By this statement, I refer only to resident tax-payers.

		£	s.
The aggregate valuation in 1774 was	2504	3
" " " " 1775 "	1605	6
" " " " 1776 "	1906	19
" " " " 1777 "	38819	16
" " " " 1778 "	18841	16
" " " " 1779 "	19688	3
" " " " 1780 "	4915	
" " " " 1781 "	3006	3
The rating of Abner Smith, in 1774 "	138	4
" " " " " " 1775 "	83	9
" " " " " " 1776 "	119	15
" " " " " " 1777 "	1273	
" " " " " " 1778 "	702	2
" " " " " " 1779 "	625	17
" " " " " " 1780 "	139	4
" " " " " " 1781 "	31	6

In 1781, he was by far the richest man in town.

DEPRECIATED PAPER CURRENCY.

During the larger part of this period Murrayfield was suffering, with the rest of the country, the evils of a depreciated and depreciating paper currency. To make this more clear, I take the liberty of quoting from the eighteenth edition of Prof. Perry's "Political Economy," page 382, the following: "In June, 1775, a week after Bunker Hill, the Continental Congress began its fiscal career by voting to emit $2,000,000 in new bills of credit issued on the faith of the 'Continent,' but referred as to payment to the separate colonies in the ratio of their supposed gross population. The best excuse for this action is the one urged by the Congress itself to the French minister:

"*America, never having been much taxed, nor for a continued length of time, being without fixed government & contending against what was once the lawful authority, had no funds to support the war; and, the* contest being upon the very question of taxation, the levying of imposts, unless from the last necessity, would have been madness. To borrow from individuals without any visible means of repaying them, while the loss was certain from ill success, was visionary. A measure, therefore, which had been early adopted, and thence became familiar to the people, was pursued. This was the issuing of paper notes representing specie for the redemption of which the public faith was pledged.'

"One phrase only of this clear passage is cloudy—'paper notes representing specie.' John Law cast some haze over the Continental Congress; the wording of the notes is curiously obscure: '*This bill entitles the bearer to receive ten Spanish milled dollars;*' the notes in no sense *represented* specie; they virtually *promised to pay* it to the bearer; unluckily, the party issuing the promise was not the party bound to pay; the continent promised while the colonies were expected to fulfill; unluckily, also, no good provision was made by either party for the *fulfillment* of these promises; and consequently the vice of the continental money was, that there was no economical limitation of their supply. The notes were not amenable to the law of supply and demand in the ordinary way, and hence they could not long maintain a steady value. In a certain remote sense they were indeed amenable to that law, which presided over the decline and final extinction of their value. These issues, too, came into competition with the revolutionary issues of eleven separate colonies, New Hampshire and Georgia issuing none, the total of which in 1775–83 was $209,524,776. So that this further increase of supply depreciated in comparison with silver both classes of notes. Eighteen months, however, had passed, and $20,000,000 continental had been authorized, besides large local issues, before a marked depreciation began.

"As the issues increased, as it became evident to all that no provision was made to keep the promises, and as Burgoine was prosperously advancing from Canada towards New York, the middle of 1777 saw a general fall of the notes, not the same in all the States at the same time, and not at all in strict ratio with the increase of the notes. At the close of 1777, the average depreciation from silver was not far from three to one; at the close of 1778, it was not far from six to one; at the end of 1779, it was about twenty-eight to one; the press then rested, after Congress had put out nominally $200,000,000; but actually about $40,000,000 more than that, though the ceasing of issue did not arrest the cascade of discredit. Early in 1780, Congress advised the States to repeal their laws making the bills a legal tender for debts, and devise the scheme of 'new tenor,' by which the old bills might be taken up in a new paper bearing interest at six per cent. in a ratio of forty to one, to which the old bills had now sunk in comparison with silver, and $88,000,000 of the old paper were thus redeemed, New York and Massachusetts and Rhode Island taking up their entire quota in this way; but the 'new tenor' money never came into much circulation, and old and new alike dropped out altogether in the spring of 1781, when the old notes, if passed at all, were passing at about three hundred to one. The Continental army in camp at Newburgh, combined to refuse to receive them on any terms; and President Reed gives a pleasing picture of the way in which they passed out in Pennsylvania:

"'At once, as if by that force which in days of ignorance would be ascribed to enchantment, all dealings in paper ceased; necessity brought out the gold and silver, a fortunate trade opened at the same time to the Havana for flour, all restrictions were taken off, and the Mexican dollars flowed in by thousands; this supported the sinking spirits of those who would have been discontented and uneasy, and in a few days specie became the universal medium and so continues.'

"The country found no more lack of silver for money than Massachusetts had found in 1749. Assuming that only $200,000,000 Continental had been issued, Jefferson estimated that the nation realized from them $36,367,720 in specie value, or eighteen per cent. of the nominal value. Ill effects of every kind came in the wake of this poor money. Rising prices are ever the gauge of a falling money; rising prices then as ever gave birth to rash speculations; committees of safety undertook angrily to punish, under the names of 'forestallers' and 'engrossers' the speculators who bought commodities for a further rise; there was the confusion of contracts usual under variable money, gains for the artful and unscrupulous, and envy and sufferings for the poor. Shays' Rebellion in Massachusetts, in 1786, was a national outgrowth of this fearful injustice; debtors availed themselves of the legal tender quality of the bills to pay only one-twentieth or one-fortieth of what was due; the morals of all classes of the people became corrupted through constantly calling things that were not as though they were; peculations pervaded society; Congress itself used wretched sophistries in resolving that the money '*ought to pass current in all payments, trade and dealings, and be deemed equal in value to the same nominal sums in Spanish dollars,*' and in lauding the papers as the only kind of money '*which cannot take to itself wings and fly away! It remains with us, it will not forsake us, it is always ready at hand for the purposes of convenience, and every industrious man can find it.*' John Jay, and many others who knew better, helped to make current such nonsense as this; and then, a little later, swallowing all its brave words, Congress repudiated for its part, and advised in effect the States to repudiate, all obligations to redeem these bills. Their volume had been swelled both by native and by British counterfeiters, and there was almost no crime to which their issue and depreciation did not contribute. Noah Webster, a clear headed essayist of the time, said of this paper money: *'We have suffered more from this cause than from every other cause or calamity. It has killed more men, corrupted the choicest interests of our country more, and done more injustice, than even the arms and artifices of our enemy.'*

"Washington, himself as a creditor the victim of that form of social robbery involved in a depreciated legal tender, unfortunately did not understand the mysteries or rather the simplicities of paper money, and thus vented his wrath towards the wrong objects: *'It gives me sincere pleasure to find that the Assembly is so well disposed to second your endeavors to bring those murderers of our cause, the monopolizers, forestallers, and engrossers, to condign punishment. It is much to be lamented that each State, long ere this, has not hunted them down as pests to society, and the greatest enemies we have to the happiness of America. I would to God that some one of the more atrocious in each State was hung on gibbets upon a gallows five times as high as the one prepared for Haman! No punishment, in my opinion, is too severe for the man who can build his greatness upon his country's ruin!*"

COUNTY CONVENTION TO FIX PRICES FOR NECESSARIES OF LIFE.

A county convention was held at Northampton in September, 1779, for fixing the prices of the necessaries of life. The town sent Timothy Lyman as a delegate to this convention, and at the town meeting held October 18th, voted to abide by the doings of the convention, and chose Deacon Samuel Matthews, Lieutenant William Moore, and Ensign Stephen Lyman a committee "to see that the doings of the convention are not violated."

CONTROVERSY WITH OTHER TOWNS CONCERNING QUOTAS.

At the March meeting 1779, Deacon Samuel Matthews, Ensign Stephen Lyman, and Lieutenant William Moore were chosen to be the committee of safety. One article in the warrant was, "To see what method the town will take in order to defend themselves against the unreasonable claims of other towns respecting the Continental soldiers which the town has hired into the service, and to pass such vote respecting the article above mentioned as they shall judge best." What these "unreasonable claims of other towns" were does not appear. Perhaps Murrayfield had hired men who were residents of other towns to help fill its own quota. This would naturally lead to controversy. Ensign Stephen Lyman was chosen to go to Northampton "to defend the town against the unjust claims of other towns concerning the Continental soldiers."

The nature of this controversy is made more clear from the following entry upon the record book of the town: "Murrayfield, April 13th, 1779. Then the town of Murrayfield met upon the desire of the selectmen and consulted what method the town shall take in order to make a new return of the Continental men. Voted there shall be a return made of all the men that have been enlisted from the town, and likewise of all those that have been hired from other towns into the continental service, and that all the light that can be given shall be put in." In this connection the following from a muster roll of this year will not be uninteresting. The roll contained the following memoranda of men put in by Murrayfield:

"Francis Thompson, age 17, height, 5 feet 6 inches; complection brown. Ebenezer Smith, age 18, height, 5 feet 7 inches; complection dark."

They were in Captain Black's company in the regiment of Colonel Mosley. On the back of the muster roll was the following endorsement:

"Springfield, 31st July, 1779. Received of Justin Ely, Esq., commissioner for the State of Massachusetts Bay, the men mentioned in the within list to serve for nine months in the Continental Army agreeable to a resolution of General Court of said State of June 8. THEOPHALUS CLARK."

PROPOSED NEW CONSTITUTION.

A town meeting was held May 17, at which the town was called upon to consider "whether they choose at this time to have a new Constitution or Form of Government made, and whether they will give their Representatives power to do anything to make one;" Thirty-four voted in favor and none against. This was in response to the resolve passed by the General Assembly of the State, as follows:

"In the House of Representatives, Feb. 19, 1779.

Whereas, The Constitution or Form of Civil Government, which was proposed by the late Convention of this State to the People thereof, hath been disapproved by a majority of the inhabitants of said State.—

And Whereas, It is doubtful from the Representations made to this Court, what are the sentiments of the major part of the good People of this State, as to the expediency of now proceeding to form a new Constitution of Government.—

Therefore Resolved, That the Selectmen of the several towns within this State cause the Freeholders and other Inhabitants in their respective towns, duly qualified to vote for Representatives, to be lawfully warned to meet together in some convenient place therein, on or before the last Wednesday of May next, to consider of, and determine upon the following questions:—

First.—Whether they choose, at this time, to have a New Constitution or Form of Government made.

Secondly.—Whether they will empower their Representatives for the next year to vote for the calling a State Convention, for the sole purpose of forming a New Constitution; provided it shall appear to them, on examination, that a major part of the People present and voting at the meetings, called in the manner and for the purpose aforesaid, shall have answered the first question in the affirmative.

And in order that the sense of the People may be known thereon.—

Be it further *Resolved*, That the Selectmen of each town be and hereby are directed to return into the Secretary's Office, on or before the first Wednesday of June next, the doings of their respective towns, on the first question above mentioned, certifying the numbers voting in the affirmative, and the numbers voting in the negative, on said question."

A majority of the people in the state voted in favor of calling the convention, and in accordance with the advice of the General Court, precepts were issued for the choice of delegates to meet at Cambridge in the month of September. The result of this convention was the drafting of a constitution and a declaration of rights which the people, by more than a two-thirds vote, approved. The town meeting held in Murrayfield to act upon the constitution was appointed to be held May 2d, 1780. The first action taken by the town was choosing a committee of three from each school district to consider the proposed Constitution and declaration of rights and report at an adjourned meeting. This committee consisted of the following persons: Samuel Jones, John Jones, Benjamin Eggleston, Deacon James Hamilton, Lieutenant William Moore, Deacon Jesse Johnson, Doctor David Shepard, Ensign Stephen Lyman, Deacon Samuel Matthews, William Bell, Lieutenant John Newton Parmenter, Aaron Bell, Ebenezer Stowe, Lieutenant James Clark, Captain James Black, Jonathan Webber, Gershom Rust, Reuben Woolworth, Benjamin Converse, Robert Proctor, and Daniel Twadwell. The meeting then adjourned to May 16th, at which eight voted for and the remainder against the proposed constitution. But another meeting was called and held May

26th, to further consider and vote upon the proposed constitution, with the following results:

"On the second article of the Constitution, Section one, Chapter two, page 17, objected against by fifteen." A proposed "alteration that the governor instead of being of the Christian Religion it should be inserted that he shall be of the Christian & Protestant Religion, voted by fifteen."

"Article ten, page 32 objected against as it stands now by twelve votes." The provision objected to was as follows: "The Captains and subalterns of the militia shall be elected by the written votes of the train-band & alarm list of their respective companies, of twenty-one years of age & upwards;" &c. The town "voted for the alteration following, viz.: 'That all persons that are in the train-band & alarm list above the age of sixteen shall have liberty to vote for their captains & subalters,'" by a vote of thirteen.

"Part second, Chapter one, Section one, Article four was voted for by ten, objected against by two." The reason offered was "that those articles that have duties & excises laid on them will come dearer to the purchaser." This article defined the power and authority of the General Court. The part of it particularly objected to reads as follows: "And also to impose, & levy reasonable duties & excises, upon any produce, goods, wares, merchandize, & commodities whatsoever, brought into, produced, manufactured, or being within the same."

"Chapter six, voted for a revision of the Constitution in ten years if the people have a mind for it."

"Voted that all the other articles in the Constitution shall stand as they be, or that we are willing that they should stand without any alteration."

June 16th, 1780, the Constitutional Convention passed a resolve that the first General Court under the new constitution should be holden on the last Wednesday in October. "And in order thereto, there shall be a meeting of the Inhabitants of each Town & Plantation in the several Counties within this State, legally warned & held, on the first Monday of September next, for the purpose of electing a Governor, Lieut. Governor, & persons for Councillors & Senators." A meeting was also required to be held in October following for the choice of representatives to the General Court. In pursuance of this resolve the Selectmen of Murrayfield called a meeting for September 4th. Twenty-seven votes were cast for John Hancock for Governor. At the October meeting David Shepard was elected to represent the town in the General Court.

A town meeting was held in Murrayfield, January 31st, 1780. John Newton Parmenter was chosen moderator, and the meeting then adjourned to Landlord White's and finished its business. This adjournment was probably in consequence of the weather being too cold to hold the meeting in the meeting-house. At this meeting the town voted "to give those who furnished wool &c for soldiers' blankets twenty-four fold from the year 1774 for what they furnished."

At the March meeting Ensign Stephen Lyman, Deacon Samuel Matthews, and Ebenezer Stowe were chosen to be the committee of safety. The election of committees of safety was now required by law.

The law also required towns to provide for the support of soldiers' families, and the town, in 1780, raised six hundred pounds for that purpose.

SUPPORT OF SOLDIERS' FAMILIES AND CLOTHING FOR SOLDIERS.

Clothing the soldiers and furnishing them transportation was put upon the towns. At the March meeting, 1781, the town voted "that those persons that found the clothing for the soldiers the year past shall have the money allowed for the same by the General Court."

PAY OF SOLDIERS.

A committee was chosen "to procure money for the soldiers that had, & were about to enlist; & that the committee borrow one hundred & fifty dollars silver & one half of it in paper according to the exchange;" also "to raise twelve hundred silver dollars in order to hire or pay the men that have inlisted or may inlist into the Continental Army for three years, & that the said sum of money be assessed immediately & that the whole be paid into the town treasury by the first of May next." But a part of this action was reconsidered at a meeting held April 2d; and the town then voted "to raise six hundred hard dollars & six hundred hard dollars more or an equivolent in paper money or specie according to the exchange." Also voted that said sum "be paid into the treasury by the 7th of April inst."

RAISING ADDITIONAL MEN FOR THE ARMY.

At a meeting held July 25th, the town voted "to raise five men for three months' service to go into the Continental Army;" and "to give them fifty hard dollars each, and paying each man ten hard dollars before he marched, & the town to draw their wages." Stephen Lyman was chosen "a committee to buy & sell cattle enough to purchase the money to pay the soldiers their ten dollars a man."

In April, 1782, the town chose a committee to procure two more Continental men recently called for; and in June the town voted "to raise fifty pounds to pay for two Continental men, & to borrow the money for a few days;" and Edward Wright, Jr., was appointed "a committee" to try to borrow the money. At a meeting held February 3d, 1783, the town voted "that the selectmen provide two shirts for Samuel Brewer now in the Continental Army."

BEEF FOR THE ARMY.

In 1780 a requisition was made by the General Court upon the town of Murrayfield to furnish a certain quantity of beef for the army. At a meeting held October 16th of that year the town voted "to purchase 3,840 weight of beef, and to raise five thousand pounds for the above use;" and Captain Joel Seaward, Timothy Lyman and Captain James Black were chosen a committee to make the purchase. In December the General Court called for more beef for the army; and a town meeting was called and held January 9th, 1781, in the meeting-house; but it was so cold that as soon as a moderator was chosen the meeting adjourned to the house of Doctor Shepard, and then voted "to raise eight thousand pounds to purchase this town's proportion of beef; and that the money should be paid in by the 20th of February next." A committee of three was then chosen to purchase "the beef & grain that is sent for by the General Court as reasonable as they can, & deliver the same at the place appointed by the County's Committee, & all their reasonable costs shall be allowed them." Later on other requisitions for beef were made: July 10th, 1781, the town voted " to raise a sum of money sufficient to purchase 3,044 pounds of beef, to be assessed upon the inhabitants, non-residents, and absentees of Murrayfield at the current price that the superintendent shall say the price is through the county, & that the assessors be directed to assess the same as soon as they can or shall receive the amount from the superintendent;" and on the 30th of July, "seventy pounds in silver money," were raised to pay for the beef.

POVERTY OF THE TOWN.

'Finally, at a meeting held August 26th, 1782, more beef having been called for, the town decided that it could not purchase "any beef for Mr. Phelps or the Army." The town had become very poor; its aggregate valuation was but three thousand and six pounds. It may be an interesting fact to the reader, that at a town meeting held July 5th, 1781, the town instructed the constables—who were also the tax collectors at that time—"not to take any more paper money towards what they were indebted to the town at present for taxes."

A HISTORY OF MURRAYFIELD.   137

Raising Men for the Army.

Inasmuch as many of the men who went into the army, either volunteered or were raised by the payment of bounty through the efforts of private individuals actuated either by pure patriotism, or, which was more frequently the case, by a desire to escape personal service in the army, the records of the town give very little light as to who went, how they were induced to serve, when they went, or where they served. But toward the last of the war, as might be expected, the records of the town show some action by the town in its corporate capacity. In December, 1780, the General Court called upon Murrayfield to furnish some more men for the Continental Army. At a meeting held January 30th, 1781, the town voted "to raise six men for the army for three years or during the war;" and "Capt. Abner Smith, Lieut. William Campbell, Ebenezer Stowe, Lieut. James Clark, Capt. John Kelso, & Abner Smith, Jr., were chosen a committee to hire six men, & their reasonable charges shall be allowed."

Averaging and Equalizing the War Burden.

Some disagreements arose among the inhabitants of Murrayfield as to the equal sharing of the burdens of the war. This was perfectly natural in a struggle like our war for independence. It was not a war carried on by an established government for its own aggrandizement, but it was the struggle of a people to establish a government of their own which it was fondly believed would shower equal blessings upon all; and it was expected and justly demanded that each individual should do his proportionate share of the common duties, and bear his proportionate share of the common burdens, as he expected to enjoy his share of the common blessings which would be the reward of success.

At a town meeting held July 5th, 1780, it was voted, "that the town will come into an average of what they have done before with respect to the service done in the war if the town will pass the following vote, viz.:

"1st. That every month's service that a person has done in the present war shall be estimated alike in every year. 2d. That those persons that are behind in the service, estimating it by polls & estates, shall be obliged to hire or go into the service until they are on an equality with those that have done the most according as they stand in the town valuation."

The town also passed the following votes:

"Voted to choose a committee to adjust the service of each man in the present war.

"Voted to choose five to join with the officers. Chose Doct. David Shepard, Mr. Ebenezer Stowe, Timothy Lyman, Lieut. Newton Parmenter & Samuel Bell."

When the committee came to the work of adjusting and equalizing the service, they found difficulties growing out of the claims and demands of individuals touching the services they claimed to have rendered. So at a meeting held on the 4th of September, the town voted to submit these differences to a committee of three persons not residents of the town, and selected for this committee, Col. Timothy Roberts, Maj. Warham Parks, and Capt. David Mosely of Westfield. Ebenezer Stowe, Lieut. John Newton Parmenter, and Doct. Shepard were chosen to represent the town before the committee. There were several persons with whom these differences had arisen; but Ensign Stephen Lyman was one whose name appeared in the records of the town.

At a meeting held April 2d, 1781, the town voted that "every month's service should be estimated equally alike from the beginning of the war until this day;" and also voted that Sergeant John Blair, Sergeant John McIntire, and Lieut. William Campbell be a committee to make the average, and they were given a month's time to do it and make their report to the town. But the differences were not settled to the satisfaction of all concerned; and a meeting was called for September 7th, "To hear the petition of Timothy Smith & others respecting the average sum the court allowed them." Also, "To see if the town will come into any method that there may be an average made of past services in the war." But the town voted, "not to give those persons that hired the six & three months' men the average sum ordered by the General Court." The town then voted to choose a committee consisting of five: Capt. James Black, Doct. David Shepard, Lieut. William Campbell, Ensign Stephen Lyman, and Thomas Elder, "to make an average of past services in the present war;" and also voted, "that every month's service be estimated at forty shillings per month, that has been done in the present war."

Another meeting was held September 17th, for the purpose of trying to adjust the differences between Timothy Smith and others on the one hand and the town on the other, without going to court; and it was voted that, "the town will come to an average of all past services as near as may be in the present war by the last of November next upon the rules of justice and equity and leave it to a committee of one man out of town for a chairman and two men that the town shall pitch upon in the town; and said committee shall lay the same before the town as soon as completed, & if the town agrees to the average it shall be binding, saving that if any individual thinks himself aggrieved he or they shall have liberty of an appeal to indifferent men out of town, he or they paying the cost if they are not injured, and if the committee out of town finds him or them injured by the first average the town shall pay the cost. Chose Col. Timothy Robertson, chairman of the committee, & Doct. David Shepard & Mr. Timothy Lyman for the committee." This committee made a report to the town at a meeting held June 10th, 1782; and the town voted, "to accept the average that Capt. Shepard read." The town then chose a committee consisting of Capt. Sloper of Blandford, Deac. Brewster of Worthington, and Deac. Wares of Norwich, "to settle with the aggrieved party." But what this settlement was, or whether it was to the satisfaction of the aggrieved party, does not appear. It probably ended the controversy; and this was of more consequence to all concerned than that it should be settled to the exact line of equity.

Deacon Jesse Johnson and others appear to have been another group of aggrieved persons; but evidently they were less persistent than Timothy Smith and his friends, for at a town meeting held July 10th, 1781, the town "voted not to allow to Deac. Johnson & others what the average sum was that was allowed them by the General Court for the six & three months' men;" and here this case apparently ended. Stephen Lyman and Timothy Lyman appear to have made some claim which the town disposed of by a vote passed December, 1780, "to allow the Lymans three-fourths of the service of those three years' men." These were probably men sent by the Lymans as substitutes.

I will now give the names of those who served in the war for the town of Murrayfield, as they appear upon the enrollment lists now in the office of the Secretary of the Commonwealth. The minute men who marched to Cambridge in Col. Seth Pomeroy's regiment in April, 1775, were the following: David Shepard, James Clark, Gershom Rust, John McIntire, Russell Dewey, George Williams, Nathan Wright, Benjamin Wright, John Blair, Asa Gould, Benjamin Eggleston, James Geer, Archelus Anderson.

Col. Seth Pomeroy was a Northampton man, a gunsmith by trade, and served as major in the French and Indian War, in 1745, and was in the battle of Crown Point. He also served at the siege of Louisburg. At the time of the battle of Bunker Hill he had been appointed a brigadier-general. Of his conduct at the battle of Bunker Hill, Bancroft speaks as follows: "The veteran Seth Pomeroy, of Northampton, an old man of seventy, once second in rank in the Massachusetts army, but now postponed to younger men, heedless of the slight, was roused by the continuance of the cannonade, and rode to Charlestown Neck; there, thoughtful for his horse, which was a borrowed one, he shouldered his fowling-piece, marched over on foot, and amidst loud cheers of welcome took a place at the rail-fence." At the retreat he "walked backward facing the enemy & brandishing his musket till it was struck & marked by a ball." He was elected a brigadier general by Congress; but perceiving some distrust of his capacity on account of his age, he retired from the camp before receiving his commission. Well might our Murrayfield minute men have felt proud to serve under such a man.

The following named Murrayfield men enlisted and went in Col. David Brewster's regiment, 9th Continental, April 24th, 1775: Capt. Malcom Henry, Sergeant William French, William Spencer Smith, Joseph Henry, William Foot, John Elder, and Ezekiel Snow; and they were discharged October 7th, 1775. The name of William French does not appear among the discharged.

John Laccore, David Blair, George Black, William Moore, Thomas Elder, and Thomas Smith went into the army in 1775, for a short service. Thomas Smith again enlisted in August, 1775. Aschel Johnson enlisted in Capt. Hastings' Company, May 20th, 1775, and was discharged September 24th, 1775. George Black and Thomas Smith were discharged at Roxbury, October 6th, 1775. They had served in Col. Davidson's regiment and in Capt. Ferguson's company. In 1776, David Bolton, William Smith, and Eli Woolworth went into service under Capt. Reuben Munn in the regiment commanded by Col. Nicholas Dike.

October 21, 1776, the men named below joined Col. John Mosley's regiment and marched to Mount Independence under command of Lieut. Col. Timothy Robertson: Capt. Enoch Shepard, Lieut. William Campbell, Sergeant Gershom Rust, Sergeant John McIntire, Sergeant Nathan Wright, Corporal John Elder, Edward Wright, a fifer, and the following privates: Alexander Partridge, James Bentley, Ebenezer Freeman, Allen Geer, Thomas Elder, William Elder, Ebenezer Stowe, John Smith, Lemuel Laccore, Abner Smith, and Jonathan Wait. Their term of service was twenty-eight days.

March 1st, 1777, Jehiel Eggleston and James Fobes enlisted for three years or during the war. December 19th, 1778, Patrick King enlisted and went into the 9th regiment; and in July, 1780, Elijah Brewer* enlisted and went into the 7th regiment. Joseph Winter, age 17 years, Francis Thomas,† aged 17 years, described as five feet six inches in height, and of brown complexion, and Ebenezer Smith age 18 years, described five feet seven inches in height and of brown complexion, enlisted July 9th, 1779, for nine months.

John Thompson was drafted and went into Col. John Mosley's regiment.

In 1780, the persons named below served in Capt. Black's company and Col. Mosley's regiment for three and six months: John Carlile, William Carlile, Alexander McCullen, William Harris, Timothy Smith, Jesse Wright, Elijah Brewer, James Moore, Daniel Babcock, Abraham Converse, Isaac Converse, Jude Jones, Samuel Woolworth, Nathan Matthews, Nathaniel Babcock and Primus Hill.

The following names appear as of the new levies for six months from Massachusetts, under date May 29th, 1780: Joseph Gilbert, Patrick King, Leonard Pigne, Noah Wilson, Moses Barr, John Carlile, William Carlile, Alexander McCullen, Joseph Winter, Timothy Smith, Jesse Wright and William Harris.

The following named persons enlisted April 16th, 1781: Justin Rust, Samuel Rust, Quartus Rust, Edward Taylor, Archelus Anderson, and on June 5th, 1781, Elijah Stanton. At another time in the same year Alexander Mecla, Timothy Smith, William Harris, John Curtis, Elijah Brown, Jesse Wright and Joseph Witter went together. Witter was 17 years of age, five feet eight inches in height and of dark complexion.

Timothy Smith, Jesse Wright, John Carlile, William Carlile, Winter, and Daniel Babcock appear on an enrollment list in 1780 as six months men; also, on another enrollment list, Alexander McCullen and William Harris.

I give the above lists as I find them on the several enrollment lists on file in the office of the Secretary of State.

Excise Duties.

At a town meeting held in January, 1782, the town voted to instruct its representative to "do his endeavor" to get the duties taken off sundry articles. Spirituous liquors, rum, tea and indigo were specifically named with an etc.

---

* It does not appear that Brewer was a Murrayfield man. He is referred to in the town records as "Samuel Brewer."
† In one enrollment list his name is Francis Thompson, which is probably correct

Action Touching the Northwest Corner of the Town.

A special town meeting was called to be held March 29th, 1779, and one article in the warrant was: "To see if the town will consent to have the northwest corner of this town set off to join with Worthington and Becket corner in order to make a society or town." This was in response to the following petition:

"MURRAYFIELD, February 18th, 1779.

Whereas we, the inhabitants of the north west parts of the town of Murrayfield being convened together with the inhabitants of the north east part of Becket & south west part of Worthington, unanimously think it best to be set off as a town: Wherefore we request & desire to be set off from this town & adjoin those forementioned inhabitants; our living so remote from the middle of the town makes it very tedious attending any town business especially the preaching of the Gospel. Therefore we whose names are underwritten do humbly petition to this town to set us off near as far as Thomas Elders.

       (Signed) SAMUEL JONES,
              JOHN TAYLOR,
              JOHN THOMPSON,
              JOHN JONES,
              BENJAMIN EGGLESTON,
              BIGOTT EGGLESTON,
              LEBANON ISHAM."

The town voted not to grant the request. But sometime after the name of the town was changed to "Chester," the legislature took such action that the northwest corner of the town became part of the town of Middlefield, by an act passed March 21st, 1783.

Change of Name.

As early as December, 1775, action was taken with a view to changing the name of the town. There was a town in Hampshire county called Myrifield, afterward incorporated under the name of Rowe. The similarity of the names caused great confusion in various ways; so the selectmen of the town of Murrayfield inserted an article in the warrant "To see if the town will vote to alter the name of the town, & if so, to vote what name they would have it called." The town voted to have the name changed to "Mount Asaph," and chose a committee, consisting of Lieutenant Enoch Shepard, Deacons Jesse Johnson and James Hamilton, "to petition the General Court for the alteration." The reason for this proposed change as given in the "History of the Connecticut

Valley" is not only misleading, but it is absurd. John Murray, to be sure, became a tory and left the country; but not, probably, until after the declaration of independence. At any rate, the act by which he and others were forbidden to return was not passed until 1778. If the reason for making the change was that John Murray had become odious as a tory, there was no objection to the fact being named in their petition. There is no evidence that a petition to change the name to "Mount Asaph" was ever presented to the General Court pursuant to the vote of the town. No further action was had upon this subject until, at the November meeting 1782, the town voted "to petition the General Court to have the name of this town altered, & to have it called 'Mountfair,' or any other name the court shall see fit;" and "that the town clerk be directed to send a petition to the General Court with the spirit of the above vote included therein." A petition was accordingly sent to the General Court for a change of name. But a meeting was called for February 10th, 1783, for the purpose of reconsidering the vote to call the town "Mountfair," and the vote was reconsidered, and a vote passed that the town be called "Fairfield." But for some reason the General Court would not grant this name, and the name "Chester" was selected. The act changing the name reads as follows:

"Whereas, from the great similarity between the names of said town called Murrayfield & a plantation called Merryfield* in this commonwealth, many difficulties & inconveniences have arisen, & the inhabitants of the former pray that the name of the said town may be altered.

Therefore, Be it enacted by the Senate & House of Representatives, in General Court assembled, & by the authority of the same, that the land lying in the county of Hampshire, formerly incorporated into a town by the name of Murrayfield, shall no longer bear that name; but henceforth shall be called & known by the name of Chester, the aforesaid incorporating act notwithstanding. And all officers in the said town shall hold & exercise their offices respectively, in the same manner as they would have done had not the name of said town been altered."

This act was passed February 21st, 1783, but as it did not go into effect immediately upon its passage, the March meeting was called under the old name and also a meeting in April.

March Meeting, 1783.

The March meeting was held the 3d of the month. Stephen Lyman was chosen moderator, and David Shepard was chosen town clerk.

---
* This name was sometimes spelled "Myrifield," and sometimes "Merryfield." It was, a few years later, incorporated under the name of "Rowe."

But it was too cold to continue the meeting in the meeting-house, so it was adjourned to meet "down to William Stowe's house." At this meeting the last election was had of town officers for the town under its old name. They were as follows:

Selectmen and Assessors.—John Blair, William Campbell and Timothy Lyman.

Treasurer.—Stephen Lyman.

Constables.—Benjamin Converse for the south end of the town and Timothy Smith for the north end.

Tythingmen.—Gideon Matthews and Andrew Henry.

Wardens.—Reuben Woolworth, Samuel Moore, David Shepard, Deacon James Hamilton.

Surveyors of Highways.—Joseph Abbott, Jr., Edward Wright, Jr., Thomas Smith, James Core, William Foot, Samuel Moore, Captain Alexander, John Clark and Robert Smith.

Fence Viewers.—James Moore and Robert Smith.

Hog Reeves.—Jonathan Waite, Jr., William Smith and Jonathan Draper.

Sealer of Weights and Measures.—William Stone.

Sealer of Lumber.—Deacon Matthews.

Pound Keeper.—William Foot.

Sealer of Leather.—Isaac Bissell.

The collection of taxes was put up to the lowest bidder, and it was struck off to Timothy Smith at fourpence on the pound. Eighty pounds were raised for repairs of highways, and three shillings was fixed as the price of a day's work.

At the April meeting some roads were accepted; and this was the last town meeting held under the name of Murrayfield.

APPENDIX.

No records of births were kept by the town until Doctor David Shepard was chosen clerk of the town of Murrayfield. To him we are indebted for such records of births, deaths and marriages as appear in the record book of the town prior to 1790. It appears that he took pains to gather such facts as he could, and write them out in the last part of the one book that was kept to record all the doings of the town in. They are little more than memoranda jotted here and there without much regard to order or arrangement. Although extending later than the time of the foregoing history, I have ventured to gather up and arrange in this appendix all the facts for the convenince of the reader and especially for the convenience and information of persons who are interested in the families of the early settlers of Murrayfield. Some of the births recorded took place in other towns, some before the parents came here, and in some cases the mothers went to their old homes and remained until confinement.

The births were as follows:

To Abiel and Sarah Abbott: Joseph, June 11, 1783; Nathan, November 1, 1784; Sally, April 4, 1787; Atcksa, July 28, 1789.

To Ebenezer and Anna Abbott: Rufus, January 31, 1784; Anna, December 4, 1786; Tryphena, May 24, 1789.

To John and Louis Abbott: Phebe, November 23, 1777; John, March 10, 1783; Dolly, March 17, 1785; Billa, February 10, 1788.

To Joseph J. and Hannah Abbott: James P., July 16, 1779; Hannah, July 19, 1781; Betsey, October 26, 1784.

To Nathaniel and Mary Adams: Eliphel, August 18, 1786.

To Nathaniel and Eunice Alexander: Eunice, August 28, 1782; Gaius, October 14, 1784; Anna, October 14, 1786.

To Samuel and Rebecca Allis: Lemuel, July 9, 1784.

To Archelus and Sarah Anderson: Susannah, February 8, 1770; Sarah, November 5, 1771; Lucretia, November 29, 1773; John, October 19, 1777.

To Daniel Barnard and wife: Samuel, February 3, 1786; Sophia, October 2, 1789.

To the Rev. Aaron and Theodosia Bascom: James, April 16, 1773; Samuel Ashley, February 10, 1780; Theodosia, September 11, 1781; Aaron, April 19,

1783; John, December 23, 1784; Fanny, November 8, 1786; Charlotte, March 18, 1789.

To Aaron and Mary Bell: Mary, February 27, 1774, born at Weston; Aaron, December 29, 1775; John Cheney, January 2, 1777; James, June 17, 1780; John Cheney, 2d, May 20, 1783.

To William and Margaret Bell: Mary, March 1, 1772; Justus, February 2, 1774; Simpson, March 19, 1779.

To John and Persa Bigelow: Polly, December 23, 1788.

To Elijah and Mary Blackman: William, February 4, 1787; John Hall, March 22, 1784.

To John and Elizabeth Blair: Molly, June 7, 1771; Solomon, January 30, 1773; James, August 10, 1774; Anna, April 5, 1776; John, February 4, 1778; Sally, October 15, 1779; Betsey, October 15, 1782; James, June 22, 1784.

To Matthew and Sarah Campbell: Mary Wallis, February 27, 1774, born at East Windsor; Cephas, April 19, 1776; Ira, March 4, 1778; Ethan, April 26, 1780; Alvin, November 22, 1782; Sally, January 25, 1785; James Marr, April 13, 1788.

To William and Marah Campbell: Polly and Stella, April 7, 1768; Jane, June 24, 1770; Lucinda, ———, 1772; Billy Young, November 1, 1775.

To John and Sarah Carlile: Sophia, March 10, 1781; Francis, March, 9, 1784.

To James and Dolla Carlile: Eben Smith, February 19, 1789.

To William and Levonia Carlile: Joel, March 31, 1790.

To Eliakim and Pamelia Clapp: Pamelia, April 11, 1787; Rachel, December 8, 1788; Eliakim, August 1, 1790.

To James and Sarah Clark: John Scott, April 1, 1762; Royal, November 21, 1763; Tilas, June 28, 1766; James and David, April 25, 1768; Orin, March 24, 1773; Royal, December 17, 1782.

To James and Ruth Clark: Ruth, July 17, 1769.

To Timothy and Rebecca Cooley: Margaret, April 21, 1788; Chester, March 28, 1790.

To Robert and Mary Crawford: John, September 8, 1783; Russell, April 11, 1786; Polly, February 14, 1788.

To James and Phebe Crow: Isabel, June 6, 1779; Hulda, March 21, 1782.

To John and Anna Crow: Jean, February 23, 1767; John, 3d, July 13, 1769.

To Joshua and Molley Draper: Bethenel, August 27, 1774; Lucy, January 22, 1776; Hazar Enan, September 6, 1777; Rufus, January 22, 1779; Abijah, September 3, 1781; Sylvester, May 14, 1783.

To Thomas and Margaret Elder: Thomas, June 12, 1774; Samuel, March 5, 1776; Kata, April 9, 1778; James, January 30, 1780; Charlotte, January 27, 1782; John, March 9, 1784; Artemas, October 14, 1785.

To Thomas and Nabby Elder: Laura, July 27, 1789.

To William and Sarah Elder: Samuel, March 9, 1785; Norrid, May 22, 1787; William, May 5, 1789.

To Samuel and Stella Ellis: John, June 9, 1763; Samuel, February 11, 1765; Margaret, January 4, 1767; Noah, June 14, 1769; Sally, April 26, 1771; Ebenezer, November 23, 1773; Sally, April 5, 1777.

To James and Thankful Fairman: Frederick, May 15, 1770; Amaza, November 3, 1771.

To Thaddeus and Abigail Ferry: Abigail, July 30, 1788.

To Solomon and Rhoda Ferry: Orra, July 6, 1788.

To Gershom and Editha Flagg: Mary, February 4, 1783; Ebenezer, June 14, 1785; Edith, July 17, 1786.

To Thomas and Nancy Flint: Esquire, April 3, 1784; Lucy, December 18, 1785.

To Nathan and Rebecca Fobes: Jabez, September 27, 1784; Sally, July 1, 1786; Justin, October 20, 1788.

To William and Ruth Foot: Eunice, November 8, 1778; Ruth, November 26, 1780; Asa W., August 4, 1786.

To Jacob and Elizabeth Fowle: Betsey, December 13, 1780; Nancy, September 5, 1782; Polly, February 27, 1784.

To Silas and Mary Freeman: Brewster, March 27, 1765, born at Preston, Conn.; Freeman, March 29, 1767, born at Preston, Conn.; Edmon, August 5, 1769, born at Preston, Conn.; Joseph, September 8, 1771, born at Preston, Conn.; Benjamin White, March 1, 1773, born at Canterbury, Conn.; Charles, December 10, 1775, born at Preston, Conn.; Nathaniel, May 25, 1778; Samuel Dweller, February 12, 1780; Sylvanus, February 14, 1783.

To Samuel and Susannah French: Azael, May 12, 1778.

To Alexander and Martha Gordon: John, May 6, 1769.

To Samuel and Olive Gould: Patty, February 19, 1777; Molly, September 15, 1779.

To Lewis and Tersa Hancock: Polly, June 18, 1788.

To Malcom and Dolly Henry: Mary, July 5, 1763; Isabel, April 12, 1765; Susanna, January 20, 1767; Andrew, March 16, 1769; Dolly, September 23, 1771.

To Oliver and Elizabeth Hitchcock: Levi, October 9, 1786.

To Zadock and Christiana Ingall: James, June 26, 1783; Zadock, October 16, 1784.

To Jesse and Sarah Johnson: Eunice, January 23, 1769; Roxana, July 28, 1770; Isaac, March 10, 1772; Sybil, December 30, 1773; Mabel, November 3, 1775; Roxana, July 14, 1777; Daniel, March 22, 1779; Louis, October 30, 1780; Lucy, May 18, 1785.

To John and Hannah Jones: Arba, April 24, 1775; Cynthia, April 3, 1778; Hannah, February 10, 1781.

To John and Anna Kirtland: Mary, December 14, 1770.

To Samuel and Betty Knight: Samuel, February 11, 1771.

To John and Sarah Laccore: Sally, February 18, 1774; Cynthia, August 16, 1775; Roxana, September 15, 1777; Phebe, September 15, 1780; John, April 8, 1783; Anna, November 21, 1785; Ranseler, April 8, 1788.

To Lemuel and Edith Laccore: Edith, March 23, 1771; Lemuel, November 8, 1772; Margaret, August 31, 1775; John, October 9, 1777.

To Stephen and Anna Lyman: Crispus, March 27, 1773; Gaius, July 15,

1774; Clarissa, October 10, 1776; Noah, October 2, 1778; Burnham, April 22, 1780; Chester, March 22, 1782; Stephen, July 25, 1783.

To Timothy and Dorothy Lyman: Susanna, November 6, 1770; Achsa, February 27, 1774; Theodosia, November 16, 1775; Dorothy, April 24, 1780; Timothy, August 30, 1782; Asael, April 3, 1785.

To Nathan and Jane Mann: Sarah, November 12, 1764; Nathan, October 19, 1766; Prudence, June 11, 1769.

To Gideon and Esther Matthews: Esther, October 5, 1763; Gideon, May 20, 1766; Lucy, September 14, 1768; Lucy, April 18, 1771; Benjamin, May 19, 1776; Nathaniel Eggleston, October 10, 1780; Osee, March 14, 1784.

To Reuben and Adah Matthews: Hannah, October 19, 1769.

To John and Anna McIntire: Oliver, March 3, 1763, born at Pelham; Roxana, July 25, 1765; Deidamia, February 10, 1766; Salva, August 2, 1768; John, August 16, 1770; Levi, June 2, 1773.

To Isaac, Jr., and Zerina Mixer: Elizabeth, April 6, 1768.

To Ebenezer and Rachel Meacham: Jeremiah, October 14, 1760, born at Enfield, Ct.; Mary, May 28, 1764; Enoch, July 5, 1766; Stephen, November 20, 1767; Luther, May 7, 1770; Hannah, May 2, 1772.

To James and Molly Moore: Dolley, March 28, 1783; James, November 19, 1784; Polly, August 26, 1786; John, June 19, 1788.

To John and Elizabeth Moore: Lucy, November 2, 1780; Levi, June 15, 1782; Elizabeth, September 1, 1786.

To John, Jr., and Elizabeth Moore: John, April 16, 1786.

To Samuel and Elizabeth Moore: John, January 17, 1780; Asa, December 10, 1781; Theodosia, March 7, 1784; Betsey, March 21, 1786; Clara, September 25, 1789.

To Robert and Dolly Moore: Artemus, March 13, 1786; Ezra, May 3, 1787; Sarah, February 25, 1789.

To David and Eunice Palmer: Eunice, December 24, 1770.

To John David and Abigail Palmer: Ocren, November 18, 1770; David, September 13, 1788.

To John Newton and Hannah Parmenter: Arthusa, February 18, 1778; Melinda, August 23, 1779; John, March 18, 1781; Azel, November 15, 1784; Jonas, July 29, 1787.

To Amasa and Martha Pomeroy: Roxa, June 11, 1780; Abigail, February 22, 1782; Martha, March 12, 1784; Nice, April 20, 1786; Asa, April 7, 1788.

To Luther and Rhoda Pomeroy: Nancy, September 8, 1786; Rhoda, September 29, 1787, born at Northampton; Sally, November 10, 1788; Luther, October 21, 1790.

To Robert and Ruth Proctor: Jonathan, October 1, 1765; Betsey, June 26, 1768; Robert, January 10, 1771; Elijah, August 29, 1773; Molly, September 16, 1775; Jeremiah, October 14, 1777; Ruth, March 6, 1780.

To William and Elizabeth Prior: Elizabeth, June 5, 1783; Daniel, February 15, 1785; Ziphar, February 19, 1787.

To Israel and Eunice Rose: Joseph, June 1, 1760, born at Granville; Olive,

A HISTORY OF MURRAYFIELD. 149

October 20, 1762; Israel, December 7, 1764; Eunice, May 8, 1767; Benjamin, September 5, 1770.

To Nathan and Sarah Rose: Roxana, May 2, 1768; Nathaniel, April 6, 1770.

To Zebulon and Olive Rose: Sabay, August 10, 1769; Anna, October 10, 1770.

To Gershom and Mary Rust: Polly, September 9, 1772; Patty, March 12, 1776; Cooley, February 28, 1778; Joseph Ashley, April 27, 1779.

To Justin and Margaret Rust: Dolly, September 17, 1788.

To Sylvanus and Charlotte Sanderson: Calvin, February 23, 1787.

To David and Mary Scott: William, October 22, 1764; James, July 19, 1767; Mary, May 6, 1770.

To Noadiah and Sarah Seaward: Jesse, April 26, 1784; Calvin, October 5, 1786; Cathrine, December 26, 1788.

To David and Lucinda Shepard: Martha, March 19, 1774; David, June 8, 1777; Lucinda, June 12, 1782; Harriet, May 17, 1785; Fanny, May 20, 1787; Horace, February 5, 1789.

To Daniel and Kezia Smith: Anna, September 3, 1780; Phineas, February 10, 1782.

To John and Abigail Smith: Eunice, March 2, 1765; Abigail, August 6, 1767.

To John and Lydia Smith: Caleb, August 27, 1782; Patta, July 28, 1784; Lydia, March 17, 1786; Russell, October 20, 1788.

To Daniel and Pruda Smith: Parmelia, August 8, 1787.

To Ebenezer and Nice Smith: Bernice, May 23, 1785.

To Joab and Elizabeth Smith: Ira, October 17, 1784.

To Thomas and Submit Smith: Timothy, May 25, 1762, born at Wallingford, Ct.; Eben Blakely, September 10, 1763, born at Wallingford, Ct.; Dollither, November 29, 1765; Esther, September 6, 1767.

To Ezekiel and Phebe Snow: Damaris, April 19, 1768; Oriandatus, July 26, 1770; Ezerias, April 13, 1772; Hezekiah, February 4, 1774.

To Daniel and Jane Stone: Mary, February 14, 1781; Susa, October 22, 1783; Nathaniel, December 17, 1785.

To William and Hetty Stone: Harvey, March 13, 1783; Sally, November 29, 1786; Sophia, September 1, 1788.

To Ebenezer and Content Stowe: Ebenezer, September 6, 1777; Lydia, December 17, 1778; Esther, June 19, 1780; Cephus, March 10, 1782.

To William and Lois Tanner: William, April 23, 1786.

To Jonathan and Margaret Wait: Samuel, March 26, 1779.

To Jonathan and Mary Wait: Lucy, May 5, 1781.

To James and Achsa Warner: James, September 19, 1787; Henry, May 10, 1789.

To Ebenezer and Keziah Webber: John, April 13, 1870.

To Ebenezer and Renia Webber: Liddah, April 23, 1768.

To Jonathan Hart and Keziah Webber: Pela Hart, January 15, 1773; Clarica, April 24, 1775; Molly, August 30, 1777; Keziah, September 3, 1779.

To Peter and Sarah Williams: Eunice, February 3, 1768; Elisha, June 24, 1770.

To Phineas and Molly Wheeler: Betsey, April 11, 1784.
To Abner Witt and wife: Polly, February 10, 1788.
To William Witt and wife: William, October 9, 1783.
To Edward and Cloe Wright: Edward, June 8, 1775; Cloe, April, 1777; John, April 5, 1779.
To Joshua and Triphena Wright: Joshua, October 15, 1771.
To Joseph and Elizabeth Wright: Joseph, January 16, 1787; Daniel, February 16, 1789.
To Nathan and Mary Wright: Polly, April 8, 1784; Nathan, August 26, 1786; Sibil, October 16, 1788.
To Henry and Sabbahis Vadekin: Henry, September 10, 1783; Philip, May 25, 1786.

MARRIAGES.

Very few entries of actual marriages appear upon the town records of Murrayfield. They were kept no doubt by the clergymen who performed the service, and possibly many appear upon the church records. The intentions of marriage were required to be published three times "at some public lecture or town meeting, in both the towns where the parties or either of them do ordinarily reside, or be set up in writing upon some post of their meeting house door in public view, there to stand so as it may easily be read, by the space of fourteen days." The parties to the marriage were required to produce to the minister or the magistrate performing the service, a "certificate of such publishment under the hand of the town clerk or constable of such towns respectively." A record of intentions of marriage was required to be kept by town clerks. The statute also required that "all marriages shall be registered by the town clerk of the same town where they are consummated." The absence of records of marriage of Murrayfield men may be explained by the assumption that many of them married women residing in adjoining or in distant towns, so that only their intentions of marriage would appear.

Below is a list of intentions of marriage that appear in the first record book of the town, arranged in alphabetical order, and with them the marriages, so far as they appear of record, between the following named persons:

January 13, 1783: Abiel Abbott and Sarah Mann. They were married January 23.

March 19, 1781: Ebenezer Abbott and Anna Wright. Married December 31, 1781.

May 18, 1784: Isaac Averet and Bethiah Fuller of Norwich.

January 8, 1771: Samuel Buck of Chesterfield and Susanna Palmer of Murrayfield.

January 8, 1772: John Barnard of Westfield and Deliverence Holaday of Murrayfield. They were married January 16.
June 15, 1780: Samuel Bell and Elizabeth Campbell.
October 13, 1780: Roswell Benjamin of Norwich and Thankful Cooley of Murrayfield.
January 16, 1773: Patrick Bulkley and Anna Williams.
April 24, 1773: Samuel Boyes, Jr., of Blandford and Elizabeth Black of Murrayfield.
April 29, 1774: George Black and Anna Boyes of Blandford.
December 25, 1790: Daniel Bigelow and Mercy Wood. They were married January 27, 1791.
April 3, 1791: Elijah Bacon of Whitestown, N. Y., and Lucy Sizer of Chester.
September 30, 1787: John Bigelow and Persa Wright. They were married November 29, 1787.
May 10, 1778: James Campbell and Lorena Smith.
January 27, 1783: James Campbell of Blandford and Isabel Elder of Murrayfield. Married December 18, 1783.
January 25, 1789: Matthew Campbell and Isabel Lindsey of Blandford.
January 9, 1790: Matthew Campbell and Sarah Bell of Oakham.
December, 1786: Joseph Campbell and Jemima Moore. They were married November 6, 1787.
June 24, 1780: John Carlile and Sarah Smith.
July 13, 1788: James Carlile and Dorothy Smith.
May 7, 1789: William Carlile and Lovina Cooley. They were married May 28
September 28, 1782: John Clark and Sela Anderson of Chesterfield.
April 19, 1789: Joseph Clapp of Easthampton and Susanna Lyman of Chester. They were married May 28, 1789.
October 19, 1788: Daniel Collins and Anna Williams of Worthington.
July 29, 1787: Timothy Cooley and Rebecca Smith. They were married September 12.
December 6, 1770: David Crow and Hulda Button.
March 4, 1771: Timothy Culver and Margaret Williams.
November 20, 1770: Ebenezer Dowd and Sarah Dunn.
October 20, 1781: Isaac Dowd and Elanor Osborn of Lower Salem.
October 28, 1787: Abraham Drake of Worthington and Susanna Hamilton of Chester. Married December 24.
November 4, 1789: Vester Edwards of Northampton and widow Polly Smith of Chester.
February 19, 1774: Samuel Eggleston and Mary Taylor.
October 9, 1774: Benjamin Eggleston and Mary Gordon.
November 16, 1772: Thomas Elder and Margaret Moore.
March 8, 1784: William Elder and Sarah Campbell.
March 2, 1788: Thomas Elder and Nabby Fellows. Married April 17.
September 26, 1778: John Elder and Sarah Moore of Rutland.
March 13, 1791: Samuel Ellis and widow Dolly Tracy.

A HISTORY OF MURRAYFIELD.

May 31, 1779: Deodatus Ensign of Westfield and Abigail Woolworth of Murrayfield. Married February 9, 1780.
November 25, 1773: Samuel Fairman of Norwich and Joanna Williams of Murrayfield.
August 10, 1786: Ozias French and Elizabeth Dayton of Blandford. They were married August 24.
January 17, 1790: Jabez French and Sarah Johnson: Married April 1, 1790.
September 29, 1771: Joseph Geer of Worthington and Lydia Bell of Chester.
July 13, 1777: Allyn Geer and Perimelia Daniels of Worthington.
July 13, 1783: David Gleason and Sarah Gleason.
June 21, 1784: John Grims of Chatham and Esther Shepard.
August 28, 1790: Luther Granger and widow Ruth Goodwill.
September 18, 1790: Nathan Goodwill and Lucy Fairbanks of Mendham.
March 31, 1791: Nathaniel Goodwill and Molly Bell.
December 8, 1781: Aaron Hale and Martha Loomis.
February 10, 1788: Samuel Hamilton of Chesterfield and Susanna Hamilton of Chester. Married March 6.
January 25, 1789: John Hamilton and Sarah Fleming of Palmer.
May 25, 1772: John Haskel and Debora Meacham.
January 8, 1771: Jonas Henry of Murrayfield and Margaret Henry of Blandford.
October 6, 1780: Andrew Henry and Jael Elder.
March 3, 1783: Joseph Henry and Lydia Kelso. Married March 10.
April 9, 1781: Solomon Hingham of Becket and Molly Wright of Murrayfield.
January 23, 1791: William Holland and Polly Moore.
October 12, 1780: Samuel Hulbert of Kent, Conn., and Lucy Smith of Murrayfield.
October 1, 1780: Zebulon Isham and Rose Ellis of Hebron, Conn.
August 7, 1790: Selathial Judd and Irena Day.
November 16, 1772: Daniel Kirtland and Theodosia Mixer.
May 3, 1779: Jethro Kenney and Ruth Jackson of Spencer.
March 22, 1784: Phineas King of Southampton and Lola Smith of Chester.
October 15, 1773: John Laccore and Sarah Smith.
August 9, 1778: Capt. Daniel Lamb of Springfield and widow Martha Jones of Murrayfield.
November 15, 1777: Noah Leonard of West Springfield and Lydia Taylor of Murrayfield.
August 25, 1770: Stephen Lyman and Anna Blair of Weston.
July 3, 1786: Deac. Stephen Lyman and widow Hannah Clark of Southampton.
April 4, 1790: Lucas Matthews and Polly Brooks.
December 14, 1786: Ebenezer Nathan Messenger of Becket and Sally Campbell of Chester. Married December 14.
July 25, 1778: William McIntire and Roxana Campbell.
July 8, 1787: Oliver Millard and Zillar Lee.

January 30, 1791: Oliver Miller and Cynthia Black.
August 20, 1773: Samuel Moore of Rutland and Elizabeth Elder.
July 25, 1781: James Moore and Mary Henry of Becket.
December 28, 1787: Robert Moore and Dorothy Abbott.
July 7, 1771: Moses Moss of Preston and Anna Mixer.
December 14, 1786: Benjamin Mussey and Elizabeth Ingall. Married January 4, 1787.
July 20, 1777: Reuben Parks of Westfield and Betty Clark.
March 7, 1790: Tabor Pelton of Middlefield and Anna Moore.
December 7, 1782: William Prior and Elizabeth Ellis.
September 20, 1789: Heman Prior and Mitte Sanderson. Married October 15.
March 15, 1789: Hugh Quigley and Molly Mulhollan. Married July 12, 1789.
November 24, 1781: William Russell and Penelope Northrop.
January 24, 1790: Gershom Rust and Sally Matthews. Married April 1, 1790.
April 22, 1787: Justin Rust and Margaret Shepard. Married August 31, 1787.
July 25, 1785: Tyrol Sanderson of West Springfield and Elizabeth Smith of Chester.
October 7, 1787: William Scott of Norwich and Lovisa Miller.
July 1, 1787: Job Searle of Southampton and Esther Matthews. Married July 2.
October 2, 1786: Noadiah Seward, Jr., and Diadema McIntire. Married October 2.
December 25, 1772: Dr. David Shepard and Lucinda Mather. Married January 7, 1773.
March 13, 1791: Asa Slayton and widow Sarah Anderson.
November 10, 1767: John Smith and Abilene Core were married.
August 13, 1775: Abner Smith, Jr., and Abigail Pomeroy of Southampton.
January 4, 1780: Daniel Smith and Keziah Pomeroy.
April 9, 1781: John Smith and Lydia Seward.
April 12, 1781: William Smith and Lucy Converse.
April 3, 1784: Jacob Smith and Elizabeth Lunnon.
November 14, 1784: Ebenezer Smith and Nice Pomeroy. Married November 25.
April 1, 1787: Enos Smith and Lucy Bently. Married August 16.
April 1, 1787: Ebenezer Smith and Damoras Snow. Married April 19.
March 11, 1787: Daniel Smith, 3d, and Prudence Wood. Married April 12.
January 23, 1791: William Smith and Sally Anderson.
January 17, 1790: John Stevenson and Nella Walker.
November 2, 1789: Gershom Sylvester of Chesterfield and Polly Durger French. Married November 18.
December 4, 1773: Ebenezer Tillotson of Farmington, Conn., and Roxana Laccore.
November 9, 1788: Samuel Augustus Thorp and Polly Hamilton.
December 30, 1771: Daniel Twadwell and Martha Crow. Married January 9, 1772.
January 26, 1784: Daniel Twadwell and Abigail Tracy.

May 3, 1778: Jonathan Wait, Jr., and Margaret Smith.
July 24, 1774: John Ward and Susanna Beard of Hartwood.
December 22, 1771: Jonathan Hart Webber and Keziah Cooley of Springfield.
November 17, 1781: Jude White and Roxa Loomis of Southampton.
May 29, 1784: John Williams and Relief Abbott.
April 26, 1784: Eli Woolworth and Sally Olds.
July 26, 1786: Samuel Woolworth and Bersheba Crossman.
May 25, 1772: Edward Wright, Jr., and Cloe Pomeroy.
July 14, 1776: Bezeliel Wright and Sarah Whitney of Waltham.
May 20, 1786: Joseph Wright and Elizabeth Parmenter.

DEATHS.

I am certain that the records of the town of Murrayfield fail to show all the births or all the marriages; and I feel certain that they do not show all the deaths in the town during the period of time covered by the records. It is probable that some deaths of inhabitants of the town occurred outside of the town and were not for that reason recorded. I give below a list of deaths so far as they appear in the records, and the date of their occurrence.

Joseph Abbott, January 30, 1770.
Phebe, daughter of John and Louise Abbott, June 22, 1779.
John Cheney Bell, son of Aaron and Mary, May 10, 1781.
James Blackman, October 31, 1787.
William Campbell, January 19, 1782.
Sarah Campbell, wife of Matthew, May 6, 1788.
Margaret Elder, wife of Thomas, October 20, 1785.
Ebenezer Flagg, son of Gershom and Edith, July 7, 1785.
Lucy French, April 29, 1781.
Eunice, daughter of Samuel and Susanna French, October 2, 1776.
Susa, daughter of Samuel and Susanna French, September 26, 1776.
Aaron, son of James and Mary Holland, age 7 years, November 16, 1777.
Roxana, daughter of Jesse and Sarah Johnson, September 27, 1776.
Mabel, daughter of Jesse and Sarah Johnson, October 1, 1776.
Nathan Mann, December 21, 1770.
John, son of Samuel and Elizabeth Moore, September 12, 1780.
―――― an adopted son of Samuel Matthews, March 29, 1777.
Nice Pomeroy, May 27, 1787.
Patty, daughter of Gershom and Mary Rust, December 29, 1789, age 14 years.
Russell, son of Gershom and Mary Rust, March 26, 1776.
Abigail, wife of John Smith, August 12, 1767, aged 37 years.
David Smith, aged 78 years, January 6, 1771.
Patty Smith, daughter of John and Lydia Smith, May, 1785.
Nice, wife of Ebenezer Smith, January 2, 1785.

A HISTORY OF MURRAYFIELD.   155

Bernice, son of Ebenezer and Nice Smith, January 9, 1785.
Ezekiel Snow, January 28, 1776.
Triphena, daughter of Edward and Triphena Wright, October 8, 1775.
John, son of Edward and Triphena Wright, October 11, 1775.
Jonathan, son of Edward and Triphena Wright, September 17, 1776.
Pela Hart, son of Jonathan Hart and Keziah Webber, November 8, 1775.
Olive Witt, wife of William Witt, January 3, 1789.

HIGHWAYS.

The surveys of the highways approved at the March town meeting in 1769, being of interest in several respects are given in full: "Worthington road through Murrayfield to Westfield, beginning at Worthington south line at a hemlock tree marked on east side of the highway, S. 5 deg. E. 20 rods, S. 8 deg. E. 38 rods, S. 5 deg. E. 29 rods, S. 15 deg. E. 53 rods, E. 22 deg. S. 90 rods, E. 41 deg. S. 20 rods, S. 15 deg. E. 90 rods, S. 30 deg. E. 40 rods, S. 25 deg. E. 12 rods, S. 45 deg. E. 24 rods, S. 20 deg. E. 100 rods, S. 90 deg. E. 60 rods, S. 20 deg. E. 90 rods, E. 30 deg. S. 90 rods, S. 16 deg. E. 90 rods, two miles from Worthington; S. 16 deg. E. 100 rods, S. 7 deg. W. 100$\frac{20}{100}$ rods, S. 11 deg. E. 180 rods, S. 4 deg. W. 20 rods, S. 28 deg. W. 60 rods, S. 20 deg. W. 100 rods, S. 15 deg. W. 9 rods, S. 5 deg. W. 36 rods, S. 31 deg. W. 90 rods, S. 31 deg. W. 60 rods to a small beech tree on a ridge marked 4 miles from Worthington; then same course 7 rods to a small beech tree near the Middle Branch east side of the branch, then southeasterly by the east bank by Mr. Wait's mill by said east bank to the road that crosses the fordway westerly of Mr. Timothy Smith's one mile and 50 rods by said branch, then E. 10 deg. S. by Mr. Smith's house 30 rods, S. 31 deg. E. 8 rods, S. 5 deg. E. 68 rods; thence southerly to a hemlock tree near bank of said branch, thence by said branch to the fordway a little west of Mr. Taggart's; thence S. 21 deg. E. by Mr. Rose's house, S. 38 deg. E. by Mr. Scott's land on the ridge against Mr. Fobes', E. 29 deg. S. across the river by Mr. Fobes'; thence east side of the river on the bank by Mr. Mixer's 70 rods, S. 15 deg. E. 132 rods, S. 4 deg. E. 32 rods, E. 30 deg. S. 26 rods, E. 35 deg. S. 20 rods, E. 30 deg. S. 6 rods, S. 19 deg. E. 39 rods, S. 36 deg. E. 90 rods, S. 25 deg. E. 98 rods, S. 45 deg. W. 32 rods, S. 18 deg. W. 16 rods, E. 27 deg. S. 99 rods, S. 14 deg. W. 19 rods, S. 20 deg. E. 26 rods, S. 25 deg. E. 36 rods, E. 40 deg. S. 46 rods, E. 45 deg. N. 20 rods, E. 22 deg. N. 42 rods, S. 25 deg. E. 8 rods, E. 34 deg. N. 46 rods by Mr. King's house, E. 10 deg. S. 58 rods, E. 33 deg. S. 16 rods, S. 38 deg. E. 64 rods, S. 44 deg. E. 40 rods, S. 33 deg. E. 120 rods, S. 45 deg. E. 100 rods, E. 45 deg. S. 30 rods,

S. 5 deg. E. 50 rods, S. 5 deg. W. 40 rods, S. 20 deg. E. 28 rods, S. 37 deg. E. 32 rods, E. 12 deg. S. 26 rods, E. 45 deg. S. 54 rods, S. 17 deg. E. 40 rods, S. 30 deg. E. 40 rods, E. 21 deg. S. 30 rods, E. 30 deg. S. 18 rods to Hampton line on Westfield mountain from Worthington line through Murrayfield eleven miles and one hundred and seventy-six rods to trees marked on the east side of the highway." The present highway from Norwich Bridge in Huntington to Westfield through Montgomery past the meeting-house is a part of the same highway.

Another is as follows: "Road to the meeting house from the fordway west of Mr. Timothy Smith's by Mr. Ebenezer Webber's thence northerly as the river runs west side of the branch 110 rods, W. 16 deg. N. 8 rods, N. 30 deg. W. 80 rods, N. 10 deg. W. 50 rods—2 rods south of Mr. Ebenezer Webber's house; thence W. 14 deg. N. 29 rods, W. 40 deg. N. 40 rods, W. 35 deg. N. 50 rods, W. 5 deg. N. 68 rods, W. 5 deg. S. 16 rods, N. 40 deg. W. 19 rods, W. 35 deg. S. 14 rods, W. 55 deg. S. 8 rods, N. 40 deg. W. 16 rods, W. 25 deg. N. 100 rods, N. 35 deg. W. 18 rods, W. 25 deg. N. 22 rods, W. 16 deg. S. 123 rods, from Mr. Ebenezer Webber's to the meeting house 1 mile and 286 rods."

Another is as follows: "Beginning at a hemlook tree 8 rods north from the meeting house, W. 5 deg. N. 20 rods, W. 31 deg. S. 198 rods, S. 25 deg. W. 8 rods, W. 16 rods, W. 10 deg. S. 176 rods between Lyman and McIntire's; thence N. 30 deg. W. 90 rods, N. 15 deg. W. 66 rods, N. 31 deg. W. 119 rods, W. 38 deg. N. 39 rods, N. 20 deg. W. 60 rods, W. 21 deg. N. 20 rods, W. 15 deg. N. 20 rods, W. 42 deg. N. — rods, N. 41 deg. W. 26 rods, N. 10 deg. W. 64 rods, N. 25 deg. W. 30 rods, W. 45 deg. N. 90 rods, N. 3 deg. W. 20 rods, N. 13 deg. E. 30 rods, N. 10 deg. W. 89 rods, to Mr. James Brown's from the meeting house 2 miles and 270 rods. Trees marked on the southwesterly side of the road, laid four rods wide."

Also: "From Mr. James Black's to the above-laid road: Beginning at the west end of Mr. Black's house, N. 8 deg. E. 90 rods, N. 10 deg. E. 100 rods, N. 30 deg. E. 100 rods, N. 8 deg. E. 60 rods, N. 19 deg. E. 30 rods, N. 30 deg. E. 70 rods, N. 35 deg. W. 90 rods, N. 45 deg. E. 40 rods, E. 19 deg. S. 20 rods, E. 23 deg. N. 19 rods, E. 18 deg. S. 26 rods to road north of Mann's."

Another: "From Mr. Gordon's by Mr. Laccore's to the meeting house: Beginning a little east of Mr. Gordon's house, N. 22 deg. E. 20 rods, S. 45 deg. E. 156 rods, to the road from David Blair's; from Blair's S. 5 deg. W. 32 rods, S. 23 deg. W. 28 rods, S. 10 deg. W. 520 rods, S. 35 deg. E. 40 rods, S. 30 deg. E. 100 rods, S. 40 deg. E. 8

rods, S. 10 deg. E. 20 rods; to the meeting house from Gordon's 3 miles and 16 rods."

Another: "From William Campbell's by Matthew and Abner Smith's to the meeting house: Beginning east side of Mr. Campbell's house, S. 5 deg. W. 20 rods, S. 10 deg. E. 40 rods, S. 20 deg. W. 20 rods, S. 3 deg. W. 20 rods, S. 21 deg. E. 40 rods, S. 20 deg. E. 160 rods, S. 19 deg. W. 76 rods, S. 15 deg. W. 60 rods, S. 5 deg. W. to Laccore's road; to the meeting house 1 mile and 316 rods. Trees marked on east side of road."

Another: "From meeting house by Henry's to the fordway against Fobes': Beginning on Webber's road from the meeting house 90 rods, then S. 30 deg. E. 30 rods, S. 15 deg. E. 40 rods, S. 30 deg. E. 90 rods, S. 12 deg. E. 35 rods, S. 40 deg. E. 25 rods, E. 35 deg. S. 27 rods, S. 10 deg. E. 1 mile and 31 rods, E. 14 deg. S. 46 rods, E. 45 deg. N. 14 rods to a little hemlock tree, thence E. 36 deg. N. 4 rods, S. 45 deg. E. 22 rods, E. 32 deg. S. 14 rods, S. 41 deg. E. 30 rods, 22 deg. S. 44 rods, S. 44 rods, S. 20 deg. E. 23 rods, S. 18 deg. E. 60 rods, E. 38 deg. S. 16 rods, S. 2 deg. W. 22 rods, S. 25 deg. E. 42 rods, E. 6 deg. S. 16 rods, E. 41 deg. S. 10 rods, S. 20 deg. E. 42 rods. E. 35 deg. S. 14 rods, S. 16 deg. E. 10 rods, S. 34 deg. E. 22 rods, E, 5 deg. N. 24 rods, S. 13 deg. W. 30 rods, E. 14 rods, E. 2 deg. S. 40 rods, E. 140 rods, N. 23 deg. E. 14 rods, N. 21 deg. W. 26 rods, thence northerly by Mr. Scott's to the road from Worthington against Mr. Fobes' 4 miles and 288 rods. Trees marked on the east side of road."

This is the road from Chester Center by the Brunley place to Norwich Bridge.

Another: "Beginning at Worthington road above Mr. Wait's mill east side of the [middle] Branch, N. 30 deg. W. 50 rods, W. 40 deg. N. 50 rods, N. 15 deg. W. 40 rods, then across the Branch W. 35 deg. N. 4 rods, then north on the west bank of the Branch 160 rods, N. 19 deg. W. 20 rods, W. 30 deg. N. 25 rods, W. 5 deg. N. 35 rods, W. 27 deg. N. 23 rods, W. 25 deg. S. 40 rods, W. 20 deg. N. 20 rods, N. 14 deg. W. 30 rods, W. 30 deg. N. 160 rods, S. 30 deg. W. 20 rods, W. 10 deg. S. 40 rods, W. 20 deg. S. 70 rods to Abner Smith's house 2 miles and 130 rods from Worthington road. Trees marked on westerly side of road."

Another: "Beginning at a chestnut stump a little east of Peter Williams' house, S. 24 deg. W. 52 rods to the bank of the brook, thence on said bank to the river;* on the bank of said river 140 rods,

* West Branch.

S. 43 deg. W. 60 rods, W. 15 deg. S. 28 rods, W. 8 deg. N. 4 rods, W. 38 deg. S. 38 rods to Blandford line to John Bolton's 323 rods; then W. 30 deg. N. 70 rods, W. 13 deg. N. 36 rods to east bank of the West Branch; on said Branch northerly 138 rods to Blandford line. Beginning at Blandford line on said bank 132 rods, N. 11 deg. W. 40 rods, W. 13 deg. N. 34 rods, W. 30 deg. N. 30 rods, W. 45 deg. N. 180 rods, N. 40 deg. W. 20 rods to the bank of said Branch 60 rods to a beech tree marked facing the river from Blandford line to the bank of the Branch, N. 30 deg. E. 15 rods, W. 35 deg. N. to the fordway above David Bolton's by said bank, then down the east bank to Mr. Bolton's 8 rods, N. 8 deg. W. 100 rods, N. 6 deg. W. 40 rods, N. 25 deg. E. 24 rods, N. 6 deg. W. 16 rods, N. 10 deg. W. 141 rods, N. 5 deg. W. 80 rods, N. 10 deg. W. 96 rods, W. 5 deg. N. 10 rods, N. 20 deg. W. 136 rods to Col. Chandler's saw mill to his house, N. 14 deg. E. 32 rods, E. 45 deg. S. 14 rods, E. 23 deg. N. 14 rods, E. 31 deg. N. 20 rods to Smith's house from the meeting house S. 28 deg. E. 50 rods, S. 35 deg. E. 20 rods, S. 10 deg. E. 20 rods, S. 22 deg. E. 40 rods, S. 10 deg. E. 50 rods, S. 20 deg. E. 8 rods, S. 15 deg. E. 6 rods, S. 10 deg. W. 20 rods, S. 10 deg. E. 40 rods, E. 42 deg. S. 20 rods to Smith's house; then to the road from Henry's E. 40 deg. S. 20 rods, S. 40 deg. E. 66 rods, E. 40 deg. S. 104 rods to the road from Henry's."

Another: "To Col. Chandler's saw mill from McIntire's corner by Lyman's, S. 2 deg. W. 60 rods, S. 34 deg. E. 26 rods, S. 24 deg. E. 76 rods, E. 10 deg. S. 20 rods, E. 35 deg. S. 68 rods, E. 18 deg. S. 30 rods, S. 40 deg. E. 40 rods, S. 16 deg. E. 20 rods, S. 4 deg. E. 30 rods, S. 45 deg. E. 10 rods, S. 15 deg. E. 24 rods, E. 26 deg. S. 18 rods, S. 40 deg. E. 18 rods, S. 25 deg. E. 28 rods, E. 10 deg. S. 12 rods, N. 24 deg. E. 20 rods to the saw mill."

Also: "Beginning at Chesterfield line at the highway, then southeasterly and westerly to the mouth of the East Branch, S. 45 deg. W. across the river, thence southerly on the west bank of the river 206 rods, W. 24 deg. S. 20 rods, S. 15 deg. W. 42 rods, S. 2 deg. W. 20 rods, S. 33 deg. W. 12 rods, S. 35 deg. E. 16 rods to bank of the river, on the bank 100 rods, S. 22 deg. W. 26 rods, S. 18 deg. E. 34 rods, S. 30 deg. E. 34 rods, S. 4 deg. E. 26 rods, S. 10 deg. E. 28 rods, S. 2 deg. W. 52 rods, S. 26 deg. W. 12 rods, S. 20 deg. E. 8 rods to bank of the river, 30 rods by said bank, W. 16 deg. N. 40 rods, W. 15 deg. S. 40 rods, W. 43 deg. S. 20 rods to Mr. Miller's house, S. 31 deg. W. 12 rods, W. 19 deg. S. 14 rods across Miller Branch, S. 10 deg. W. 20 rods, S. 3 deg. E. 10 rods; then southerly on the bank of the river [East

A HISTORY OF MURRAYFIELD. 159

Branch] 288 rods, W. 12 rods, W. 14 deg. S. 40 rods, W. 27 deg. S. 26 rods, S. 34 deg. W. 20 rods, S. 13 deg. W. 26 rods, S. 15 deg. W. 20 rods, S. 40 deg. W. 18 rods, W. 8 deg. N. 16 rods, W. 33 deg. S. 28 rods, S. 24 deg. W. 30 rods, S. 15 deg. W. 44 rods, W. 43 deg. S. 43 rods, W. 12 deg. S. 16 rods, W. 23 deg. S. 4 rods, S. 35 deg. W. 70 rods, S. 45 deg. W. 60 rods, W. 8 deg. S. 20 rods, W. 39 deg. N. 76 rods, W. 6 deg. S. 18 rods to the Middle Branch east of Mr. Ebenezer Webber's 5 miles and 93 rods from Chesterfield to said Branch."

These were the first highways laid out by the town, and it is probable that they were laid on the lines of paths already formed by travel. It is altogether probable that these roads were rough and difficult to travel, very unlike the roads of the present time. Teaming from one part of the town to another was done mostly by ox teams, and traveling was mostly on horse back.

John Smith's Account Book.

Below I give some specimen entries in the book of account kept by John Smith, one of the early settlers, and who was a member of the first board of selectmen chosen by the town of Murrayfield. It is interesting as a specimen of the method of keeping accounts that prevailed among these people, and as throwing light upon their ways of doing business, and also as giving the prices of some of the ordinary commodities and of labor.

The book from which I copy was bought by John Smith in October, 1775. One of the earliest entries is as follows:

		£	s.	d.
"November ye 30th: 1775	then Mr. Moses Clark Dets to me John Smith for my oxen two Days, to sled boards and logs,	0	2	5
	to: eating some meals of victuals, . . .	0	0	9"
"October ye 28, 1779	then Mr. Clark Credt by the hand of Mr. Peter Montague, 3 | 6	0	3	6"
"November ye 3, 1778	then Mr. Peter Montague Det. to: keeping your hors one week, . . .	0	1	6
	to: pastouring your hors six Days, . . .	0	1	2
March ye 16th: A. D. 1779	to: my oxen one Day to git wood, . . .	0	1	2
	to: an ox yoke, ...	0	2	0
	to: one pare of old shoes new mended up, .	0	2	9
	to: keeping your oxen five Days, . . .	0	1	6
October ye 28th A. D: 1779	then Mr. peter montague Deter for Discharging Mr. Moses Clark's acoumpt on your Desire, .	0	3	2
		1	7	9

		£	s.	d.
May ye 2	to: keeping your oxen a spell, ...	0	0	8
A. D. 1780	to: a bag of hay seed	0	0	9
Nov. ye 1:	to: keeping your calf sixteen Days, . .	0	0	6
ye 15.	to: my oxen half a Day, ...	0	0	9
January ye 22: 1781	to: my oxen and sled two Days, . . .	0	3	6
		1	7	9
	to: hay seed you had of John some years ago,	0	0	7
		1	3	6"

"February ye 22: A. D. 1781 } then reckoned with Mr. Peter Montague and find there is Due to me to ballance acoumpts by Book the old way as we say, . . . 0 7 11

PETER MONTAGUE,
JOHN SMITH."

Another one; the year not given.

"tuesday ye 5 of May Loren Weeb come at noon to board with me on Dr. Harwood's acompt and stayed till Monday ye 18th which makes two weeks wanting one Day, and throw out two Sabath days and there Remains one week and four Days to be paid for which I think comes to a bought seven and sixpence, ... 7-6."

"May ye 29, 1788, then Reckoned with Dr. Harwood on all Book acompts and find Due to me to balance two pounds twelve shillings and eleven pence.

JOHN SMITH,
FRANCIS HARWOOD."

Earlier transactions with Dr. Harwood were probably entered in some earlier pages missing from the book.

Here is another:

"April ye 22, A.D. 1785. I carried three hides to Capt. Kirtland's, wt 47 pounds each: sd Kirtland is to tan and curry sd hides to the halves as we say, and I am to have all the Leather by paying him for his half and if sd Leather is not Done well: sd : Kirtland is to Pay all Dammages to me for the same as we agreed to gether he should in his shop, JOHN SMITH."

One more will suffice:

		£	s.	d.
"November ye 15, 1778	then Mr. Samuel hulbed Dete to me for my horse to fetch you and your tools from Connecticut last Spring. I called it sixty five miles, .	0	8	1
one bushel and half of rye Mr. hulbud borrowed	to: keeping your maire colt six weeks, . .	0	6	0
June: ye 16th: 1779	Mr. Samuel hulbet came to my house with his family and put his maire and cow into my Pastour for me to keep.			

		£	s.	d.
	to: seven pounds and 3 ounces of mutton,	0	1	2
	to: one bushell and an half of rye,	0	4	6
	to: timber for a bedsted,	0	1	6
	to: half a Day moving,	0	1	3
	to: four pounds and ¼ of mutton,	0	0	10
	to: moving part of a Day,	0	1	0
August	to: one bushel and an half more of rye,	0	4	6
	to: half a bushel of wheat,	0	2	0
	to: two peaces of mutton wayed: 10: pounds,	0	1	8
	to: ten pounds and an half of mutton,	0	1	9
September	⎫ to: 28 Pounds of beef at 2: 2: y pound,	0	5	10
yᵉ: 7:	⎭ to: ten pounds and a Quarter of mutton,	0	1	9
October: 13	to: fifty pounds of beef,	0	10	0
	Mr. hulbed Dets to me for grass as it stood on the ground to be three Day's work,	0	9	0
October: yᵉ 25:	to: fifteen pounds of Pork,	0	3	6
	to· 23: pounds of choice beef,	0	5	9
	to: Pastouring your mare: 19: weeks,	1	2	2
	to: Pastouring your cow 23: weeks,	1	3	0
		5	15	2
	to: two Days work with oxen and John three Days work that I have not got Down and you had got on your book in my favor before the a Bove footing,	0	10	3
January yᵉ 7:	⎫ to: eight Pounds of choyse Pork,	0	2	6
A. D: 1780:	⎭ to: finding your firewood four weeks,	0	6	0
	to: Leather apron Part worn,	0	1	8
	to: one old Jackit A good part worn,	0	2	6
	to: four: 10: ounces of choys good beef,	0	1	0
	to: 77: feet of Cheary Bords,	0	4	0
	to: half abushel of wheet,	0	2	0
		7	5	1"
"November	⎫ Mr. Samuel hulbut Cridt			
yᵉ 15: 1778:	⎭ By Joyner work for me,	0	7	6
June: 21	⎫ Mr. hulbut credt. By his mare to ride three			
A. D: 1779:	⎭ times to Chilsons called: 15: miles,	0	2	0
July	By his mare a Journey to mountearmes: 65: milds at one penny half penny per mile,	8	2	2"
"December: yᵉ	⎫ Mr. Samuel Hulbud Dr			
1: A. D: 1785:	⎭ to: a blue brod cloth coat price forty shillings and he gave me an order on Rufus Lyman for ten shillings and there is now Du to me to wards: sd coat: thirty shillings,	1	10	0
	to: a cheese Last summer: wt 16 pounds,	0	5	4

		£	s.	d.
	to: my going with you to northamptin once,	0	3	0
	to: my old mare for Mr. Higgins to ride to Northampton for you after Jesse,	0	1	4
July ye 19. A. D: 1786.	to: one cheese: wt 6¾ pounds,	0	2	8
Nov. y. 22	to: part of a Day hooping old barrils,	0	1	6
February 16	to: two live geeas: 3: each for keeping so Long,	0	6	0
A. D: 1787:	to: one gallon of Linced oile,	0	6	6
		2	15	8"

"May: ye 12: 1789: then Reckoned with Mr. Samuel Hulbud and find Due to me By book Nineteen shillings and one penny, ... 0 19 1
"the above acompt with hulbud settled by   SAMUEL HULBUD
giving a note to Levi Smith and I solde the   JOHN SMITH."
same to Mr: Ebenezer higgins."

One transaction stands on the book thus:

"Mr. Montague hath paid 29: squares of glass and two quarts of Rum which we call five squares more the whole makes: 34: squares."

The price of half a bushel of salt was 12 shillings: the price of half a bushel of buckwheat was one shilling and threepence; and of one and a half bushel of oats two shillings and ninepence: the price of one bushel and a peck of flax seed was seven shillings; the price of 24 pounds of butter was 12 shillings.

The following is a verbatim copy of the return on a warrant for a town meeting, as it appears on the records of Murrayfield:

"Daited at murrayfield hampshire ss. June ye 25, 1768 the inhabitants of murrayfield that are qualified according to law to vote in town affairs have Been warned according to the Directions of this Warrant.
            pr me   STEPHEN LYMAN, Constable.
The above is a true copy
test pr me JOHN SMITH, town Clerk of murrayfield."

MEETING-HOUSE.

In 1785 the meeting-house was to some extent repaired and reseated. The town records show the following report, which, although it comes two years later than the limits of this history, yet, it can not but be of such interest as to recommend its insertion here:

"Chester, December 19th, 1785. The Committee appointed to dignify and seat the Meeting House report their doings as follows, viz: The two front seats in square body and the pew at the west side of the pulpit be appropriated for the use of the aged, viz: Samuel Elder, John Laccore, Timothy Smith, John Moore, Alexander Gordon, Daniel Smith, Edward Wright, Joseph Abbott, Stephen Tracy, Ebenezer Seaward, Jonathan Wait, Eliakim Cooley, Mr. Proctor, Capt. Abner Smith, James Quigley, Ebenezer Prior, William Lunnon, Noah Kingsbury, James Carlile, Reuben Woolworth, and their wives, also the widow Webber, and the widow Campbell, old Mr. Sanderson, widow Williams, and widow Henry.

"The fore-seats in the front gallery, the men's side, is seated with the following persons: William Foote, Robert Crawford, Samuel Woolworth, Jesse Wright, John Bigelow, John Hamilton, James Mulhollon, Jr., David Cross, Enos Smith, Joseph Wright.

"The following persons are seated in the fore-seat in the east or side gallery: Rufus Smith, Joseph Campbell, William Carlile, Robert Campbell, Enoch Shepard, Jr., James Wood, Ozias French, Justin Rust, John Ellis, Elijah Bacon, Thomas Hamilton, Quartus Rust, Jabez French, William Mulhollon, Silas Clark, James Bell, Noadiah Seaward, Jr., Gideon Matthews, Nathan Mann, Jesse Johnson, Brewster Freeman, James Albertus Core, Daniel Smith, 2d, Lemuel Hamilton.

"West side of the gallery, or Woman's side, the following persons are seated in the fore-seat in the front gallery: Dorothy Tracy, Pernal Smith, Marjory Laccore, Mindwell Moore, Jinna Campbell, Nauna Mulhollon, Susannah Mulhollon, Esther Matthews, Rebecca Smith, Polly Galloway, Persa Wright, Hannah Owen.

"The following persons are seated in the fore-seat on the west side gallery, viz: Sarah Johnson, Susannah Campbell, Eunice Johnson, Christiana Oliver, Lucy Sizer, Polly Blackman, Rosanna McIntire, Diadema McIntire, Lydia Carlile, Polly Campbell, Sarah Campbell, Polly Mulhollon, Margaret Ellis, Olive Lunnon, Margaret Shepard, Betsa Moore, Margaret Bell, Pruda Wood, Sarah McIntire, Elizabeth Ingall.

"May 16, 1788. The committee appointed to seat such as are not seated in the meeting house have attended to that business, and have seated the persons that are married and those that are most advanced in age below in the pews and seats as they are, or added to the respective pews they were seated in; and those that were not seated before in the gallery that are sixteen years old and upwards and all others we seat as follows: Them that are twenty-one years and upwards we seat in the fore-seats and those that are sixteen and upwards in the second seats, and we recommend to the singers to set in the front seats in the gallery and in the fore seats in the lower tier in the side gallery the men's side, by order of the committee. STEPHEN LYMAN, Chairman.

N. B.—Those persons that was seated by the last committee are added to the pews and seats as they was seated. Test. DAVID SHEPARD,
Town Clerk."

The persons assigned to the dignified part of the meeting-house, being the pews on the lower floor, except as before stated, and their estimated dignity as settled by the dignifying committee were as follows:

In Dignity first, No. 1: Joel Seaward, Capt. Enoch Shepard, Col. Oliver, Capt. John Kelso, Doctor David Shepard, Timothy Lyman, and their wives.

In Dignity first, No. 2: Capt. Nathan Wright, Isaac Bissell, Ebenezer Stowe, Lieut. Abner Smith, Samuel Moore, and their wives, and Lieut. Joel Webb.

In Dignity first, No. 3: Lieut. James Clark, William Moore, Deacon Jesse Johnson, James Mulhollon, William Bell, and their wives, Widow Jane Mann and Ebenezer Wales, Esq.

In Dignity first, No. 4: Edward Wright, Jr., John Bell, Capt. James Black, Samuel Bell, and their wives.

In Dignity first, No. 5: Lieut. James McIntire, Capt. Elijah Blackman, Capt. William Sizer, Jabez Tracy, and their wives.

In Dignity first, No. 6: Deacon Stephen Lyman, Jonathan Webber, Deacon Samuel Matthews, Deacon James Hamilton, and their wives and Capt. Toogood.

In Dignity second, No. 1: Gideon Matthews, Abiel Abbott, John Elder, John Abbott, and their wives.

In Dignity second, No. 2: Nathan Wood, William Foote, Solomon Root, Joseph Henry, and their wives.

In Dignity second, No. 3: Lieut. William Campbell, Thomas Elder, Lieut. John N. Parmenter, Gershom Rust, Robert Proctor, William Elder, and their wives, and Lieut. Ephraim Miller.

In Dignity second, No. 4: John Moore, Robert Smith, Thomas Smith, Noadiah Seaward, Widow Patience Smith, Jonathan Miller, James Core, and their wives.

In Dignity second, No. 5: Samuel Ellis, James Moore, Daniel Smith, Elijah Fobes, William Tanner, and their wives.

In Dignity second, No. 6: Jonathan Waite, Capt. Alexander, Lieut. Crossman, Samuel French, Amasa Pomeroy, and their wives, and William Collins.

In Dignity second, No. 7: Andrew Henry, Zadock Ingall, James Campbell, William Stone, and their wives.

In Dignity second, No. 8: Ebenezer Abbott, Jacob Fowle, Nathan Fobes, James Geer, and their wives, and John Billings, Daniel Smith, and John Gambol.

In Dignity second, No. 9: Dea. John Blair, Abraham Fleming,

Silas Freeman, Capt. Reuben Stanton, and their wives, and Zenas Searles.

In Dignity second, No. 10: Simeon Mulhollon, Oliver Hitchcock, Robert Moore, John Laccore, Jr., and their wives, Maj. Crafts, and David Cross.

In Dignity third, No. 1: John S. Clark, John Carlile, Zebulon Isham, Joab Smith, Daniel Twadwell, Abner Witt, Sylvanus Sanderson, and John Sanderson.

In Dignity third, No. 2: James McHerrin, John Grimes, Gershom Flagg, William Hunt, James Melvin, John Smith, Abner Eggleston, and their wives, also Widow Wheaton, John Bigelow, John Torry, Daniel Barnard, and Ozias French.

In Dignity third, No. 3: Robert Crawford, Nehemiah Day, Ebenezer Dowd, Lemuel Ellis, Thomas Flint, and their wives; also William Quigley, William Lee, Nathan Tanner.

In Dignity third, No. 4: Eliakim Clapp, Luther Pomeroy, John Quigley, Josiah Draper, and their wives; also Mr. Walker.

In Dignity third, No. 5: Aaron Bell, Matthew Campbell, Joseph Abbott, Gideon Parsons, and their wives; also Sylvester Bemas, and Nathaniel Adams.

In Dignity third, No. 6: Henry Vaderkin, John Williams, Ebenezer Stanton, and their wives; also Widow Sarah Anderson, Joseph Wright, James Warner, Timothy Cooley.

In Dignity fourth, No. 1: Daniel Stone, Ebenezer Smith, Phineas Wheeler, Robert Bartlett, Enos Smith, Samuel Woolworth, Solomon Ferry, and Thaddeus Ferry.

In Dignity fourth, No. 2: Samuel Smith, Solomon Cooley, John Smith, 2d, Widow Bently, Datis Ensign, Roswill Benjamin, and Joseph Mann.

In Dignity fourth, No. 3: William Smith, Benjamin Stewart, Oliver McIntire, James Quigley, Marshal Wheaton, Peter Whitney, Reuben Warfield, Ephraim Wheaton.

In Dignity fourth, No. 4: Henry Brass, Timothy Bacon, Justin Rust, John Hamilton, Jr., Elisha Stanton, Zebulon Tanner.

In Dignity fourth, No. 5: Samuel Lee, William Prior, Solomon Noble, Tryal Sanderson, Samuel Perkins, Elizabeth Smith, Anna Brown, Amanda Core, Samuel Gould, and Ebenezer Freeman.

The committee to "seat and dignify the meeting house" was chosen at a town meeting held in November, 1785, and the vote directed that "in seating the committee shall have regard to age, estate and usefulness."

PLAN OF THE LOWER FLOOR, AS SEATED AND DIGNIFIED BY THE
COMMITTEE IN 1785.

```
┌──────────┬──────────┬───┬─────────┬────────┬──────────┬──────────┐
│ Dignity3ᵈ│Dignity1ˢᵗ│Rev│         │  For   │Dignity1ˢᵗ│Dignity3ᵈ │
│  Nº.2.   │  Nº.4.   │Aaron│ Pulpit│  aged  │  Nº.3.   │  Nº.1.   │
│          │          │Bascom's│     │ people.│          │          │
│          │          │Pew │         │        │          │          │
├──────────┼──────────┴───┴─────────┴────────┴──────────┼──────────┤
│ Dignity2ᵈ│                                            │Dignity2ᵈ │
│  Nº.8.   │                                            │  Nº.7    │
├──────────┼──────────┬──────────┐        ┌──────────┬──────────┐  ├──────────┤
│          │For aged people.     │        │ For aged people     │  │          │
│ Dignity3ᵈ│Dignity2ᵈ│Dignity1ˢᵗ│  B     │Dignity1ˢᵗ│Dignity2ᵈ│  │Dignity3ᵈ │
│  Nº.6    │  Nº.2.  │  Nº.6.   │  r     │  Nº 5    │  Nº.1.  │  │  Nº.5.   │
│          ├─────────┼──────────┤  o     ├──────────┼─────────┤  │          │
│          │Dignity3ᵈ│Dignity2ᵈ│  a     │Dignity2ᵈ│Dignity3ᵈ│  │          │
│          │  Nº.4.  │  Nº.10  │  d     │  Nº.9.  │  Nº.3   │  │          │
├──────────┤         │          │        │          │         │  ├──────────┤
│ Dignity2ᵈ│         │          │  A     │          │         │  │Dignity2ᵈ │
│  Nº.4    │Dignity4ᵗʰ│Dignity2ᵈ│  l     │Dignity2ᵈ│Dignity4ᵗʰ│  │  Nº.3.   │
│          │  Nº.2.  │  Nº.6   │  l     │  Nº.5.  │  Nº.1    │  │          │
│          │          │          │  e     │          │         │  │          │
│          │          │          │  y     │          │         │  │          │
├──────────┼──────────┼──────────┘        └──────────┼─────────┤  ├──────────┤
│Gallery   │Dignity4ᵗʰ│Dignity4ᵗʰ│Dignity1ˢᵗ│        │Dignity1ˢᵗ│Dignity4ᵐ│Gallery   │
│Stairs.   │ Nº.5    │  Nº.4.  │  Nº.2.   │        │  Nº.1    │  Nº.3   │Stairs.   │
│          │          │          │          │Front Door.│         │          │
└──────────┴──────────┴──────────┴──────────┴──────────┴──────────┴──────────┘
```

INDEX.

Abbott, Abiel, 88, 102.
" Ebenezer, 102, 106.
" John, 88, 102.
" Joseph, 102.
" Joseph, Jr., 144.
Account book of John Smith, 150.
Adams, Nathaniel, 145, 165.
Additional grant to the proprietors, 40.
Agawam River, 26, 49.
Alexander, Nathaniel, 106, 144.
Allen, David, 102.
Allis, Samuel, 145.
Anderson, Archelus, 64, 113.
Angell, Christian, 80.
Appropriations in 1768, 58.
Arbitration to fix places for preaching, 66.
Armes, Thomas, 104.
Armstrong, George, 63.
Army, beef for, 136.
Averet, Isaac, 150.

Babcock, Benjamin, 106.
" Daniel, 103, 106.
" Ebenezer, 103.
" Rodolphus, 103.
Bacon, Elijah, 151.
" Timothy, 165.
Baker, Charles, 28, 56.
Baldwin, Abel, 109.
" Abial, 104.
" Rev. Mr., 66, 73.
" Samuel, 106.
Ballentine, Rev. John, 65, 73.
Barnard, Daniel, 145, 165.
" John, 80.
Bartlett, Robert, 165.
Bascom, Rev. Aaron, 67, 102.
" ordination of, 73.

Bascom, salary of, 90.
" his firewood, 73, 89.
" Caleb, 74, 81, 83.
Beaumont, Capt., 102.
Beef for the Army, 136.
Belknap, Job, 106.
" Samuel, 64.
Bell, Aaron, 88, 92, 106, 133.
" Abraham, 106.
" James, 163.
" John, 103, 106.
" Samuel, 102.
" William, 64, 133.
Bemas, Sylvester, 165.
Benjamin, Roswell, 151.
Bennett, Nathaniel, 80.
Bentley, James, 106.
Berkshire County, 24.
Bidwell, John, 10.
Bigelow, Daniel, 151.
" John, 146, 151, 165.
Billings, John, 164.
Bills of Credit, oath concerning, 59.
Births, 145.
Bissell, Isaac, 104, 144.
" Israel, 109.
Black, George, 81.
" James, 31, 33, 114, 133, 136.
" James, Jr., 81.
Blackman, Elijah, 106.
Blackstone's Commentaries, 28.
Blair, Absolom, 30, 33, 45, 63.
" Anna, 33,
" David, 57.
" John, 62, 127, 138, 144.
" Robert, 30, 33, 57, 63.
" Solomon, 80.
Bolton, David, 24, 30, 42, 53, 64.
" James, 24, 31, 42.

Bolton, John, 19, 34.
" John's pet. to the General Court, 19.
Bolton grant, 19.
Boyes, John, 30, 33, 34.
" Samuel, Jr., 151.
Brass, Henry, 165.
Break-neck Hill, 17.
Brewer, John, 9.
Brewster, Deacon of Worthington, 139.
Bridge, Norwich, 43.
Bridges, 62. Conduct of the original proprietors concerning, 41.
Brockett, Joshua, 106.
Brown, James, 57, 63.
" John, 30.
" William, 106.
Buck, Samuel, 64.
Bulkley, Patrick, 151.
Bunda, B. G. Peter, 80.
Burt, Noah, 19.
" Samuel, 20.

Campbell, James, 103, 151.
" James, of Blandford, 151.
" Joseph, 151.
" Matthew, 57, 103, 151.
" Robert, 103.
" William, 31, 83, 110, 127, 137, 138, 144.
Carlile, James, 146.
" John, 105, 146.
" William, 146.
Carter, Asa, 14, 64, 80.
" William, 14, 64, 80.
Cemetery, 91.
Chandler, John, 23, 38, 48, 75, 102, 126.
" Samuel, 109.
Chester, 142.
" Center, 47.
" Factories, 31.
" Village, 19.
Church discipline, 74.
" organization of, 69.
Clapp, Ebenezer, 14.
" Elijah, 14.
" Eliakim, 146.
" Job, 35.

Clapp, Jonathan, 50.
" Joseph, 151.
" Samuel and Mary, 13.
Clark, James, 24, 30, 42, 46, 53, 58, 83, 92, 101, 112, 113, 115, 116, 127, 133, 137.
Clark, James, Jr., 62.
" James of Norwich, 18, 63, 75, 80.
" Job, 105, 109.
" John, 104, 144.
" John S., 165.
" Moses, 159.
" Silas, 163.
Clothing for the Soldiers, 125.
Cochran, Glass, 31, 33, 34.
Collins, Daniel, 151.
" Ebenezer, 103.
" William, 164.
Committee of Correspondence, 112.
Confession of faith and names subscribed thereto, 72.
Constitution, form of, sent to the towns for approval by the General Court, in 1778, but rejected by the towns, 116, 118.
Constitution, A new draft of in 1779, 132.
Conventions to fix prices of necessaries, 131.
Converse, Benjamin, 12, 133, 144.
" Samuel, 106.
Conveyances of real estate, the earliest, to wit:
  Bolton to Burt and Lyman, 20.
  Bolton to Taylor, 20.
  Brewer to Weller, 10.
  Clapp to Wait, 51.
  Clapp to Wells, 14.
  Foye to Bolton, 19.
  Green to Kirtland, 15.
  Ingersoll to Brewer, 9.
  Ingersoll to Webb, 9.
  Johnson to Sprague, 13.
  Johnson to Tobb, 12.
  Kirtland to Clark, 18.
  Matthews to Rose, 11.
  Matthews to Matthews, 11.
  Sheldon to Strong, 13.
  Strong to Carter, 14.
  Webb to Clapp, 35.

Webb to Taylor, 12.
Weller to Bidwell, 10.
Weller to Lyman, 11.
Weller to Matthews, 10.
Weller to Mixer, 11.
Williams to Kirtland, 17.
Cook, John, J., 36.
" Mace, 80.
" Pearley, 36.
Cooley, Eliakim, 104.
" George, 105.
" Keziah, 34.
" Solomon, 105.
" Timothy, 146.
Core, Abeline, 33.
" James, 104, 144.
Crafts, Edward, 103.
Crawford, Aaron, 106.
" John, 31, 48.
" Robert, 103.
Crekle, Patrick, 80.
Crooks, John, 31, 33, 34.
Cross, David, 103.
Crossett, John, 80.
Crossman, William, 103.
Crow, David, 12, 80.
" James, 80.
" John, Jr., 57, 60.
" Thomas, 12, 63, 75, 80.
Culver, Timothy, 62.
Cummings, John, 21.
Cushing, Anna, 18.
" Jacob, 18.

Dana, Daniel, 80.
Day, Nehemiah. 165.
Dean, Joshua, 21.
Deaths, 154.
Debts of the town in 1768, 59.
Declaration of Independence, vote in favor of, 115.
Deer-Reves, 54.
Depreciated Currency, 91, 128.
Dewey, Russell, 106
Dickinson, Amaziah. 34.
Difficulties that beset the early settlers, 27, 35.
Distribution of the early settlers by the proprietors, 31

Division of Murrayfield, 75, 76, 77.
Drake, Abraham, 151.
Draper, Jonathan, 144.
" Joshua, 87.
Dunham, Calvin, 106.
Dwight, Josiah, Esq., 29.

Early custom of granting townships to tenants in common, 21.
Early settlers, their difficulties, 27, 35.
" " distribution of, 31.
" " where they came from, 33.
Edwards, Vester, 151.
Eggleston, Abner, 165.
" Benjamin, 101, 133, 151.
" Bigott, 57, 58, 83.
" Jebial, 57, 80.
" Samuel, 151.
Elder, John, 63, 103.
" Samuel, 30, 53, 83.
" Thomas, 63, 138.
" William, 103.
Ellis, John, 163.
" Samuel, 57, 58, 92.
English, Andrew, 30, 33.
" William, 30, 33.
Ensign, Deodatus, 152.
Excise duties, 141.

Fairman, James, 31, 58, 80.
" Samuel, 57, 58, 80.
Faith, confession of, agreed upon, 72.
Falley, Richard, 105.
Falley's x Roads, 19.
Farnsworth, Zadreus, 104.
Ferry-boat proposed, 62.
Ferry, Solomon, 147, 165.
" Thaddeus, 147, 165.
Field, Robert, 81.
Financial condition of the country in 1779, 126.
Firewood for Mr. Bascom, 73, 89.
First division of lots, 28.
" gristmill, 50.
" Justice of the Peace, 95.
" meeting house, 53.
" meeting of the proprietors, 29.
" town controversy, 55.

First town meeting, 53.
" town meeting after the division of the town, 82.
First valuation list, 57.
Flagg, Gershom, 105.
Flemming, Abraham, 24, 42, 47, 48, 54, 74.
Flint, Thomas, 103.
Fobes, Caleb, 57, 58, 64, 73, 75, 79, 80.
" Elijah, 80.
" Nathan, 147.
" Simeon, 105.
" William, 57, 80.
Foot, John, 19.
" William, 88, 144.
Fowle, Jacob, 103.
Fowler, Bildad, 105, 109.
Foye, John, 19, 34.
Freeman, Brewster, 163.
" Ebenezer, 80, 99.
" Silas, 104.
French, Jabez, 152.
" Ozias, 152.
" Samuel, 105, 147.
" William, 80.
Fuller, Zebulon, 24, 31, 42, 80.

Gambol, John, 104.
Geer, Ebenezer, 63, 75, 80.
" Elijah, 63, 75, 80.
" Eunice, 99.
" James, 81.
" Joseph, 152.
" Silby, 81.
Gibbs, Isaac, 64.
Gilmore, David, 24, 30, 42, 47.
" James, 57, 80.
" John, 24, 30, 42, 63.
Glasgow, 24.
Gleason, David, 103.
Goodwell, Nathan, 152.
" Nathaniel, 152.
Gordon, Alexander, 30, 48, 54, 99.
" Ebenezer, 63.
" Samuel, 63.
Goss Hill, 34, 46.
Gould, Asa, 106.
" Samuel, 88.
Granger, Luther, 152.

Grants prior to sale of township, to wit:
Bolton grant, 19.
Green and Walker grant, 14.
Ingersoll grant, 7.
Sheldon and Clapp grant, 13.
Williams grant, 17.
Graves, Moses, 15.
Green, Allyn, 99.
" Anna, 15.
" George, 15.
" John, 15.
" Joseph, 14, 15.
Green mountain range, 24.
Grims, John, 152.
Griswold, John, 80.
Grout, Capt. 103.

Halberd, David, 80.
Hale, Aaron, 152.
" Moses, 24, 31, 42, 63.
Halliday, Hiram, 14.
" Job, 14.
Hamilton, James, 57, 66, 73, 83, 92, 99, 127, 133, 142, 144.
Hamilton, John, 104.
" Thomas, 163.
" Samuel, 152.
Hampshire County, 24.
Hancock, Lewis, 147.
Hannum, John, 30, 33.
Harkell, John, 63.
Hart, Rev. Mr. Ashel, 65, 66.
Harwood, Dr., 160.
Haskell, John, 152.
Hawley, Joseph, 24, 59, 79.
Hedges, David, 105.
Henry, Andrew, 81, 144.
" Jonas, 152.
" Joseph, 81, 152.
" Malcom, 34, 53, 55, 101, 112, 113, 114.
Henry, William, 81, 82.
Higgins, Ebenezer, 162.
Highways laid out in 1769, 61, 155.
Highways, 96, 155.
Hill, William, 103.
Hingham, Solomon, 152.
Hitchcock, Oliver, 105.

Holland, James, 154.
" William, 152.
Holyday, Josiah, 64.
" Solomon, 64, 80.
" Solomon, Jr., 64, 80.
Homes, Jabez, 80.
Hooker, Mr., 65.
Houses of the first settlers, 35.
Hubbard, Elisha, 15.
Hubbard, Mr., 63.
Hubbill, Silas, 14.
Hulbert, Samuel, 152, 160, 162.
Hunt, William, 105, 109.

Ingall, Zadock, 104.
Ingersoll grant, 7.
Ingersoll, David, 7, 9.
" Thomas, 7, 14.
Interval lands, 26.
Isham, Lebanon, 101, 142.
" Zebulon, 103

Johnson, Jesse, 31, 33, 66, 67, 68, 73, 83, 90, 112, 115, 116, 127, 133,139, 142.
Johnson, John, 9, 12.
Jones, Cornelius, 21.
" Elisha, 21.
" John, 101, 133, 142.
" Nathan, 21.
" Samuel, 92, 101, 103, 133, 142.
" Zebulon, 64.
Judd, Rev. Jonathan, 73.
" Selathial, 152.
" Sylvester, 105.
" Thomas, 106.
Justice of the Peace, first, 95.

Kellogg, Samuel, 103.
Kelso, Hugh, 105.
" John, 99, 137.
Kennedy, Thomas, 24, 30, 42, 46, 47, 48, 53.
Kennedy, William, 24, 31, 42.
Kenney, Jethro, 106.
" Thomas, 106.
King, Ebenezer, 12, 34, 54, 58, 80.
" Phineas, 152.
Kingsbury, Noah, 105.
Kingsley, Ebenezer, 17.

Kingsley, Nathaniel, 67.
Kingston, Paul, 31.
Kinney, Dorothy, 33.
Kirtland, John, 15, 18, 63, 64, 67, 68, 73, 75, 76, 79, 80, 98.
Kirtland, Daniel, 18, 63, 80.
Knight, Samuel, 63, 80.

Laccore, John, 30, 58, 66.
" John, Jr., 81.
" Lemuel, 57.
Lamb, David, 152.
Lamberton, Henry, 106.
Lathrop, Rev. Joseph, 73.
Lawrence, Abel, 21.
Law-suits, 56.
Lee, William, 105.
Leonard, Nathan, 67.
" Noah, 152.
Loomis, Luther, 109.
Lots, first drawing of, 30.
Lunnon, William, 106.
Lyde, Byfield, 15.
Lyman, Elias, 30, 33.
" John, 20, 30, 33.
" Nathan, 11.
" Stephen, 33, 42, 54, 58, 65, 67, 73, 92, 98, 100, 114, 115, 127, 131, 132, 133, 135, 138, 139, 143, 144.
Lyman, Timothy, 33, 73, 99, 100, 127, 136, 138, 139, 144.

Mahan River, 17.
Mann, Joseph, 105.
" Nathan, 30, 47, 53, 63.
" William, 24, 30, 42, 53.
March meeting, 1769, 60.
Marriages, 150.
Mathar, David, 103.
Matthew, Benjamin, 10, 30, 33, 34.
" Gideon, 12, 31, 33, 42, 53, 58, 66, 116, 144.
Matthew, Lucas, 152.
" Reuben, 60, 63.
" Samuel, 60, 63, 68, 73, 98, 99, 112, 114, 115, 127, 131, 133, 135, 144.
McHenry, Lieut., 81.
McIntire, John, 30, 54, 74, 87, 89, 138.
" Thomas, 31.

McIntire, William, 88.
McKnight, James, 57.
Meacham, Ebenezer, 24, 31, 33, 42, 54, 58, 64, 80.
Meeker, Daniel, 57.
Meeting-house, care of, 87.
" manner of seating, 88.
" plan of, 86, 106.
" seating of in 1773, 84.
" seating of in 1785, 162.
Melvin, James, 165.
Memorial of John Kirtland to the Court, 76.
Messenger, Ebenezer N., 152.
Middlefield, southeast corner of, 101.
Millard, Oliver, 152.
Miller, Ephraim, 104.
" Jonathan, 104.
" Oliver, 153.
" Roger, 17.
" Rev. Simeon, 66.
" William, 24, 31, 34, 42, 53, 58, 60, 73, 80.
Mill lot, 51.
Minister lot, 37.
Mixer, Isaac, 11, 54, 58, 64, 65, 73, 75, 80, 82.
Mixer, Isaac, Jr., 57, 75, 80.
Mixer's tavern, 11, 68, 75.
· Montague, Peter, 159.
Moore, James, 103.
" John, 103.
" John, Jr., 148.
" Robert, 105.
" Samuel, 105, 144.
" William, 31, 58, 80, 127, 131, 133.
Moose Meadow, 8.
Moreton, Thomas, 30.
Morgan, Abner, 43.
Morse, John, 99, 106.
" Samuel, 104.
Moseley, David, 10, 138.
" John, 35.
Moss, Moses, 24, 31, 42.
Mulhollon, James, 63, 103.
" Simeon E., 103.
" William, 103.
Murray, John, 23, 38, 47, 49, 56, 75, 102, 126.

Murrayfield, 39. Incorporation of, 52.
Mussey, Benjamin, 153.
Myrifield, 142.

Name of town changed, 142.
Napping, George, 81.
Nash, Noah, 21.
New Glasgow, 27.
New Hingham, 24.
New Settlers in 1769, 62; in 1770, 63.
Newton, Obediah, 81.
" Thaddeus, 81, 101, 126.
Noble, Asa, 30.
" John, 64.
" Solomon, 105.
" Thomas, 30.
Nooney Brook, 48.
Nooney, James, 104.
Northrop, Emanuel, 99, 106.
" Joseph, 99, 105.
Norwich Bridge, 43, 51.
Norwich Hill, 47.
Norwich incorporated, 78.
Norwich, names of taxpayers in 1773, 80.
Norwich Pond, 14.
Norwich, relations with Murrayfield, 99.

Old account book of John Smith, 159.
Old road up East Branch, 12.
Old road up Moose mountain, 45.
Orcutt, Moses, 106.
Original proprietors of Township No. 9, 23.
Otis, Allen, 109.
" Col. James, 102.
" James, 38, 44, 47, 49, 102.
" Joseph, 102.

Paine, Timothy. 23, 38, 47, 49, 56, 75, 102, 109.
Palmer, David, 63, 68, 73, 75, 80.
" David, Jr., 63, 80.
" John D., 80.
Paper currency, depreciation of, 128.
Parks, Reuben, 153.
" Warham, 109, 138.
Parmenter, John N., 92, 103, 107, 133, 134, 138.

Parsons, Joseph, 18.
" Moses, 21.
" Sarah, 18.
Partridge, Abel, 99, 106.
" Oliver, 15, 17.
Pease, Abner, 57, 63.
Pelton, Tabor, 153.
Perkins, Samuel, 165.
Pomeroy, Amasa, 103, 148.
" Ebenezer, 7, 14.
" Joseph, 106.
" Luther, 148.
" Samuel, 63.
Poor of the town, 95.
Pound, town, 94.
Pratt, Benjamin, 24.
Pratt, Othiel, 106.
Preaching, action touching, 65, 66, 67.
" controversy about, 75.
" towns required to support, 69.
Prices of necessaries, convention to fix, 131.
Prior, Ebenezer, 103.
" Heman, 153.
" William, 103.
Proctor, Robert, 57, 92, 133.
Proprietors' complaint to the General Court, 39.
Proprietors' records, beginning of, 28.
Province, general condition of, in 1762, 27.
Province lands, leasing of, 24.

Quigley, Hugh, 153.
" James, 163.
" John, 165.
" William, 165.
Quotas of men for the war, 107; controversy with other towns concerning, 131; additional called for, 135, 137.

Representatives to General Court, 98, 114.
Revolutionary war, 110.
Rhodes, Isaac, 104.
" William, 104.
Riley place, 46.

Roberts, Timothy, 138, 139.
Rock House Corner, 9, 65.
Root, Solomon, 104, 164.
Rose, Eunice, 11.
" Israel, 11, 24, 30, 33, 42, 53, 58, 66.
Rose, Nathan, 31, 33, 58.
" Zebulon, 57, 80.
Rude, John, 63, 80.
Russell, Jonathan, 63.
" William, 104.
Rust, Gershom, 64, 92, 133.
" Justin, 149.
" Quartus, 163.

Sale of township No. 9, 21.
Sanderson, John, 165.
" Sylvester, 105, 109.
" Tyrol, 153, 165.
Schools, 62, 91.
School lands, leasing of, 92.
School houses, 94.
Scotch settlers, 27.
Scott, David, 24, 30, 42, 45, 47, 64, 75, 79, 80, 83, 98, 114.
Scott, John, Jr., 30, 33.
" William, 153.
Searle, Job, 153.
" Zenas, 165.
" Zopher, 105.
Second meeting of the proprietors, 47.
Settlers before 1762, names of, 23.
" upon Ingersoll grant, 34.
Seward, Ebenezer, 163.
" Joel, 81, 101, 115, 136.
" Noadiah, 104.
" Noadiah, Jr., 163.
Shelden, Ebenezer, 13.
" Ephraim, 104.
Shepard, Dr. David, 63, 64, 83, 92, 96, 99, 100, 107, 112, 114, 127, 133, 134, 138, 139, 143, 144.
Shepherd, Enoch, 81, 89, 92, 93, 98, 99, 101, 107, 114, 127, 142.
Sizer, William, 106.
Slayton, Asa, 153.
Sloper, Capt. of Blandford, 139.
Small-pox and inoculation, 95.
Smith, Abner, 30, 33, 48, 64, 65, 74, 83, 92, 98, 99, 100, 101, 102, 113, 114, 137.

Smith, Abner, Jr., 81, 137.
" Daniel, 104.
" Daniel, Jr., 105.
" Ebenezer, 104.
" Enos, 153.
" Jacob, 153.
" Joab, 100, 153.
" John, 30, 33, 42, 53, 55, 56, 58, 60, 63, 150.
Smith, John, 2d, 105.
" John, 3d, 106.
" Levi, 162.
" Thomas, 60, 144.
" Timothy, 34, 53, 55, 56, 58, 60, 74, 76, 83, 99, 100, 113, 138, 144.
Smith, Robert, 48, 63, 144.
" Rufus, 163.
" Samuel, 165.
" William, 105, 144.
Snow, Ezekiel, 57.
Soldiers, clothing for, 125.
" money for, 115.
" names of, 139.
" pay of, 135.
" support of families, 135.
Sprague, John, M. D., 13.
Stanton, Ebenezer, 165.
" Elijah, 104.
" Elisha, 165.
" Joseph, 80.
" Reuben, 165.
Stebbins, Joseph, 105.
" Joseph J., 105.
Stevenson, John, 153.
Stewart, Benjamin, 165.
Stoddard, John, 7, 14.
Stone, Daniel, 104.
" William, 88, 144.
Story, Jabez, 80.
Stowe, Ebenezer, 105, 133, 135, 137, 138.
Strong, Caleb, 13. 14.
" Simeon, 56.
Sylvester, Gershom, 153.

Taggart, James, 12, 57.
Tanner, William, 149.
" Zebulon, 165.
Taxes, difficulty of collecting during the War of the Revolution, 106.

Taxes, complaint of non-resident taxpayers, 109.
Taylor, Eldad, 12, 20, 28, 52, 53, 56.
" John, 64, 81, 101, 142.
Third meeting of the proprietors, 48.
" town meeting, 58.
Thomas, Solomon, 14.
Thompson, John, 81, 101, 142.
" John, Jr., 81.
Tiffany, John, 64, 80.
Tillotson, Ebenezer, 104.
Tobb, Nicholas, 12.
Toogood, Capt., 164.
Torry, Calvin, 106.
" Jabez, 64.
" John, 165.
Town, change of name, 142.
" division of, 75, 76, 77.
" lines, 64.
" meeting in March, 1783, 143.
" northwest corner of, 142.
" poverty of in 1782, 136.
Township No. 9, 23.
" " original proprietors of, 23.
Township No. 9, topography of, 24.
Tracy, Jabez, 92, 106.
" Stephen, 163.
Tud, Rev. Mr., 65.
Tupper, Benjamin, 67.
Twadwell, Daniel, 57, 133.
" David, 99.

Vadekin, Henry, 150.
Valuation list in 1768, 57.
" " 1772, 64.
" lists in 1775, 1776, 1777, 1780, 1781, 1782, 101.
Valuation list, controversy about, 55, 56.
Valuation, fluctuation of during the war, 128.
Voters, list of qualified in 1770, 63.

Wade, John, 81,
Wait, Jonathan, 51, 54, 57, 74.
" Jonathan, Jr., 144.
Wales, Ebenezer, 164.
Walker, Isaac, 14, 15.

War charges, 115; Equalizing the burdens of, 137.
Ward, John, 104.
" Samuel, 102, 109.
Ware, Jonathan, 80.
Wares, Deacon, of Norwich, 139.
Warfield, Reuben, 165.
Warner, James, 149.
Warrants for town meeting, 95.
Washburn, Miles, 63, 75, 80.
Webb, Joel, 164.
" Thomas, 9.
" Samuel, 12, 34, 54, 63.
Weeb—or Webb—Loren, 160.
Webber, Ebenezer, 24, 80, 42, 47, 54, 58, 60, 66.
Webber, John, 24, 30, 42.
" Jonathan Hart, 24, 30, 33, 42, 48, 58, 60, 66.
Webber, Jonathan, 30, 66, 133.
Weller, Nathaniel, 10, 34, 63.
Wells, Joseph, 14.
Westfield River Branches, 11, 25, 34.
Wheat, Samuel, 64.
Wheaton, Ephraim, 165.
" Marshall, 165.
Wheeler, Phineas, 150.
White, Elijah, 104, 106.
" Jude, 154.
" Nathan, 106.
Whitney, Benjamin, 63.
" John, 63.
" Peter, 165.
Willard, Aaron, 21.
" Abijah, 23, 38, 47, 48, 56, 75, 102, 126.
Willard's heirs, 109.
Williams, Charles, 80.
" Daniel, 63, 80.

Williams, Davenport, 106.
" Elijah, 15.
" George, 106, 113.
" Isaac, 63.
" Job, 8.
" John, 104.
" Rev. John, 47.
" Larkin, 106, 116.
" Nathan, 18.
" Peter, 57, 58, 75, 80.
" Rodman, 106.
" Rev. Stephen, 17.
" William, 21, 23.
Wilter, Joseph, 106.
Winslow, Joshua, 8.
Witt, Abner, 106, 150.
" William, 150.
Wolves, 95.
Wood, James, 163.
" John, 31, 33, 34.
" Nathan, 164.
Woods, John, 30, 34.
" Levi, 30, 33, 34.
Woodworth, Abigail, 18.
" Samuel, 18.
Woolworth, Eli, 105.
" Reuben, 57, 58, 66, 74, 80, 133, 144.
Woolworth, Samuel, 154.
Worthington, John, 24.
Wright, Bazelial, 81.
" Edward, 63.
" Edward, Jr., 63, 136, 144.
" Jesse, 104.
" Joseph, 150.
" Joshua, 150.
" Jude, 104.
" Nathan, 81, 150.
" Thomas, 57, 63.

www.ingramcontent.com/pod-product-compliance
Lightning Source LLC
Chambersburg PA
CBHW020258170426
43202CB00008B/423